Critical Essays on
Ivan Turgenev

Critical Essays on
World Literature

Robert Lecker, General Editor
McGill University

Critical Essays on
Ivan Turgenev

David A. Lowe

G. K. Hall & Co. • Boston, Massachusetts

Library of Congress Cataloging-in-Publication Data

Lowe, David Allan, 1948–
 Critical essays on Ivan Turgenev / David A. Lowe.
  p. cm. — (Critical essays on world literature)
 Includes index.
 ISBN 0–8161–8842–4
 1. Turgenev, Ivan Sergeevich, 1818–1883—Criticism and
interpretation. I. Title. II. Series.
PG3443.L6 1988
891.73′3—dc19   88–16312
                                                      CIP

This publication is printed on permanent/durable acid-free paper
MANUFACTURED IN THE UNITED STATES OF AMERICA

CONTENTS

Introduction

Turgenev and the Critics

As an artist, Ivan Turgenev has long since acquired the reputation of an apostle of moderation. As Dmitry Merezhkovsky noted in a presentation delivered in 1909, "In Russia, in a land of every sort of maximalism, revolutionary and religious, a land of self-immolations, a land of the most frenzied excesses, Turgenev is practically our only *genius of the right measure* after Pushkin. . . ."[1] Predictably, however, especially in a Russian context, Turgenev's perceived moderation and minimalism evoked extreme responses in his lifetime and continue to produce partisan reactions even today.

The major issues in Turgenev criticism revolve around a few fundamental polarities, most of them interrelated and several of them having perhaps more to do with Turgenev's biography than with his art. One area of dispute concerns Turgenev's perceived, alleged, or proclaimed geopolitical stance with regard to Russia's centuries-old uncertainty about her national identity. The question may be summarized as Turgenev the Russian versus Turgenev the European. During Turgenev's lifetime, Western Europe generally saw him as piquantly Russian, while as far as someone like Dostoevsky was concerned, Turgenev compromised himself all the way around by showing a slavish devotion to Europe, especially to Germany. By regularly emphasizing Russia's status as a European nation, Turgenev himself strove for a synthesis on this point, but few of his critics have shown a desire to erase any boundaries, metaphoric or real, between Europe and Russia.

Although Turgenev always described himself as apolitical, a second, related motif in the literature about him emphasizes his political sympathies. Dostoevsky, for instance, saw Turgenev as an archetypical Westernizing Russian liberal of the 1840s. As part of his dramatization of the thesis that the liberals of Turgenev's generation had given metaphoric birth to the radicals and revolutionaries of the 1860s, Dostoevsky lampooned Turgenev in at least two characters in *The Possessed*—Karmazinov, the "famous writer," and the elder Verkhovensky, an amoral, fatuous windbag. A quite contrary view of

1

Turgenev's politics informs a Soviet article from the 1950s, wherein the author maintains that Soviet children should not be encouraged to read a novel as reactionary as *Fathers and Sons*.[2]

In his remarks on Turgenev, Merezhkovsky makes use of one of his favorite devices, the paradox, to explain the contradictory readings of Turgenev's political stance: "Turgenev, as opposed to our great creators and destroyers Tolstoy and Dostoevsky, is our only guardian, our only conservative, and like any true conservative, is at the same time a liberal" (58). Few other of Turgenev's critics have attempted to see both sides of this question, and much commentary on Turgenev, especially in the nineteenth century, assigns the writer praise or blame on the primary basis of the presumed political judgments expressed overtly or implicitly in specific works.

Whether Turgenev even lends himself to discussion in terms of geography or politics depends on the resolution of another major question in Turgenev criticism, namely, that of the nature of his subject matter. Critics tend to operate from one or the other of two presumptions—either that Turgenev's works reproduce Russian reality or that his writings reflect and treat universal, timeless human concerns. In the past century, critics of virtually all stripes paid the greatest heed to those works inviting or at least permitting discussion based on perceived similarities or discrepancies between the world portrayed in them and Russia at large. In practice, that meant a primary focus on the cycle *Notes of a Hunter* and on Turgenev's six novels. Few critics took cognizance of Turgenev's poetry, short stories, and plays, all of which offer relatively ungrateful material for interpreters who see literature as a branch of photojournalism.

An allied topic contrasts Turgenev the novelist with Turgenev the short story writer, poet, or playwright. During his lifetime, Turgenev's acclaim, though certainly due in no small part to *Notes of a Hunter,* ultimately rested on his novels. Since then, however, many of his stories and at least one of his plays, *A Month in the Country,* have captured the serious attention of both the critics and the public. Indeed, in the twentieth century, as influential a critic as D. S. Mirsky has argued that the sociopolitical aspect of Turgenev's oeuvre, the "stuffing" in his novels, has grown more and more stale, while the essential poetry and lyricism, especially of the stories, emerge with a freshness and purity that earlier critical stances and readers' attitudes in fact hindered.[3] Not everyone would agree with that assessment, of course, and Turgenev's novels continue to generate studies with such titles as "Turgenev: The Politics of Hesitation."[4]

A fifth major controversy in the literature about Turgenev arises from disagreement over whether Turgenev's manner of writing represents realism or something other than realism. In the Anglophone world, such influential critics as William Dean Howells and Henry

James promoted Turgenev as a founding father of realism. Until quite recently, Soviet criticism, which made a fetish of realism and treated romanticism as an ideological malady not far removed from outright sedition, also proclaimed Turgenev one of the fountainheads of Russian realism. Many of Turgenev's contemporaries, however, observed that his art had deep roots in romanticism, a fact that Western scholarship has begun emphasizing in the last twenty years or so. Meanwhile, at the beginning of the twentieth century several Russian poets and prose writers of the modernist persuasion cited Turgenev as an important influence on their styles or themes. Contemporary Turgenev scholarship continues to try to distinguish the romantic or symbolist from the realistic elements in Turgenev's style. As a consequence, few critics nowadays, even in the Soviet Union, label Turgenev a realist without swathing that epithet in several layers of qualifications.

Although modern literary theory has considerably discredited the notion of style and content as discrete entities, much Turgenev criticism continues the nineteenth-century tradition of distinguishing the medium from the message in Turgenev's works. Radical critics in Turgenev's day almost completely discounted questions of style, while the so-called aesthetic critics discussed the perceived apparatus of Turgenev's art. In the early decades of this century, the Russian Formalists penned several important studies of Turgenev's poetry, plays, stories, and novels that evince little or no interest in hermeneutics, while post-Formalist criticism has tended to concern itself with the political, sociological, historical, or philosophical contexts of Turgenev's writings. In short, Turgenev criticism remains divided over what matters more in Turgenev's oeuvre—the "how" or the "what." Turgenev himself wanted it both ways. In the foreword to his novels he maintains that in art the question of how is always more important than the question of what, but he also averred that there were times in the life of a nation when art had to give way to other, more important considerations.

A final major point of contention concerns Turgenev's general merit as a writer. Although his reputation both at home and abroad fluctuated dramatically during the major part of his career, by the end of his life the world at large had declared Turgenev a classic. Almost immediately upon his death, however, voices began to question the scale and relevance of Turgenev's art. Merezhkovsky summed up the situation in the early years of the twentieth century: "Turgenev, they say, is outmoded. The two gigantic caryatids of Russian literature—Tolstoy and Dostoevsky—really have overshadowed Turgenev for us. Forever? For long? Aren't we fated to return to him through them?" (58). Merezhkovsky's queries remain very much to the point today. Critics continue to argue about whether Turgenev belongs to the ranks of the geniuses or the journeymen.

All the polarities that shape discussion of Turgenev have their precedents in nineteenth-century criticism. Twentieth-century histories of Russian literary criticism generally identify three major groupings or schools of Russian criticism in the last century: radicals, conservatives, and aesthetic critics. These designations, a product of Russian cultural history and Soviet literary historiography, clearly demonstrate the confusion between political journalism and literary art characteristic of much nineteenth-century Russian writing about belles lettres. Furthermore, these conventional labels conceal important similarities between the radicals and conservatives and differences within individual camps. Nonetheless, as with the equally problematic terms *realism* and *romanticism,* the notion of nineteenth-century Russian critics as radicals, conservatives, or aesthetes has become such a fixture of literary discussion that it makes more sense to draw on it, albeit with reservations and disclaimers, than to attempt an entirely new system of classification.

In Soviet parlance the tag "radical democrats" almost always accompanies the radical critics. By and large, these literary commentators exerted the greatest influence of any critics of the age, and their views and general approach to literature have played a decisive role in the evolution of Soviet criticism as well. Few Soviet sources make any attempt to conceal the favored status granted the radicals. On the contrary, reference works often force the radicals upon the reading public in the same unsubtle way that Stalin made the poet Vladimir Mayakovsky a secular icon by dubbing him the "best and most talented poet" of the era and declaring indifference to his memory a crime. In Ye. Yefimov's *I. S. Turgenev: Seminar,* for instance, a standard guide for teachers, mention of nineteenth-century criticism of *On the Eve* is accompanied by the following unambiguous note of caution: "The treatment of the question of the appraisal of *On the Eve* by reactionary and liberal critics is to be limited to a few examples. The main attention is to be devoted to the criticism of the revolutionary democrats."[5]

The radical critics generally continued a mode and style of civic-minded criticism founded by Turgenev's friend and mentor, Vissarion Belinsky (1811–48). In Turgenev's mind, and not only in his, Belinsky represented many of the noblest strivings and best traits of the "men of the 1840s." That term, crucially important for any survey of the evolution of Russian culture in the last century, refers to the educated Russians of Turgenev and Belinsky's generation, men who helped shape modern Russian culture. Although the generation of the 1840s embraced both conservatives and revolutionaries, Slavophiles and Westernizers, theologians and atheists, virtually all the movers and shakers of the era shared a gentry provenance (the plebeian Belinsky being a major exception) and a dual commitment to art and the life of the mind. Thanks to their immersion in German idealism, the men of the 1840s in fact viewed art as the primary vehicle for describing and understanding the world.

Belinsky occasionally showed remarkable acumen, especially in spotting the talent of Lermontov, Dostoevsky, and Turgenev early on. One cannot overlook several lamentable aspects of his legacy, however. He boasted a leaden style, and as Mirsky observed, "It was Belinsky, more than anyone else, who poisoned literature by the itch for expressing ideas, which has survived so woefully long" (175). Mirsky means the Russian tendency, especially pronounced in the nineteenth century, to attempt to compensate for the lack of a free press by using writing about literature as an Aesopian forum, or even pulpit, from which to address the burning issues of the day. In this connection, a remark that Pushkin made in 1820 bears repeating: "We have literature of a sort, but we have no criticism."[6] Pushkin's complaint remained largely valid for the rest of the century. Russia's literary criticism, particularly in the nineteenth century and especially as practiced by Belinsky and his heirs, often reads like what the rest of the world would probably consider heavily politicized journalism on mostly nonliterary topics.

In his "Recollections of Belinsky," Turgenev had the following to say about Belinsky's attitude toward his works: "As for me, I have to say that after the first salute that he made to my literary activity, he rather soon—and quite rightly—grew cold toward it; he could not have encouraged me in the composition of those verses and narrative poems which I had given myself up to at that time."[7] Turgenev is referring here to Belinsky's initial enthusiasm for such works as *Parasha* (1843), which the critic praised for their appeal to the intellect (the dread "ideas" to which Mirsky alludes) and for their "hints at Russian life."[8]

As for Belinsky's reaction to Turgenev's first efforts in prose, Turgenev recalls: "Although he was more satisfied with my prose works, he placed no special hopes on me" (Vol. 14, 52). Turgenev somewhat understates the case here. Belinsky in fact identified the initial sketches of *Notes of a Hunter* as among the best works of 1847 and argued that in them Turgenev had "approached the people [the peasantry] from a side from which no one before him had yet approached them."[9] Moreover, said Belinsky in a letter to Turgenev, the sketch "Khor and Kalinych" showed Turgenev's "true forte."[10] In the final analysis, however, Belinsky left no significant critical writing about Turgenev, and his views had no appreciable influence on the poetry and short stories that Turgenev produced during Belinsky's sadly short life. In his novels, however, whose appearance Belinsky did not live to see, Turgenev clearly heeded Belinsky's implicit demand for a socially conscious art. Turgenev admitted as much when he dedicated his supreme novelistic achievement, *Fathers and Sons,* to Belinsky.

While Belinsky distinguished art from bald propaganda, such was not the case with his spiritual progeny of the 1850s and 1860s, Nikolay Chernyshevsky (1828–89), Nikolay Dobrolyubov (1836–61), and Dmitry Pisarev (1840–68), who lacked Belinsky's grounding in German idealism. The evolution of the radicals' views on art, from the stingy utilitarianism propounded by Chernyshevsky in his notorious M.A. thesis, "The Aesthetic Relation between Art and Reality," to the wholesale destruction of aesthetics undertaken by Pisarev, follows an ascending curve of violence to the very concept of art as a legitimate form of human expression. Chernyshevsky launched the assault on art by declaring it at best a substitute for reality, and Pisarev brought the naive savagery to a simple-minded logical conclusion by declaring chemists always more useful than poets.

The arrival of the radicals on the literary scene in the late 1850s produced a dramatic change in the critical reception of Turgenev's works. Until then his stories and novels had garnered generally admiring reviews, but as a consequence of the radicalization of educated Russian society, Turgenev's works suddenly became the subject of vituperative polemical articles. Chernyshevsky's major contribution to the fray, a review of the story "Asya" (1858), bore the title "A Russian at the *Rendezvous.*"[11] Although Chernyshevsky sometimes showed himself capable of genuine insights into specific works of literature, especially Tolstoy's trilogy, *Childhood, Boyhood,* and *Youth,* "A Russian at the *Rendezvous*" sheds no light at all on Turgenev's story. Instead, in a manner typical of Russian literary criticism at its most irrelevant, this classic article uses Turgenev's utterly apolitical story as an opportunity to flail liberals in general and Turgenev in particular.

René Wellek points out that Chernyshevsky's junior colleague and protégé, Dobrolyubov, applied Chernyshevsky's views on aesthetics more systematically than did the senior critic himself.[12] As a consequence, Dobrolyubov occupies a position, modest, to be sure, in the evolution of a sociology of literature. In his articles he often dwelt on the differences between two generations of the Russian intelligentsia: the men of the 1840s and those of the 1860s. In Dobrolyubov's opinion, the representatives of Turgenev's generation suffered from a fatal attraction to endless and pointless philosophizing, while the radicals of the 1860s felt that the time had come to translate words into acts. In just that spirit Dobrolyubov wrote his most famous piece on Turgenev, a review of the novel *On the Eve* bearing the title "When Will the Real Day Come?"[13]

The hero of *On the Eve*, Insarov, is a Bulgarian freedom fighter. Reading Turgenev's novel as a documentary record of social history,

Dobrolyubov accuses Turgenev's generation of an inability to produce men of action and resolve such as Insarov. In a passage that invites interpretation as a call to revolution, Dobrolyubov predicts the imminent appearance of a Russian Insarov:

> We shall not have to wait long for him; the feverishly painful impatience with which we are expecting his appearance in real life is the guarantee of this. We need him; without him our lives seem to be wasted, and every day means nothing in itself, but is only the eve of another day. That day will come at last! At all events, the eve is never far from the next day; only a matter of one night separates them. (226)

Of the radical critics of the 1850s and 1860s who addressed themselves to Turgenev's works, Pisarev alone demonstrated genuine insight. For all his usual extremism and iconoclasm, Pisarev's "Realists" and "Bazarov," both about *Fathers and Sons,* offer observations about the novel and its protagonists that even today may be accepted almost without reservation.[14] Pisarev understands, for instance, that as personalities, the nihilist Bazarov and the aristocrat Pavel Petrovich "are made of the same material."[15] More importantly, Pisarev sees what escaped many of his contemporaries—that the question of where Turgenev's sympathies lie in the novel lacks a pat answer.

All in all, in fact, Pisarev's articles on *Fathers and Sons* rank among the best nineteenth-century criticism of the work. Nevertheless, it should be noted that by their very perspicacity, "Realists" and "Bazarov" represent an exception within Pisarev's oeuvre, most of which sacrifices profundity for effect. Generally speaking, the radicals' criticism of Turgenev tells one much more about Russian cultural history than about Turgenev's works. However, an acquaintance with Chernyshevsky's and Dobrolyubov's otherwise irrelevant pieces on Turgenev serves as a valuable introduction to twentieth-century Turgenev criticism, much of which either continues the traditions of civic criticism or, conversely, rejects them in a frankly polemical manner.

The refusal to treat Turgenev's works as sociopolitical documents had its advocates among Turgenev's own contemporaries. By concentrating on Turgenev's stories of the 1850s and 1860s, the most important of the aesthetic critics, Alexander Druzhinin (1824–64), Vasily Botkin (1810–69), and Pavel Annenkov (1812–87)—all friends of Turgenev's—tried to divorce his art from politics. Druzhinin's major effort in that direction, the long article *"Stories and Tales by I. Turgenev"* (1857), attempts to counter earlier readings of Turgenev by radical critics or critics close to the radicals. Drawing on the nineteenth-century cliché that inanely dubbed Alexander Pushkin (1799–1837) an art-for-art's sake poet devoid of a civic conscience and Nikolay Gogol (1809–52) a nitty-gritty realist, Druzhinin maintains that critics writing before him

> . . . see a realist artist in the most charming idealist and dreamer
> who has ever appeared among us. They hail a creator of objective
> works in a person full of lyricism and impetuous, uneven subjectivity
> in his art. They dream of a continuer of Gogol in a person raised
> on Pushkin's poetry and too poetic to seriously tackle the role of
> anyone's continuer. . . . They expected from him what he could
> not give; they were not satisfied with what of his could and should
> have given true pleasure. . . .[16]

In Druzhinin's conception, then, Turgenev emerges as a pure artist unsullied by and unsuited for any sociopolitical orientation.

Annenkov shares with Druzhinin a determination to disassociate Turgenev's art from any burning social issues. In spite of the title of his "About Thought in Works of Fiction (Remarks on the Latest Works of Turgenev and Tolstoy)" (1855), Annenkov's article in fact analyzes Turgenev's poetics. Focusing on the stories from the 1850s, Annenkov distinguishes a new subtlety in Turgenev's art, a transformation that Turgenev himself was to describe as a move away from his "old manner" to "a new one." Annenkov finds the growing sophistication of Turgenev's narrative technique especially apparent in rounded characterization, gentle humor, and all-embracing lyricism.[17] Annenkov's observation has since become a cliché of Turgenev criticism, as has the remark, made in another article from 1855, that Turgenev's lyricism bears comparison with that of the poet Fyodor Tyutchev (1803–73): "He [Turgenev] is a poet of the sun, summer, and only somewhat of autumn, just like Mr. Tyutchev, with whom he has much in common in his view of nature and his understanding of it."[18]

Unlike aesthetic critics such as Druzhinin and Annenkov, who rejected the notion of Turgenev as an ideological writer, conservative critics did not dispute the radicals' contention that Turgenev's works encapsulated specific ideas and ideologies. The most important of these conservative critics, Apollon Grigoriev (1822–64) and Nikolay Strakhov (1828–95), represented a school of thought known as *pochvennichestvo*. This term, created from the Russian word *pochva*, "soil," lacks any reasonable English equivalent but suggests links both with nature and with one's native soil. Attempting to reconcile Westernizing and Slavophile strands in Russian culture, the theorists of *pochvennichestvo*, who included Dostoevsky, drew on Belinsky's organic view of aesthetics, itself a heritage of German idealism, in their conception of a work of art as a biological organism of sorts, and of art in general as a way of understanding life and the world.[19]

Despite its considerable longueurs, Grigoriev's classic *"A Nest of Gentlefolk* by Ivan Turgenev" remains one of the most insightful nineteenth-century articles on the writer.[20] In charting the evolution of Turgenev's art, Grigoriev identifies important early influences on the writer, especially romanticism and the so-called natural school. Of the Russian romantics, Grigoriev points to Mikhail Lermontov and his hero Pechorin, from the novel *A Hero of Our Time* (1840), as especially significant sources of inspiration for Turgenev. The natural school, its role, and, indeed, its very existence, have become topics open to considerable debate among twentieth-century scholars and critics. Nonetheless, for Grigoriev the term clearly refers to Russian writers of the 1840s whose works echoed Gogol's. First among them, at least as far as posterity is concerned, is Dostoevsky, and Grigoriev anticipated twentieth-century scholarship that has drawn attention to the links between Turgenev's early works and Dostoevsky's.

The ideologist in Grigoriev comes to the fore when he analyzes Lavretsky, the hero of *A Nest of Gentlefolk*. In Grigoriev's treatment, Lavretsky's return from abroad to his family estate represents an instance of *pochvennichestvo* in action. All in all, Grigoriev sees Lavretsky as an authentic and positive Russian type. Both conservative and radical critics indulged in a nearly fanatical pursuit of positive heroes in works of literature, by the way, and they bequeathed this naive but potentially dangerous sport to socialist realism and its commentators.

Strakhov made his most important contribution to Turgenev criticism with a brilliant analysis of *Fathers and Sons* originally published in Dostoevsky's journal *Time*.[21] In his lengthy review, Strakhov insists that Turgenev's poetic novel treats life, not politics, that it rises out of the particular to address the universal. Strakhov does not deny that Turgenev's poetry has ideological overtones, however. True to *pochvennichestvo*, Strakhov sees *Fathers and Sons* as a dramatization of the triumph of living life over arid theory: "Turgenev stands for the eternal foundations of human life, for those basic elements which may perpetually change their forms, but in essence always remain unchanged."[22] Here Strakhov admires both Turgenev's artistry and his ideological commitments, but that was not always so. Elsewhere Strakhov applauds the novelist's talent but deplores his Westernizing Weltanschauung.[23]

The division of critics into radicals, aesthetes and conservatives reflects the overheated political climate of the 1860s. In that decade and atmosphere, Turgenev's determination to remain an ostensibly objective artist-observer made him enemies on virtually all sides. The publication of *Fathers and Sons* in 1862, a novel now generally regarded as one of the supreme masterpieces of Russian literature, spelled the end of Turgenev's popularity in Russia for nearly two decades, until the very last years of his life.

While Turgenev's reputation suffered in his homeland, however, it gained considerably abroad. Turgenev in fact was gaining an international following—the first Russian writer ever to do so. In 1869, writing to Pyotr Vasiliev, the compiler of *A Bibliographical Note on Translations of I. S. Turgenev's Works into Foreign Languages* (Kazan, 1868), Turgenev noted:

> Almost everything that I have written has been translated into *French,* under various titles. Besides *Notes of a Hunter, A Nest of Gentlefolk,* about ten stories, as well as *Smoke,* have been translated into German; the bookseller Behre in Riga has begun an edition of selected works of mine—the first volume includes *Fathers and Sons,* the second—"An Unfortunate Girl" and three other stories. *Notes of a Hunter, Smoke, Fathers and Sons,* and *A Nest of Gentlefolk,* have been translated into *English. . . . Smoke* and *Fathers and Sons* have been translated into *Dutch; Smoke, A Nest of Gentlefolk,* and several stories—into *Swedish;* a few stories have been translated into *Czech, Serbian,* and Hungarian. I have also been informed that *Notes of a Hunter* has been translated into *Spanish* and will soon be published. . . .[24]

Toward the end of his life, Turgenev was gratified to see his reputation in Russia recover. By the late 1870s, Russian readers, critics, and the public in general reacted to his person and works at least with respect, and often with exaltation. On his visits to Russia in 1879, 1880, and 1881, Turgenev found large, enthusiastic crowds turning out for his readings. Upon his death, commentators both at home and abroad mourned the passing of one of the very greatest writers of the age.

In France, where Turgenev had enjoyed cordial relations with the literary community, especially in the last two decades of his life, Melchior de Vogüé's *Le roman russe* (1886) served to alert the non-Russian world in general to the virtues of Russian novelists, Turgenev not the least among them. The French critic especially admired the compassion that Turgenev demonstrated in his works and which seemed so lacking in French works of the era.[25] Writing at approximately the same time, Paul Bourget, in his *Essais de psychologie contemporaine,* generally agreed with de Vogüé about the essential healthiness of Turgenev's literary world. True, Bourget saw Turgenev as disillusioned, weak-willed, and pessimistic, but not decadent and despairing.[26]

In the Anglophone world, the evolution of American and English critical attitudes toward Turgenev displayed an affinity to the contrapuntal pattern known as contrary motion. The elevation of Turgenev to the ranks of the classics occurred first of all thanks to American critics. As Royal Gettmann has demonstrated, until the mid-1880s, English critics either remained indifferent to Turgenev or treated his writings not as works of literature but as sources of documentary information about Russian life.[27] Meanwhile, in the United States, critics took an intense interest in Turgenev from the early 1870s on. Gettmann observes: "They approached the novels . . . as serious, artistic narratives. . . . In the effort to refine public taste and to raise the level of fiction, a group of writers associated with W. D. Howells deduced from the works of Turgenev a form of the novel they called 'dramatic.' This anticipated in several respects—withdrawal of the author, singleness of theme, restriction of time and place—the 'well-made' or 'dramatic novel' described by Percy Lubbock and J. W. Beach" (185).[28] Adding to the American chorus of praise for a great realist, Henry James, in the 1880s and 1890s, published several famous appreciations of Turgenev. Summing up his art, which James admired for its subtle combination of moral vigor and refined technique, James wrote: "Turgenev is in a peculiar degree what I may call the novelists' novelist,—an artistic influence extraordinarily valuable and ineradicably established."[29]

In spite of the advocacy of such an influential figure as James, however, Turgenev's reputation in the United States began to slip from the 1890s on, as the novels of his great contemporaries—first Tolstoy, then Dostoevsky—became generally known. Meanwhile, in England, as though to make up for earlier ill-use, and no doubt taking the lead from James, critics and fellow novelists created a veritable Turgenev cult. To quote Gettmann again: "The English were compelled to admit the sickly condition of their fiction, and they could no longer deny the existence of French realism. Using Turgenev as a shield against the French, the English moved toward what I have called the post-Victorian compromise—an ideal which accommodated Flaubert's care for art with Russian concern for the spirit" (186). As examples of the reverence with which Turgenev was treated, one might cite Arnold Bennett, who applauded Turgenev for having "uttered the last word of pure artistry,"[30] or Ford Madox Ford, who opined: "We are pretty certain that Turgenev was greater than Shakespeare . . . his characters are more human than Shakespeare's were."[31]

In the years following World War I, the English at last joined in the reappraisal long since under way in America. Turgenev was measured against other Russian writers and found wanting. Often asking of him and his art what neither could give or even intended to, critics expressed doubts about Turgenev's reliability as a social historian, a hunger for richer subject matter, and objections to Turgenev's pessimism.

A reevaluation of Turgenev's art by Russian critics paralleled the one that occurred abroad. This reorientation was accomplished in two stages, both of which went against the traditional notion of

Turgenev as a realist concerned with depicting Russian social reality. In the first, critics and writers associated with the turn-of-the-century phenomenon known in Russian cultural history as decadence or symbolism, claimed Turgenev as their own.[32] In a famous programmatic article, "On the Reasons for the Decline of and the New Currents in Contemporary Russian Literature" (1893), Merezhkovsky identified three basic elements of the new art—mystical content, symbols, and a wider vision of reality—that are foreshadowed in Turgenev's works.[33] The poet Konstantin Balmont declared that symbolist poetry owed its primary inspiration to Turgenev:

> The path from Pushkin to the refined and tender poetry of our days runs not so much through Lermontov and Nekrasov, not so much even through the sternly nocturnal Tyutchev and the starry-glowing Fet, as precisely through Turgenev, who educated our language, our singing reverie, who taught us to understand, through beautiful lover, that the best and truest essence . . . in art is the Maiden-Woman.[34]

Other critics noted an affinity between symbolist prose and Turgenev's *Poems in Prose* and so-called mysterious tales. In general, symbolism and decadence proclaimed Turgenev a kindred spirit by focusing on his stories and ignoring the novels.

The second stage of reorientation came with Russian Formalism, a school of criticism that came to the fore at approximately the time of World War I and exerted an overwhelming influence on Russian criticism until the mid-1930s.[35] Generally speaking, the Formalists went against the nineteenth-century tradition of literary criticism as civic-minded journalism. In place of politicized commentary more or less totally divorced from the text, the Formalists hoped to forge an exact science based on close—even microscopic—attention to the text. In the process, the Formalists made many important contributions to the fields of literary theory, literary history, comparative literature, and the sociology of literature. In the case of Turgenev criticism, the Formalists and critics closely allied to the Formalists adopted a frankly polemical stance toward one of the most sacred tenets of nineteenth-century Turgenev criticism by flatly denying that Turgenev pursued political goals in his art. Having attempted to sweep that notion aside, Formalist critics went on to produce landmark studies of Turgenev's technique in the novel and short story and magisterial works on Turgenev's place in the evolution of Russian and European literature.

In the years since World War II Turgenev criticism, both in the Soviet Union and abroad, has proceeded along the parallel tracks of formal analysis and more or less traditional literary scholarship. The formal studies have forced a reappraisal of the nature of Turgenev's realism and an accompanying reinterpretation of many of this works. Scholars have made tremendous strides in the areas of textology and biography. The major achievements in this regard are the *two* complete editions of Turgenev works and letters undertaken by Leningrad's Institute of Russian Literature (Pushkin House), the first completed in 1968, the second in progress. Such scholarly largesse is entirely unprecedented, even for the Soviet Union. It testifies, however, to the continuing vitality of Turgenev criticism and scholarship in the late twentieth century. Turgenev's reputation may not be what it once was, but to judge by both the quantity and the quality of criticism published in the major European languages over the last few decades, the awareness that Turgenev is not a Tolstoy or a Dostoevsky has hardly spelled an end to the attraction that one of Russia's finest artists holds for critics. On the contrary, the healthy state of Turgenev criticism merely confirms the accuracy of Mirsky's assessment that it is "impossible to imagine a time when 'The Singers,' 'A Quiet Spot,' 'First Love,' or *Fathers and Sons* will cease to be among the most cherished of joys to Russian readers" (208). One can only assume that Mirsky did not consciously intend to exclude non-Russians from the ranks of Turgenev's future admirers, because as we approach the twenty-first century, Turgenev's appeal has never seemed more univeral and timeless.

Vanderbilt University   DAVID A. LOWE

Notes

1. D. S. Merezhkovsky, "Turgenev," vol. 18, *Polnoe sobranie sochinenii* (Moscow: Sytin, 1914), 58; hereafter cited in the text.

2. V. Arkhipov, "K tvorcheskoy istorii romana I. S. Turgeneva *Ottsy i deti*," *Russkaya literatura* 1 (1958):132–62. For a discussion of Arkhipov's article and published responses to it by Soviet critics and scholars, see Zbigniew Folejewski, "The Recent Storm around Turgenev as a Point in Soviet Aesthetics," *Slavic and East European Journal* 6, no. 1 (1962):21–27.

3. See D. S. Mirsky, *A History of Russian Literature*, ed. Francis J. Whitfield (New York: Knopf, 1958), 207; hereafter cited in the text.

4. Irving Howe, "Turgenev: The Politics of Hesitation," in *Politics and the Novel* (New York: Horizon Press, 1957), 129–33.

5. Ye. Yefimov, *I. S. Turgenev: Seminar* (Leningrad: Gosuchpedizdat, 1958), 131.

6. A. S. Pushkin, *Polnoe sobranie sochinenii*, vol. 10 (Moscow: AN SSSR, 1956–58), 145.

7. I. S. Turgenev, *Polnoe sobranie sochinenii i pisem*, vol. 14 (Moscow-Leningrad: AN SSSR, 1960–68), 52; hereafter cited in text.

8. See Turgenev, vol. 1, 506, 515.

9. See Turgenev, vol. 4, 494, 511.

10. V. G. Belinsky, *Polnoe sobranie sochinenii*, vol. 12 (Moscow: AN SSSR, 1956), 336.

11. An English translation of Chernyshevsky's "A Russian at the *Rendez-vous*" is

included in Belinsky, Chernyshevsky, and Dobrolyubov, *Selected Criticism,* ed. Ralph Matlaw (New York: Dutton, 1962), 108–29.

12. René Wellek, *A History of Modern Criticism,* vol. 4, (New Haven, Conn.: Yale University Press, 1965), 249.

13. An English translation of Dobrolyubov's "When Will the Real Day Come?" may be found in Belinsky, Chernyshevsky, and Dobrolyubov, 176–226; hereafter cited in the text.

14. A substantial excerpt from "Bazarov," translated into English by Lydia Hooke, may be found in Ivan Turgenev, *Fathers and Sons,* edited with a substantially new translation by Ralph Matlaw (New York: Norton, 1966), 195–218.

15. D. I. Pisarev, "Realisty," in *Bazarov; Reality* (Moscow: Khodozhestvennaya literatura, 1974), 109.

16. Alexander Druzhinin, *"Povesti i rasskazy I. Turgeneva," Sobranie sochinenni,* vol. 7 (St. Petersburg: Tip. Imp. Akademii nauk, 1865–67), 288.

17. See Pavel Annenkov, "O mysli v proizvedeniyakh izyashchnoy slovesnostyi (Zametki po povodu poslednikh proizvendenii g. Turgeneva i. L. N. T.)," *Sovremennik* (1855): section 3, 10–11.

18. Annenkov, in *Sovremennik* no. 1 (1855), quoted in *Sobranie kriticheskikh materialov dlya izucheniya proizvedenii I. S. Turgeneva* vol. 1, ed. V. Zelinsky (Moscow: Tipografiya Malinskogo, 1884), 111. For Annenkov in English, see the memoirs *The Extraordinary Decade,* ed. Arthur Mendel, trans. Irwin Titunik (Ann Arbor: University of Michigan Press, 1968), and the 1858 article "The Literary Type of the Weak Man (Apropos of Turgenev's Story 'Asya')," trans. Tatiana Goerner, *Ulbandus Review* 1, no. 1 (Fall 1977):90–104, and 2, no. 2 (Spring 1978):74–85.

19. On Belinsky, Grigoriev, and Strakhov as organic critics, see Victor Terras, *Belinskij and Russian Literary Criticism: The Heritage of Organic Aesthetics* (Madison: University of Wisconsin Press, 1974), 99.

20. Apollon Grigoriev, *"Dvoryanskoe gnezdo I. S. Turgeneva, " Russkoe slovo,* nos. 4, 5, 6, 8 (1859); for an English translation, see A. A. Grigor'ev, "A Nest of Gentlefolk by Ivan Turgenev," in *Literature and National Identity,* trans. and ed. by Paul Debreczeny and Jesse Zeldin (Lincoln: University of Nebraska Press, 1970), 65–118.

21. Nikolay Strakhov, *"Ottsy i deti," Vremya* no. 4 (1862); for a substantial excerpt from the article, in an English translation by Ralph Matlaw, see Turgenev, *Fathers and Sons,* 218–29.

22. Strakhov, quoted in *O Turgenev: Russkaya i inostrannaya kritika,* ed. P. P. Pertsov (Moscow: Kooperativnoe izd., 1918), 42–43.

23. The best treatment of Strakhov in English is Linda Gerstein, *Nikolai Strakhov* (Cambridge, Mass.: Harvard University Press, 1971).

24. I.S. Turgenev, *Polnoe sobranie sochinenii i pisem* (Moscow-Leningrad: Nauka, 1960–68), *Pisma* 8, no. 55. See p. 430 of the same volume for bibliographical information about the translations.

25. Melchior de Vogüé, *Le roman russe* (Paris: Plon-nourrit, 1886), 133–202.

26. Paul Bourget, "Ivan Tourguénev,"*Nouveaux Essais de Psychologie contemporaine* (Paris: A. Lemerre, 1886), 199–250.

27. Royal Gettmann, "Turgenev in England and America," *Illinois Studies in Language and Literature* 27, no.2 (1941); 185; hereafter cited in the text. For my remarks on English-language Turgenev criticism I have drawn extensively on the excellent study Gettmann compiled with Rissa Yachnin and David Stam, *Turgenev in English: A Checklist of Works by and about Him,* introduction by Marc Slonim (New

York: New York Public Library, 1962); Allan Urbanic and Barbara Urbanic, "Ivan Turgenev: A Bibliography of Criticism in English, 1960–83," *Canadian-American Slavic Studies* 17, no. 1 (Spring 1983); 118–43; and Donald Davie, "Turgenev in England, 1850–1950," in *Studies in Russian and Polish Literature in Honor of Waclaw Lednicki,* Zbigniew Folejewski et al. (The Hague: Mouton, 1962), 168–84.

28. For a detailed discussion of Howell's views on Turgenev, see Gettmann, "Turgenev in England," 53–61.

29. Quoted in Gettmann, "Turgenev in England," 131. For an extensive treatment of James's evaluation of Turgenev and of Turgenev's influence on the American novelist, see Gettmann, 66–77, and Dale Peterson, *The Clement Vision: Poetic Realism in Turgenev and James* (Longon; Pt. Washington, N.Y. Kennikat, 1975).

30. *Academy* 57 (4 November 1899); 516; quoted in Gettmann, "Turgenev in England," 156.

31. Ford Madox Ford, *The Critical Attitude* (London: Duckworth, 1911), 156–58; quoted in Gettmann, "Turgenev in England," 165.

32. For a detailed study of Turgenev's links to symbolism, see Marina Ledkovsky, *The Other Turgenev: From Romanticism to Symbolism* (Würzburg: Jal-Verlag, 1972), 125–38, to which I am greatly indebted for my own remarks on Turgenev and symbolism.

33. Merezhkovsky, *Polnoe Sobranie Sochinenii,* Vol. 12, 249.

34. Konstantin Balmont, "Rytsar Devushki-Zhenshchiny," in N.L. Brosksy, ed. *Turgenev i ego vremya* (Moscow-Leningrad: Gosizdat, 1923), 16–17.

35. The most important English-language studies of Russian formalism are Victor Erlich, *Russian Formalism: History and Doctrine* (The Hague: Mouton, 1969); Krystyna Pomorska, *Russian Formalist Theory and its Poetic Ambiance* (The Hague: Mouton, 1968); and Ewa Thompson, *Russian Formalism and Anglo-American New Criticism* (The Hague: Mouton, 1971).

Biographical Sketch   David A. Lowe

Ivan Sergeevich Turgenev, the second of Varvara Petrovna (neé Lutovinova) and Sergey Nikolaevich Turgenev's three children, all sons, was born on 9 November 1818, in Oryol.[1] Through his father Turgenev could trace his roots to Russia's ancient nobility; thanks to his mother a substantial inheritance would eventually fall to him. Both his parents exercised a strong and often perverse will that made for a tempestuous home life. Tradition holds that Turgenev's overbearing parents traumatized the boy irrevocably, sowing in him the seeds of chronic passivity and indecisiveness. One need not necessarily accept this view, especially if one has doubts about the claims of child psychology and certainly if one realizes that throughout his life Turgenev tenaciously pursued his own perceived best interests.

In 1821 Turgenev's father moved the family to Varvara Petrovna's estate at Spasskoe, a village not far from Mtsensk (a city in Oryol province). That remained the Turgenevs' primary residence until 1827, although in the years 1822–23 the family undertook a grand tour of Western Europe. Life at Spasskoe, with Varvara Petrovna's 5,000 serfs, proceeded on a scale of luxury that largely defies the twentieth-century imagination. All was not sugar and spice, however, for both with her sons and with her serfs Varvara Petrovna demonstrated an alarming capacity for psychopathic caprice and cruelty. Turgenev's implacable hatred for the institution of serfdom as well as for all forms of violence probably dates from his childhood at Spasskoe.

Turgenev received his primary education at home, at the hands of a large and odd assortment of tutors. Not too surprisingly, he read voraciously, feasting on now-forgotten classics of eighteenth-century Russian literature and on such then-contemporary Russian preromantics and romantics as Nikolay Karamzin, Vasily Zhukovsky, and Konstantin Batyushkov. In addition, the young Turgenev read Dickens, Bulwer Lytton, and the English romantic poets—all apparently in the original. (Turgenev learned French, German, English, Greek, and Latin as a child. In later life he added Polish, Spanish, and Italian to his staggering arsenal of languages.) As twentieth-century scholarship and criticism are beginning to make clear, for all his renown as a realist, Turgenev never really abandoned the romantic ethos that informed much of his childhood reading.

Early in 1827 the Turgenevs moved to Moscow, presumably in the interest of their sons' formal education. Turgenev studied at home and at various boarding schools until the fall of 1833, when he gained admittance to Moscow University. Appropriately enough, he enrolled as a student in the literature department. Although his fellow students included such future friends and intellectual luminaries as Alexander Herzen and Nikolay Stankevich, Turgenev seems not to have known them at the time. Indeed, Moscow University hardly impressed him, and when the family moved to Saint Petersburg, Turgenev soon followed suit.

In the fall of 1834 Turgenev entered the University of Saint Petersburg, where he studied history and philology. Two major events occurred in his life that autumn. First, his father died, leaving Turgenev and his brothers entirely dependent upon their mother and subject to her whims. Second, Turgenev completed his first serious bit of writing, *Steno,* a mediocre narrative poem in the Byronic mode that did not see the light of day until well after Turgenev's death.

While a student at the University of Saint Petersburg Turgenev had the good fortune to see his idol Alexander Pushkin twice, once at the home of Pyotr Pletnyov, who lectured on Russian literature at the university. In addition, Turgenev attended the premiere of Nikolay Gogol's comedy *The Inspector General* and later left an eyewitness account of the same author's brief, ludicrous tenure as a professor of history at the University of Saint Petersburg. All this time Turgenev lived at home with his mother, with whom relations were already strained.

In 1837, Turgenev graduated from the University of Saint Petersburg with the equivalent of a bachelor's degree. He and his mother then moved back to Spasskoe, where on more than one occasion he defended the estate serfs from Varvara Petrovna's wanton cruelty. Given his mother's character, Turgenev quite understandably had no desire to remain long at Spasskoe. In 1838, having obtained his mother's permission to study philosophy in Berlin for two years, he set out for Western Europe. With the exception of a few months spent in Russia in 1839, Turgenev remained abroad until 1841.

Already during his first stay in Western Europe one of the central traits of Turgenev's biography emerges: although his life did not abound in dramatic events as such, it was rich in friendships (often turning into quarrels) with some of the most remarkable personalities of the age. Of the people with whom he became close in the years 1838–41, both in Berlin and while travelling through Germany and Italy, perhaps no one had a greater influence on Turgenev than Stankevich.[2] One of the most charismatic intellectuals of his generation, he presided over a German idealist philosophical circle in Moscow. (The question of whether Turgenev and Stankevich knew each other before Stankevich went to Berlin in 1838 remains unresolved.) The force of Stankevich's personality seems to have made Turgenev shed much of his flippancy and gain interest in serious philosophical issues. Stankevich's death in 1840 quite shattered Turgenev. Several of Turgenev's other friends, associates, and heroes also died young, before they could fulfill their promise. Consequently, Turgenev concluded that a malevolent fate doomed talented young Russians to an early demise. Turgenev later dramatized that notion in several of his works.

In Berlin Turgenev often spent time with Karl Werder, an exponent of the philosophy of Georg Wilhelm Friedrich Hegel, and with Bettina von Arnim, whose claim to fame—beyond her salon— lay in her having had a juvenile affair with Johann Wolfgang von Goethe. Turgenev's closest friend in Berlin, however, proved to be none other than Mikhail Bakunin, the future anarchist. They shared lodgings and a fascination with Hegelian philosophy. In his first novel, *Rudin,* Turgenev would use his former roommate as the prototype for the title character.

At the University of Berlin Turgenev studied history, classics, and philosophy. His enthusiasm for German idealism and its jargon eventually turned into ironic bemusement, but in 1841 he felt sufficiently attracted to the subject matter to return to Russia to prepare seriously for his master's examination. Upon arriving back in Russia, Turgenev immediately headed for Moscow, and soon thereafter he and his mother traveled together to Spasskoe. During that summer of 1841 Turgenev entered into a liaison with Avdotya Yermolaevna Ivanova, one of his mother's serfs. Several years passed, however, before he took any interest in Polina (Paulinette), the daughter born of that brief and loveless union.

Turgenev's relations with women were not always so casual, however. Having no difficulties in attracting the opposite sex, Turgenev entered upon a series of romantic affairs throughout his life. With one grand exception, though, Turgenev backed out of these attachments. Since much of Turgenev's personal experience was transmuted into his art, it comes as no surprise that the motif of the aborted affair, of a man proving incapable of returning a woman's love, should figure prominently in Turgenev's fiction. The first such painful incident in Turgenev's life occurred in the fall of 1841, when he visited Pryamukhino, the Bakunin family estate. There he had a tentative romance with Tatyana, Mikhail's favorite sister. Turgenev ended it, abruptly and clumsily.

The winter of 1841–42 saw Turgenev in Moscow, where he led a very active social life. Curiously, the future Westernizer par excellence frequented the Slavophile circle that included such figures as the Kireevsky brothers, Yury Samarin, Konstantin Aksakov, and, on occasion, Gogol. On the whole, however, Turgenev and the Slavophiles did not really take to each other.

The mention of Slavophiles and Westernizers perhaps demands a note of explanation. These rival intellectual camps had their roots in the 1830s and 1840s and shared certain traits and convictions. Almost all of these thinkers came from the gentry, relied on philosophy and art for interpreting the world, and abhorred serfdom as well as the absence in Russia of the most elementary civil rights. In their views on Russia's past and future, however, the two groups differed fundamentally. The Slavophiles, passionately religious and antiurban, saw Peter the Great as the arch-villain of Russian history. With his importation of Western European culture and technology, the Slavophiles averred, Peter did violence to Old Russia, destroying its patriarchal, communal, and allegedly idyllic way of life.[3] To the Westernizers, however, pre-Petrine Russia seemed a barbaric wasteland. Russia's sole hope for the future, the Westernizers proclaimed, lay in the cultivation of Western European political institutions and cultural norms. In its most extreme varieties, Westernizing thought embraced socialism and revolution. Turgenev, one of the most moderate Westernizers, advocated the British constitutional monarchy as an appropriate model for Russia.

For a while Turgenev thought seriously about a university career. Finding his way to Moscow University blocked, he set his sights on the University of Saint Petersburg. There he took and passed his master's examination in philosophy in the late spring of 1842. All that stood between him and a university position now was a dissertation, but he soon recognized imaginative literature as his true calling and abandoned the idea of an academic career.

After a summer spent at Spasskoe in 1842 and a second trip to Germany in the fall of that year, Turgenev took up residence in Saint Petersburg. The time had come for him to find employment, and in 1843 he took a position with the Special Office of the Ministry of the Interior. The work attracted Turgenev because the Special Office was occupied with embyonic projects for the reform of serfdom. Government service and Turgenev hardly suited each other, and Turgenev soon found himself devoting much of his time to writing.

Until 1843 Turgenev had published only a few poems and a single book review. In the fall of that year, though, his narrative poem *Parasha* appeared. It earned praise from Vissarion Belinsky, an ardent Westernizer and undoubtedly the single most influential nineteenth-century critic of Russian letters.[4] He and Turgenev soon became close friends, and Turgenev subsequently heeded Belinsky's call for an engagé literature, at least in his novels, if rarely in his stories. Like Stankevich, Belinsky died young, and Turgenev revered the memory of the critic until his own dying days.

In the years 1843–44 Turgenev published a number of works in different genres: several lyric poems; a short play, *Carelessness*; a long poem entitled *A Conversation*; the story "Andrey Kolosov," and a lengthy review of a new translation of Goethe's *Faust*. The play, of distinctly marginal interest in and of itself, indicated that Turgenev was seeking to channel his talent in a new direction.

In the fall of 1843 an event occurred that decisively altered the course of Turgenev's life. The twenty-one-year-old Pauline Viardot came to Saint Petersburg to sing at the Imperial Opera.[5] She belonged to an extraordinary family of musicians. Her father, Manuel García, had created the role of Almaviva in Rossini's *The Barber of Seville*. Her older sister, whom her contemporaries knew as la Malibran, had a tragically short but highly celebrated career as the *prima donna assoluta* of her day. Pauline, married to the much older Louis Viardot, a French writer of some repute, added even more luster to the family name. By the time of her Saint Petersburg debut she had already conquered London with her voice and intelligence (if not with her looks, for she was a plain, some would even say even ugly woman). Germany and France would soon be applauding her deliriously too.

Turgenev made Pauline's acquaintance on a November morning in 1843. He instantly fell in love with her and for the rest of his life totally and unquestioningly subordinated his wishes to hers. At the outset Pauline probably found Turgenev's all-too-ardent admiration irritating and may well have told him so, because Turgenev inexplicably left Saint Petersburg before the end of the concert season and joined his mother in Moscow.

The Viardots returned to Saint Petersburg for the 1844 season, and Turgenev became a frequent guest of theirs, sometimes giving Pauline Russian lessons. When the Viardots traveled to Moscow in February 1845, Turgenev soon followed. There he persuaded his mother to attend one of Pauline's concerts. Varvara Petrovna's reaction was a model of terseness: "You have to admit it, that damned Gypsy sings well!"

By early 1845 Turgenev decided to go to Western Europe again, but first he had to petition the Emperor to allow him to retire from government service. Approval came quickly, and in May, in the company of the Viardots, Turgenev embarked for France. He spent the summer with the Viardots at their home in Courtavenel, where the guests included Pauline's close friend George Sand. Turgenev later recalled these months as the happiest of his entire life.

At the end of the summer Turgenev traveled through France with the critic and essayist Vasily Botkin. Toward the end of the year he returned to Saint Petersburg, where the Viardots were again installed. By this point Turgenev's friendship with Pauline had deepened into something like intimacy, the two of them having exchanged their first kisses by the end of the year. Louis Viardot seems to have tolerated Turgenev's presence quite well, and the two men in fact had shared interests in hunting and literature.

Late in 1845 Turgenev first met Fyodor Dostoevsky, another of Belinsky's protégés. Dostoevsky at first liked Turgenev very much, but by the end of the summer of the next year he had conceived a loathing for the man, probably because Turgenev had made fun of the swaggering and morbid young author. In the 1870s Turgenev and Dostoevsky were to quarrel royally, with grand consequences for Russian literature.

Turgenev passed the summer of 1846 at Spasskoe. The experience left much to be desired, since he and his mother argued endlessly—about Pauline Viardot and money, among other things. The strained relations helped Turgenev make up his mind to go abroad again, especially since the Viardots would not be returning to Saint Petersburg, whose climate they could no longer tolerate. Early in 1847 Turgenev left for Western Europe, where he remained for three years.

Turgenev initially went to Berlin, where the Viardots provided the primary attraction. In June, Belinsky, who had gone abroad for treatment of his tuberculosis, showed up on Turgenev's doorstep. The two friends soon set off for Dresden together, where the Viardots had taken up temporary residence. Turgenev forced Belinsky upon the Viardots, to no one's particular pleasure. Like most of Turgenev's

Russian friends, Belinsky resented the hold that Pauline Viardot had on her Russian admirer.

When the Viardots left Dresden, Turgenev and Belinsky made their way to Salzbrunn. When they separated in late July, Belinsky stayed to compose his famous letter attacking Gogol for the latter's *Selected Passages from a Correspondence with Friends,* a work that Belinsky deemed reactionary. Turgenev, meanwhile, went on to London, his itinerary dovetailing with that of the Viardots. By the fall he had settled in Paris, where he resided more or less uninterruptedly until 1850. In Paris and nearby Courtavenel Turgenev's life centered on the Viardots, a few Russian friends, and his writing.

During Pauline's frequent absences Turgenev remained very much in the thick of Viardot family life, addressing Pauline numerous lengthy letters. Whether he and she ever consummated their relationship remains a topic for seemingly endless speculation. No incontrovertible evidence pointing one way or the other exists, but a cryptic note in Turgenev's autobiographical "Memorial" invites one to conclude that he and Pauline may have made love on a few occasions in 1849 and 1850.

Turgenev's closest Russian friends in Paris were Alexander and Natalie Herzen.[6] He also spent time with the Herzens' friends and colleagues in radicalism, Georg and Emma Herwegh. Turgenev's former roommate, Bakunin, turned up in Paris for a few months in 1847. The two saw each other several times, although Turgenev later concealed these meetings from the Russian authorities.

Turgenev wrote a great deal in the period 1847–50. Most of the stories that make up *The Notes of a Hunter* (also known in English as *A Sportsman's Sketches*) date from this time, as does "The Diary of a Superfluous Man." In addition, Turgenev completed no fewer than five plays while in France. The most significant of them, the autobiographical *A Month in the Country* (originally entitled *The Student*), did not appear in print until 1855. The others works for the stage were *Lunch with the Marshal of the Nobility,* a one-act comedy; *It Tears Where It's Thinnest,* a longer one-act play; *Alien Bread,* a bitter two-act drama; and *The Bachelor,* a three-act comedy and the first of Turgenev's plays to tread the boards.

In 1850, for reasons not entirely clear, Turgenev decided, albeit reluctantly, to return to Russia. Scholars and biographers suggest, variously, that Pauline Viardot had declared an end to their intimacy and wished Turgenev to leave; that he felt compelled to leave because of the attention that Pauline was showing the young composer Charles Gounod; or that Turgenev somehow felt it his civic duty to go back to Russia. No one really knows what lay behind Turgenev's departure, although certainly his shaky finances make it imperative that he reach some sort of understanding with his mother. Sick at heart, Turgenev set sail for Russia.

At Spasskoe Turgenev rediscovered his daughter Polina (Paulinette), whose life until then had differed very little from that of any serf's. Pauline Viardot offered to raise the girl, and in late October 1850 Turgenev took his daughter to Saint Petersburg, from where she and a chaperone, a Madame Robert, made their way to Paris. At about the same time both Turgenev and his only surviving brother, Nikolay Sergeevich, broke with their mother as a result of her unwillingness to make any financial disposition for them. Before the end of the year, however, Varvara Petrovna died, leaving her sons a substantial inheritance. From then on Turgenev's income always sufficed for a comfortable existence, but his lax management of his affairs and his extraordinary generosity often worked separately or together to create temporary financial crises.

From 1850 until 1852 Turgenev shuttled back and forth between Moscow and Saint Petersburg. In Moscow he frequented the salon of Countess Sailhas de Tournemire, who wrote historical novels under the pen name Yevgenia Tur. Gatherings at her home provided a refuge for the liberal intelligentsia, of which Turgenev certainly counted himself a member. Turgenev also became close with the family of Sergey Aksakov, a Slavophile and the future author of *A Family Chronicle.*

In the years immediately following his return to Russia Turgenev published several stories: "Mumu," "The Inn," "Three Meetings," "The Singers," and "A Meeting." The last two became part of the canon of *The Notes of a Hunter.* At the request of the actress Vera Samoylova, Turgenev wrote a play, *The Provincial Lady,* which to his surprise and pleasure turned out to be a success with the public. After 1851, however, Turgenev abandoned writing for the stage, returning to the dramatic genre only much later, when he composed French-language libretti for operettas set to music by Pauline Viardot.

In March 1852 Gogol died. Turgenev, crushed by this loss to Russian literaturre, wrote an obituary that the Saint Petersburg censor refused to pass. Nikolay I ruled Russia with the proverbial iron fist in the late 1840s and early 1850s, and all mention of Gogol in print had been forbidden. Turgenev nobly but unwisely sent the obituary to friends in Moscow, asking them to try to arrange for its publication there. For neither the first nor the last time in Russian literary history, the right hand of the censorship did not know what the left was doing, and the obituary soon appeared in print. Retribution struck swiftly. The authorities put Turgenev under arrest on 28 April 1852 and exiled him to Spasskoe a month later.

Turgenev's confinement to his estate did not prevent the first publication of the collection *Notes of a Hunter,* in August 1852. The

book, which most readers interpreted as a subtle indictment of serfdom, enjoyed an unqualified success and firmly established Turgenev
as a front-rank Russian author. In later life Turgenev maintained that
the publication of *Notes of a Hunter* provoked his arrest and exile,
but the facts contradict that interpretation of events.

Life in exile did not lack comforts and pleasures. Turgenev spent
much of the time hunting, playing chess, listening to music, and
reading. He missed his close friends, however, and especially Pauline
Viardot. Indeed, for her sake he risked prison and indefinite exile
by using forged documents to make a secret trip to Moscow to see
her in April 1853. Thanks to the intercession of friends in high place,
exile came to an end in December 1853, when Turgenev received
notification that he could now travel freely and live in Moscow or
Saint Petersburg, if he pleased. He left Spasskoe within the month.

By late December 1853 Turgenev had arrived in Saint Petersburg.
There he counted among his friends and colleagues a group of writers
associated with the journal *The Contemporary,* founded by Pushkin
in 1836 and now managed by Ivan Panaev and Nikolay Nekrasov.
The writers who allied themselves with the journal included Pavel
Annenkov, who was one of Turgenev's closest friends and his most
trusted literary advisor, Botkin, Dmitry Grigorovich, Alexander Druzhinin, Ivan Goncharov, who was the future author of *Oblomov,* and
the young Lev Tolstoy. Not all of these writers fulfilled their early
promise, but still and all, they represented a formidable array of talent.[7]

In the years 1854–56 Turgenev continued writing short stories,
as indeed he did for the rest of his life. Narratives dating from this
period include "Faust," for whose overly impressionable heroine
Tolstoy's sister, Countess Maria Tolstaya, provided the model; "A
Quiet Spot," whose tragic events belie the title; and "Yakov Pasynkov," a tribute to such figures of the 1840s as Stankevich and
Belinsky. Now, however, Turgenev yearned to break with what he
called his "old manner" and to attempt a novel. In fact, in 1853 he
had completed three parts of a projected large work with the evocative
title "Two Generations." Friends who read the work in manuscript
found the writing pale in spots, and Turgenev eventually destroyed
all but one chapter and an early outline of the novel.

The turning point came with Turgenev's first completed novel,
Rudin, which he finished in 1855 but which did not appear in print
until 1856. Turgenev's original intention had been to satirize Bakunin
in the title character, but in late 1855 the Russian authorities had
arranged for the extradition of Bakunin and imprisoned him in the
Schlüsselburg Fortress. This state of affairs moved Turgenev to add
to his novel an anachronistic epilogue in which the hero acquires a
belated tragic aura.

The Crimean War had broken out in 1853, and as long as it

dragged on, Turgenev could only dream of joining the Viardots and his daughter. By April 1856, however, negotiations had resulted in a peace treaty and the authorities granted Turgenev's request for a passport for travel abroad. A few months later he set sail from Saint Petersburg for Western Europe.

Perhaps by way of celebrating his newfound freedom, or perhaps as a consequence of melancholy wanderlust, for the next few years Turgenev crisscrossed Europe, spending time, alternately, in London, Spasskoe, Berlin, and Rome. Herzen's residence in London gave Turgenev reason enough to visit that capital. Moreover, Turgenev's English acquaintances included the likes of Carlyle, Thackeray, and Macaulay. Over the years Turgenev's respect and admiration for the British grew steadily, and in time they paid him the compliment of responding warmly to his works.[8]

Turgenev passed the fall of 1856 with the Viardots at Courtavenel. This made for a supremely happy time for him, although in general he suffered from depression during the late 1850s and the early 1860s. To begin with, uncertainty about his abilities as a writer gnawed at him. As a matter of fact, from the 1850s on, threats to retire from literature become a regular motif in Turgenev's letters to friends, especially to Annenkov. The lack of a genuine family life, of his own "nest," as he called it, also grieved Turgenev. True, he had his daughter Paulinette, who was fourteen years old at the time of his arrival in Paris in 1856. His letters to her and about her, however, show that Turgenev did not feel any authentic affection for her. Their characters differed too greatly, and Paulinette's hostility toward Pauline Viardot, her legal guardian in Turgenev's absence, necessarily produced tension in the relations between father and daughter as well.

In the late 1850s a distinct chilliness in Pauline Viardot's treatment of him undoubtedly distressed Turgenev more than did anything else. His letters to her from the period breathe the same adoration as earlier, but meetings between the two became infrequent. Pauline was keeping Turgenev at a distance, both literally and figuratively.

In the summer of 1858 Turgenev returned to Russia and remained there ten months. Half the time he occupied himself with writing at Spasskoe. His recently finished story "Asya" had appeared in the January issue of *The Contemporary*, and he was entering into the most productive phase of his career. Work on his next major project, the novel *A Nest of Gentlefolk*, coincided with the peak of his friendship with the Countess Yelizaveta Lambert. The two seemingly had little in common, what with the Countess's profound religiosity, her association with the highest circles of Saint Petersburg society, and her philistine taste in literature. For all that, Turgenev sincerely liked the Countess and often shared his most intimate thoughts with her.

Turgenev had conceived the idea for *A Nest of Gentlefolk* early in 1856, but he did not finish the novel until late November 1858, writing most of it at Spasskoe. Scholars consider it likely that Turgenev drew on Countess Lambert as the prototype for Liza Kalitina, the devout young heroine of the work. Lambert applauded the novel, mistakenly seeing in it a sign that the agnostic Turgenev was undergoing a religious conversion.

Both the public and the critics greeted *A Nest of Gentlefolk* with enormous enthusiasm. Soon after its publication came the essay "Hamlet and Don Quixote," the story "First Love," and Turgenev's third novel, *On the Eve*. That novel, which recounts the tale of a Bulgarian revolutionary and his self-sacrificing young Russian wife, led to Turgenev's break with the young radicals of the day. The story of that rupture revolves around the journal *The Contemporary*.

As mentioned earlier, a number of the leading writers of the age, including Goncharov, Tolstoy, and Turgenev, had allied themselves with Panaev and Nekrasov's *The Contemporary*. Some of these supporters even went so far as to pledge all their future work to it. After 1855, however, the journal adopted an increasingly radical tone that offended many of its most distinguished contributors. The new orientation resulted from Nekrasov's hiring two young firebrands, Nikolay Chernyshevsky and Nikolay Dobrolyubov, to serve as critics and spokesmen for the journal. These two men, who actually came to the fore in the latter half of the 1850s and whose personalities and views differed in significant ways, have earned the reputation of typical radicals of the 1860s.[9]

Chernyshevsky and Dobrolyubov did not disguise their impatience with the leading Westernizers of Turgenev's generation, the so-called men of the 1840s, and the hostility soon became mutual. To reduce the issues involved here to broad generalizations, the roots of the conflict between the two generations lay primarily in matters of class, politics, and aesthetics. Turgenev and his confreres generally boasted a gentry background, whereas the radicals of the 1860s came from common stock. With such notable exceptions as Herzen and Bakunin, Westernizers of Turgenev's generation tended to favor reform over revolution, while the radical leaders of the 1860s gave at least tacit support to the violent overthrow of the existing regime, although of course they could not express such ideas openly in the press.

Turgenev and his contemporaries, nurtured on German idealist philosophy, made a veritable cult of art. The men of the 1860s, drawing on British utilitarianism and German materialism and often making hash of both, viewed art as a poor substitute for science and political action. Finally, personal style played a part in the conflict: whereas the intelligentsia that blossomed in the 1840s prided itself on its erudition, eloquence, and manners, the radicals of the 1860s considered humanistic education irrelevant and cared nothing for bon ton. The erstwhile united front of the Westernizing intelligentsia began to crumble.

In 1859 and 1860 Dobrolyubov published a number of pieces in *The Contemporary* that heaped scorn on liberals of Turgenev's stripe. Turgenev took umbrage, the more so as he believed that *The Notes of a Hunter* and his time in exile had earned him the right to a measure of respect from the younger generation. The showdown came in 1860 over Dobrolyubov's review of *On the Eve*. Turgenev read the article in proof and strongly objected to Dobrolyubov's conclusion, worded in Aesopian language, that the novel contained a call to revolution. Nekrasov ignored Turgenev's request that the journal withhold the article, and Turgenev firmly resolved to have nothing more to do with *The Contemporary*. Most of the original contributors soon followed Turgenev's lead.

Paradoxically, the radicalization of Russian youth—and of educated Russian society in general—increased at an even more rapid pace after the single greatest reform in nineteenth-century Russia, namely, the abolition of serfdom, on 3 March 1861. The conditions of emancipation placed heavy financial burdens on the peasants, however, and within a few months radical leaders were labeling the emancipation a fraudulent maneuver and a cosmetic reform. As a result, a wave of revolutionary propaganda and violence swept over Russia in 1861 and 1862, evoking repressive countermeasures on the government's part. Chernyshevsky, probably innocent of any overt political action, suffered arrest and exile.

Thus, the socio-political climate was already dangerously overcharged when *Fathers and Sons* appeared in 1862. Turgenev had begun work on his novel about the clash between the generations in 1860 but did not finish polishing and revising the work until the following year. Since *Fathers and Sons* spotlights a young radical, Bazarov, Turgenev knew that the novel might provoke controversy. He did not anticipate, however, the nearly universal outcry that *Fathers and Sons* occasioned. With precious few exceptions, critics on all sides hurled thunderbolts at Turgenev. The younger generation expressed venomous rage, seeing in Bazarov a parody of a radical. Their strongly worded criticism further wounded Turgenev, who was still smarting after his break with *The Contemporary*. His literary reputation in Russia seemed decidedly on the decline.

Along with the apparent failure of *Fathers and Sons* and rejection by Russia's young people came quarrels with several of Turgenev's oldest friends and confidants. In withdrawing from *The Contemporary*, for instance, Turgenev had simultaneously called an end to relations with Nekrasov. Sixteen years passed before a reconciliation of sorts took place, when Turgenev visited his by then mortally ill literary colleague. In early 1860 Turgenev also found himself at loggerheads with Goncharov. The latter, who suffered from an emotional instability that worsened with the years, accused Turgenev of plagiarism. Specifically, Goncharov charged that in *A Nest of Gentlefolk* Turgenev had pilfered characters and situations from Goncharov's then-unfinished novel *The Precipice.* Turgenev, who in fact seems to have borrowed some of Goncharov's ideas, finally demanded arbitration or a duel. The court of arbitration that convened to resolve the matter declared that since the two authors had drawn on Russian reality for their works, some overlapping on detail was inevitable. Furious, Turgenev announced to Goncharov that relations between the two of them were at an end, but an uneasy rapprochement was reached in 1864.

Turgenev and Tolstoy also parted ways in the early 1860s. Their friendship had blown hot and cold from the very beginning, in 1855, when Tolstoy had expressed eagerness to meet Turgenev. Between the years 1856 and 1858 their paths crossed on several occasions, both in Russia and in Western Europe, but an atmosphere of muddled recriminations often accompanied these meetings. Things took a dramatic turn for the worse in 1861, when the two writers visited the poet Afanasy Fet at his estate, Stepanovka. A silly quarrel erupted over Paulinette Turgeneva's upbringing and reached a climax with Turgenev's calling Tolstoy some sort of rude name. Fet's two distinguished guests abruptly departed for their own estates, and Turgenev immediately wrote Tolstoy a letter of apology. The letter did not arrive promptly, however, and Tolstoy, the future apostle of nonviolence, challenged Turgenev, always the advocate of moderation, to a duel. No duel transpired, and the affair had all but blown over when, a few months later, Turgenev heard gossip to the effect that Tolstoy was accusing him of cowardice. Now Turgenev, in his turn, issued a challenge to Tolstoy. That duel did not take place, either, but the two men continued to be on the outs until the late 1870s.

At about this time Turgenev broke with his old friend Herzen as well. The two engaged in spirited polemics in the years 1862–63, Herzen via his London-based Russian-language "underground" periodical *The Bell,* Turgenev through letters to his longtime comrade. Herzen considered bourgeois Western Europe a spiritual graveyard and asserted that the only hope for humanity lay with Russia and the Russian peasant. Turgenev disagreed strongly. Russia, he argued, did not differ essentially from the rest of Europe. Turgenev added that the Russian peasant was potentially just as petit bourgeois as any Paris shopkeeper. The polemic turned increasingly acrid, but it was a Senate Inquiry that actually brought relations to a temporary end.

In 1862 the Senate established a commission to examine possible links between Russian citizens abroad and Herzen's *The Bell.* Turgenev received an order to return to Saint Petersburg to appear before the commission, but he successfully petitioned for permission to answer the questions in writing, from Paris. To the extent that he played down his friendship with Herzen and concealed his meetings with Bakunin, Turgenev's replies departed from the truth. His responses did not entirely satisfy the commission, which issued a second summons to Saint Petersburg. Turgenev arrived there in January 1864, but after a brief interview his examiners fully exonerated him. Soon afterwards Herzen published a report in *The Bell* claiming that Turgenev had conducted himself ignobly before the commission, renouncing his former friends. What Turgenev told the examiners remains unknown, but he insisted that he had betrayed no one. On that note Turgenev and Herzen, too, called it quits, although a reconciliation came within a very few years.

Pauline Viardot provided the one ray of light in the generally gloomy picture that Turgenev's life presents in the decade of the 1860s. Her attitude toward her Russian admirer unaccountably thawed, and Turgenev once again enjoyed the status of a family intimate. In 1862 the Viardots moved from France, where Turgenev had also been living, to Baden-Baden. Turgenev followed soon thereafter, taking an apartment for his daughter, her chaperone, and himself not far from the Viardot villa. Unfortunately, Paulinette still nursed an unconcealed grudge against Pauline Viardot, so that before long Turgenev felt compelled to send his daughter and her companion back to Paris. In 1865 Paulinette married Gaston Bruère, an alliance that eventually proved costly for Turgenev and disastrous for the bride.

Baden and his position as virtually one of the Viardot family suited Turgenev admirably. The Viardot villa became a major social and cultural center. Frequent guests there included Clara Schumann, Johannes Brahms, European royalty, and various Russian visitors. Turgenev knew relative happiness in Baden, and his trips to Russia were few and short: three weeks in 1865 and five weeks each in 1867, 1868, and 1870.

For the first few years after the appearance of *Fathers and Sons* Turgenev wrote very little, publishing only three stories: "Phantoms," "Enough," and "The Dog." Dostoevsky printed the first two stories in his journal *The Epoch,* praising them highly in correspondence with Turgenev while privately disliking them greatly. In fact, "Phantoms" and "Enough" do not rank among Turgenev's major achievements.

In 1864, probably under the impression of his polemic with Herzen, Turgenev began work on his fifth novel, *Smoke*. One of the least successful of his works with regard to composition, *Smoke* combines a love story, a satire on Russian revolutionaries and émigrés, and didactic remarks about Russia's past, present, and future. Published in 1867, the novel offended nearly everyone. Turgenev's exposé of Russia's cultural shallowness—a stance resulting from his mixed feelings of love and hatred for his homeland—particularly enraged Dostoevsky, and at a stormy meeting in Baden in 1867 he told Turgenev as much. Moreover, in his novel *The Possessed,* conceived partially as a reply to *Smoke,* Dostoevsky produced a devastating parody of Turgenev in the figure of Karmazinov, "the famous writer." These incidents curtailed all relations between Turgenev and Dostoevsky.

In a reverse case, the appearance of *Smoke* occasioned Turgenev's reconciliation with Herzen, to whom he sent an offprint of the novel along with a letter indicating his hope that their friendship might be renewed. Herzen did not like the novel but he accepted the olive branch with alacrity. The two old friends met much later—in Paris in 1870—just a few days before Herzen's sudden death from pneumonia. As in earlier days, they got along splendidly.

Toward the end of the decade Turgenev published five stories: "The Story of Lieutenant Yergunov," "The Brigadier," "A Misfortunate Girl," "A Strange Story," and "A King Lear of the Steppes." In addition, three of the five pieces that would eventually make up *Memoirs of Literature and Life* appeared in print in 1869. None of these works received a particularly friendly reception in Russia, where the Turgenev renaissance had not yet begun. Abroad, however, Turgenev's reputation was growing steadily. By the end of the 1860s French translations of virtually everything that Turgenev had written until then existed, as did German and English versions of the majority of his writings. One could also find Dutch, Swedish, Serbian, and Hungarian translations of various stories and novels. In short, Turgenev was becoming a writer with an international following, the first Russian to do so.

Although he always asserted that as a Russian writer he could not and would not create in a language other than his native one, between 1867 and 1869 Turgenev in fact composed four French-language operetta libretti for Pauline Viardot, who set them to music. These operettas originally served as domestic entertainments for the Viardot family and their guests. One of the operettas, *The Last Sorcerer,* additionally had professional stagings in Weimar and Karlsruhe. The latter performance proved a minor scandal, earning scathing reviews for Turgenev's text. Nonetheless, as his letters attest, Turgenev treasured the collaboration.

In 1868 the Viardots, accompanied by Turgenev, moved to Karls-ruhe. The next year he returned to Baden, however. In 1870, soon after the outbreak of the Franco-Prussian War, Turgenev and the Viardots took up residence in London.

Turgenev remained in London only about a year. The Viardots' tenure there proved even shorter. While in England, Turgenev visited many of the reigning literary celebrities, including Carlyle, with whom he had very little in common, Tennyson, Swinburne, George Lewes, whom Turgenev had known in Berlin in the 1840s, and George Eliot. He also spent time with his English translator, William Ralston.

At the conclusion of the Franco-Prussian War the Viardots, by reason of Louis's political sympathies, settled in France. Turgenev moved there as well, and from then until his death he lived practically as a member of the Viardot family, spending winters in Paris and summers in Bougival. Two of the Viardot children, Claudie and Marianne, held a special place in Turgenev's affections. He surely felt closer to them than to his own daughter. He showered Paulinette with generosity, however. Most of their correspondence centers on financial matters, with Paulinette and her husband constantly asking for money and Turgenev usually supplying it.

In France, a country for which he never developed any particular admiration, Turgenev came to have close relations with many of the literary luminaries. Gustave Flaubert considered him one of his best friends, and Turgenev reciprocated the feelings. He regarded George Sand, an old friend of the Viardot family, with special warmth. Emile Zola, Alphonse Daudet, Edmond de Goncourt, Flaubert (when in Paris), and Turgenev met regularly for dinner and conversation. Turgenev and Henry James also became acquainted in Paris, in 1857. The American already held Turgenev's writings in high regard, and he yearned to meet the Russian novelist. The two men predictably proved compatible and spent time in each other's company on several occasions in the late 1870s and early 1880s.

The cosmopolitan Turgenev hardly turned his back on Russia and his Russian friends and acquaintances, however. Indeed, he had become something like a one-man clearing house for European culture. In France and Germany he propagandized at one time or another the works of Tolstoy, the playwright Alexander Ostrovsky, and even Dostoevsky. (Relations between Turgenev and Dostoevsky had not improved, and Turgenev had privately concluded that Dostoevsky was talented but quite mad.) Conversely, thanks to Turgenev's efforts, works by Flaubert, Zola, and Goncourt started to appear in Russian translation.

Turgenev's interests went beyond literature. Perhaps because of his friendship with Pauline Viardot, he had come to love music passionately. He followed Wagner's career with somewhat forced interest (whereas Pauline declared herself a Wagnerite "to her fingertips") but showed real enthusiasm for several Russian composers then just beginning to earn acclaim in Europe, especially Tchaikovsky and Borodin.[10]

Beginning with the 1870s Turgenev shifted his allegiance from Mikhail Katkov's journal *The Russian Herald,* where he had often published in the 1860s, to Mikhail Stasyulevich's new *European Herald.* Katkov's views had become distinctly right wing, and Turgenev could no longer abide any connection with the man. Similarly, for a time in the 1870s Turgenev broke off relations with his old friend Fet, whose conservatism likewise enraged him.

Turgenev's most significant work of the early 1870s, the long story "Spring Freshets," appeared in 1872. This tale of a man's betraying an ingenuous young girl because of an overwhelming passion for an older, amoral woman evoked anathemas in Russia and Germany, but French critics praised it. Other stories from the first half of the decade were "Knock, Knock, Knock!," "Punin and Babunin," and "The Watch." Turgenev also added three stories to the canon of *Notes of a Hunter:* "The End of Chertopkhanov," "Living Relics," which he had actually written in the 1840s, and "There's a Knocking!" The last he based on a rough draft from the 1840s.

In the course of three trips to Russia between 1871 and 1874 Turgenev did on-the-spot research for his sixth and last novel, *Virgin Soil,* where he treated the Populist movement in both its violent and nonviolent variants. When *Virgin Soil* came out in 1877 Russian critics initially found fault with it. In translation, however, the novel had an instant success and gained accolades from Flaubert, among others. Turgenev finished out the decade with two more short stories, "The Dream" and "Father Alexey's Story."

Toward the end of the 1870s Turgenev suddenly found himself a popular and respected figure in his homeland. During a trip to Russia in 1879 the ovations that greeted his appearance stunned and gratified him, particularly since many students contributed to the hosannas. In fact, young people frequently expressed the hope that Turgenev would return to Russia for good and become a leader of progressive opinion. All the attention and adulation quite turned Turgenev's head, but he was too set in his ways to give up life with the Viardots.

Along with belated acclaim at home came a remarkable demonstration of Turgenev's status abroad. In June 1879 Oxford University conferred on him the degree of Doctor of Civil Law. Ralston had helped arrange for this honor, which understandably delighted Turgenev.

In 1879 the twenty-five-year-old actress Maria Savina resurrected Turgenev's nearly forgotten *A Month in the Country.* Turgenev attended one of the performances in Saint Petersburg and found himself captivated both by Savina's personality and by her acting. Before long he was in love, and the chance to spend time in Savina's company provided one of the motivations for his trips to Russia in 1880 and 1881.[11] Many of his letters to her bespeak overt passion, but it is doubtful that the two actually became lovers. They shared, rather, an especially tender friendship flavored with a strong dose of eroticism. Pauline Viardot knew and disapproved of this infatuation, but it posed no real threat to her. Whatever fantasies Turgenev may have entertained about Savina, his devotion to Pauline remained constant.

During his final visits to Russia Turgenev met Tolstoy a number of times, and the two resumed their correspondence, which had broken off after the quarrel in 1861. Turgenev especially enjoyed conversation with Tolstoy, whose talent as a writer he had never ceased admiring, although he still had reservations about the man, as did Tolstoy about him.

The most exhilarating cultural event of the last decades of the nineteenth century in Russia centered on the unveiling of a monument to Pushkin in Moscow in June 1880. Many of the leading writers of the day, including Dostoevsky, Turgenev, and Alexey Pisemsky, participated in the accompanying festivities. Dostoevsky's dramatic speech, in which he used the example of Pushkin to extol the allegedly unique virtues of Russians, plunged the audience into an unbridled enthusiasm that verged on hysteria. Turgenev, who also spoke at the proceedings, later urged his publisher, Stasyulevich, to pour some cold water on Dostoevsky's speech, which he found clever but entirely wrongheaded.

In 1882 Stasyulevich visited Turgenev in Bougival and learned that for several years Turgenev had been writing his *Prose Poems,* which he considered private works not for publication. Turgenev acceded to Stasyulevich's request, however, that he make a selection of the prose poems for *The European Herald.* Perhaps aware of Turgenev's declining health, critics generally praised the collection. Tolstoy's approval of some of the pieces especially pleased Turgenev. In his final years Turgenev continued writing short stories: "The Quail," a children's story set down at Tolstoy's request, "Old Portraits," "The Desperado," "The Song of Triumphant Love," "Klara Milich," and "Une Fin" ("An End"). Turgenev, near death, dictated the last story to Pauline Viardot in French.

Turgenev never knew the true nature of his final illness, which began to plague him early in 1882. What doctors finally diagnosed as "gouty neuralgia of the heart" actually was cancer of the spinal marrow. The disease soon immobilized him and caused him increasing pain, but he apparently did not realize that he was on his deathbed until very near the end.

Problems with his daughter erupted at the same time as Turgenev's final illness. Her husband had squandered all the family's money, taken to the bottle, and turned violent. Early in 1882 Paulinette fled to Paris with her two children, and not long after that Turgenev arranged for them to live in Switzerland. Under French law a wife had no rights at all, and Paulinette, in fact, was in hiding. Turgenev gave her a substantial monthly stipend, but within a short time she was running up debts and—what Turgenev found even more outrageous—spreading gossip about Pauline Viardot. His last letter to his daughter seethes with fury: Turgenev calculated that he had provided Paulinette and her husband half a million francs, all of which they had dissipated. After Turgenev's death Paulinette lived on the interest from securities that he had left her in the Viardots' name. When his granddaughter Jeanne began working, she helped her mother financially. Jeanne, who died single in 1952, revered the memory of her grandfather. Of her brother Georges, who also died unmarried and without issue, hardly anything is known.

Turgenev passed his final weeks in agony, but the Viardot family surrounded him with care, attention, and love. Until the very end he received visitors, made literary plans, and continued his correspondence. One of his last letters he addressed to Tolstoy, who had announced his renunciation of literature. Once again revealing the profound generosity of spirit that very often characterized him, Turgenev implored "the great writer of the Russian land" to return to his true calling. In addition, Turgenev wrote of the happiness that he had derived from finding himself Tolstoy's contemporary.

Turgenev died on 15 September 1883. The story of his burial and of the probate of his estate follows typically Russian lines, with endless delays and a fulsome display of official stupidity. In the end Turgenev was laid to rest in Saint Petersburg, with a huge number of police agents in attendance to prevent radicals of all stripes from turning the impressive ceremony into a political demonstration. The legal wrangling over Turgenev's estate went on for some time. He had intended for Pauline Viardot to inherit everything, but because of a variety of wills and the problems involved in working through both Russian and French courts, by the conclusion of the litigation Viardot received no more than one-third of what Turgenev had wanted to leave her, the woman he had adored above everyone and perhaps everything on earth.

Notes

1. In the nineteenth century the Russian calendar (so-called Old Style) lagged behind the Western calendar (so-called New Style) by twelve days. All dates in the present sketch refer to the Western calendar. For information about Turgenev's life

I have relied heavily on Leonard Schapiro, *Turgenev: His Life and Times* (New York: Random House, 1978), the most accurate and detailed biography of Turgenev in any language. An invaluable Russian source is M. K. Kleman, *Letopis zhizni i tvorchestva I. S. Turgeneva* (Moscow-Leningrad: Academia, 1934).

2. The best study of Stankevich is Edward J. Brown, *Stankevich and His Moscow Circle* (Stanford, Calif.: Stanford University Press, 1966).

3. A superb work on the Slavophiles is Andrzej Walicki, *The Slavophile Controversy*, trans. Hilda Andrews-Rusiecka (Oxford: Oxford University Press, 1975).

4. Victor Terras, *Belinskij and Russian Literary Criticism* (Madison: University of Wisconsin Press, 1974), provides a thorough treatment of Belinsky's thought and influence.

5. April Fitzlyon, *The Price of Genius: A Life of Pauline Viardot* (London: John Calder, 1964), is the best available biography of one of the most remarkable women of the nineteenth century.

6. The standard work on Herzen in English is Martin Malia, *Alexander Herzen and the Birth of Russian Socialism* (Cambridge, Mass.: Harvard University Press, 1961).

7. Henri Granjard, *Ivan Turguénev et les courants politiques et sociaux de son temps,* 2nd ed. (Paris: Institut d'études slaves de l'Université de Paris, 1966), provides a detailed and now classic treatment of Turgenev's involvement with *The Contemporary.*

8. Patrick Waddington, *Turgenev and England* (New York: Macmillan, 1981), seems to leave no stone unturned with regard to its announced topic.

9. The most brilliant study in English of the radicalization of Russian youth in the 1850s and later is Abbot Gleason's *Young Russia* (New York: Viking Press, 1980).

10. A. Kryukov's *Turgenev i muzyka* (Leningrad: Gos. muzykalnoe izdatelstvo, 1963) offers a reasonably comprehensive account of Turgenev's musical interests.

11. Ivan Turgenev, *Letters to an Actress,* ed. and trans. Nora Gottlieb and Raymond Chapman (London: Allison & Busby, 1973), offers the best English-language treatment of the relations between Turgenev and Savina.

Articles and Essays

[Turgenev's Prose]

D. S. Mirsky°

Turgenev's first attempt at prose fiction was in the wake of Lermontov, from whom he derived the romantic halo round his first Pechorin-like heroes ("Andrey Kolosov," "The Duelist," "Three Portraits") and the method of the intensified anecdote ("The Jew"). In *A Sportsman's Sketches,* begun in 1847, he was to free himself from the romantic conventions of these early stories by abandoning all narrative skeleton and limiting himself to "slices of life." But even for some time after that date he remained unable in his more distinctly narrative work to hit on what was to become his true manner. Thus, for instance, "Three Meetings" (1852) is a story of pure atmosphere woven round a very slender theme, saturated in its descriptions of moonlit nights, with an excess of romantic and "poetical" poetry. "The Diary of a Superfluous Man" (1850) is reminiscent of Gogol and of the young Dostoevsky, developing as it does the Dostoevskian theme of humiliated human dignity and of morbid delight in humiliation, but aspiring to a Gogol-like and very un-Turgenevian verbal intensity. (The phrase "a superfluous man" had an extraordinary fortune and is still applied by literary and social historians to the type of ineffective idealist portrayed so often by Turgenev and his contemporaries.) At last "Mumu" (1854), the well-known story of the deaf serf and his favorite dog, and of how his mistress ordered it to be destroyed, is a "philanthropic" story of the tradition of "The Greatcoat" and of *Poor Folk,* where an intense sensation of pity is arrived at by methods that strike the modern reader as illegitimate, working on the nerves rather than on the imagination.

    A Sportsman's Sketches, on the other hand, written in 1847–51, belongs to the highest, most lasting, and least questionable achievement of Turgenev and of Russian realism. The book describes the

° From *A History of Russian Literature from its Beginnings to 1910,* Francis J. Whitfield (New York: Random House, 1958), 198–208. Copyright 1926, 1927, 1949, ©1958 by Alfred A. Knopf, Inc. Reprinted by permission of the publisher.

35

casual and various meetings of the narrator during his wanderings with a gun and a dog in his native district of Bolkhov and in the surrounding country. The sketches are arranged in a random order and have no narrative skeleton, containing nothing but accounts of what the narrator saw and heard. Some of them are purely descriptive, of scenery or character; others consist of conversation, addressed to the narrator or overheard. At times there is a dramatic *motive*, but the development is only hinted at by the successive glimpses the narrator gets of his personages. This absolute matter-of-factness and studious avoidance of everything artificial and made-up were the most prominent characteristics of the book when it appeared—it was a new genre. The peasants are described from the outside, as seen (or overseen) by the narrator, not in their intimate, unoverlooked life. As I have said, they are drawn with obviously greater sympathy than the upper classes. The squires are represented as either vulgar, or cruel, or ineffective. In the peasants, Turgenev emphasized their humanity, their imaginativeness, their poetical and artistic giftedness, their sense of dignity, their intelligence. It was in this quiet and unobtrusive way that the book struck the readers with the injustice and ineptitude of serfdom. Now, when the issue of serfdom is a thing of the past, the *Sketches* seem once more as harmless and as innocent as a book can be, and it requires a certain degree of historical imagination to reconstruct the atmosphere in which they had the effect of a mild bombshell.

Judged as literature, the *Sketches* are frequently, if not always, above praise. In the representation of rural scenery and peasant character, Turgenev never surpassed such masterpieces as "The Singers" and "Bezhin Meadow."[1] "The Singers" especially, even after "First Love" and *Fathers and Sons,* may claim to be his crowning achievement and the quintessence of all the most characteristic qualities of his art. It is the description of a singing-match at a village pub between the peasant Yashka Turok and a tradesman from Zhizdra. The story is representative of Turgenev's manner of painting his peasants; he does not onesidedly idealize them; the impression produced by the match, with its revelation of the singers' high sense of artistic values, is qualified by the drunken orgy the artists lapse into after the match is over and the publican treats Yashka to the fruit of his victory. "The Singers" may also be taken as giving Turgenev's prose at its highest and most characteristic. It is careful and in a sense artificial, but the impression of absolute ease and simplicity is exhaled from every word and turn of phrase. It is a carefully *selected* language, rich, but curiously avoiding words and phrases, crude or journalistic, that might jar on the reader. The beauty of the landscape painting is due chiefly to the choice of exact and delicately suggestive and descriptive words. There is no ornamental imagery after the manner of Gogol, no rhetorical rhythm, no splendid cadences. But the sometime poet's and poets' disciple's hand is evident in the careful, varied, and unobtrusively perfect balance of his phrases.

The first thing Turgenev wrote after the *Sketches* and "Mumu" was "The Inn." Like "Mumu" it turns on the unjust and callous treatment of serfs by their masters, but the sentimental, "philanthropic" element is replaced for the first time in his work by the characteristic Turgenevian atmosphere of tragic necessity. "The Inn" was followed in 1853–61 by a succession of masterpieces. They were divided by the author himself into two categories: novels and *nouvelles* (in Russian, *romany* and *povesti*). The difference between the two forms in the case of Turgenev is not so much one of size or scope as that the novels aim at social significance and at the statement of social problems, while the *nouvelles* are pure and simple stories of emotional incident, free from civic preoccupations. Each novel includes a narrative kernel similar in subject and bulk to that of a *nouvelle,* but it is expanded into an answer to some burning problem of the day. The novels of the period are *Rudin* (1856), *A Nest of Gentlefolk* (1859), *On the Eve* (1860), and *Fathers and Sons* (1862); the *nouvelles* "Two Friends" (1854), "A Quiet Spot" (1854), "Yakov Pasynkov" (1855), "A Correspondence" (1856), "Faust" (1856), "Asya" (1858), and "First Love" (1860). It will be noticed that the civic novels belong chiefly to the age of reform (1856–61), while the purely private *nouvelles* predominate in the reactionary years that precede it. But even "on the eve" of the Emancipation, Turgenev could be sufficiently detached from civic issues to write the perfectly uncivic "First Love."

The novels of Turgenev are, thus, those of his stories in which he, voluntarily, submitted to the obligation of writing works of social significance. This significance is arrived at in the first place by the nature of the characters, who are made to be representative of phases sucessively traversed by the Russian intellectual. Rudin is the progressive idealist of the forties; Lavretsky, the more Slavophile idealist of the same generation; Elena, in *On the Eve,* personifies the vaguely generous and active fermentation of the generation immediately preceding the reforms: Bazarov, the militant materialism of the generation of 1860. Secondly, the social significance is served by the insertion of numerous *conversations* between the characters on topics of current interest (Slavophilism and Westernism, the ability of the educated Russian to act, the place in life of art and science, and so on). These conversations are what especially distinguished Turgenev's novels from his *nouvelles.* They have little relation to the action, and not always much more to the character of the representative hero. They were what the civic critics seized upon for comment, but they are certainly the least permanent and most dating part of his novels.

There frequently occur characters who are introduced with no other motive but to do the talking, and whom one would have rather wished away. But the central, representative characters—the heroes—are in most cases not only representative, but alive. Rudin, the first in date, is one of the masterpieces of nineteenth-century character drawing. An eminent French novelist (who is old-fashioned enough still to prefer Turgenev to Tolstoy, Dostoevsky, and Chekhov) has pointed out to me the wonderfully delicate mastery with which the impression produced by Rudin on the other characters and on the reader is made gradually to change from the first appearance in the glamour of superiority to the bankruptcy of his pusillanimous breach with Natalya, then to the gloomy glimpse of the undone and degenerate man, and to the redeeming flash of his heroic and ineffective death upon the barricades of the faubourg St. Antoine. The French writer thought this delicate change of attitude unique in fiction. Had he known more Russian he would have realized that Turgenev had merely been a highly intelligent and creative pupil of Pushkin's. Like Pushkin in *Eugene Onegin,* Turgenev does not analyze and dissect his heroes, as Tolstoy and Dostoevsky would have done; he does not uncover their souls; he only conveys their atmosphere, partly by showing how they are reflected in others, partly by an exceedingly delicate and thinly woven aura of suggestive accompaniment—a method that at once betrays its origin in a *poetic novel.* Where Turgenev attempts to show us the *inner* life of his heroes by other methods, he always fails—the description of Elena's feelings for Insarov in *On the Eve* is distinctly painful reading. Turgenev had to use all the power of self-criticism and self-restraint to avoid the pitfall of false poetry and false beauty.

Still, the characters, constructed though they are by means of suggestion, not dissection, are the vivifying principle of Turgenev's stories. Like most Russian novelists he makes character predominate over plot, and it is the characters that we remember. The population of Turgenev's novels (apart from the peasant stories) may be classified under several heads. First comes the divisions into the Philistines and the elect. The Philistines are the direct descendants of Gogol's characters—heroes of *poshlost,* self-satisfied inferiority. Of course there is not a trace in them of Gogol's exuberant and grotesque caricature; the irony of Turgenev is fine, delicate, unobtrusive, hardly at all aided by any obvious comical devices. On the other side are the elect, the men and women with a sense of values, superior to those of vegetable enjoyment and social position. The men, again, are very different from the women. The fair sex comes out distinctly more advantageously from the hands of Turgenev. The strong, pure, passionate, and virtuous woman, opposed to the weak, potentially generous, but ineffective and ultimately shallow man, was introduced into literature by Pushkin, and recurs again and again in the work of the realists, but nowhere more insistently than in Turgenev's. His heroines are famous all the world over and have done much to spread a high reputation of Russian womanhood. Moral force and courage are the keynote to Turgenev's heroine—the power to sacrifice all worldly considerations to passion (Natalya in *Rudin*), or all happiness to duty (Liza in *A Nest of Gentlefolk*). But what goes home to the general reader in these women is not so much the height of their moral beauty as the extraordinary *poetical* beauty woven round them by the delicate and perfect art of their begetter. Turgenev reaches his highest perfection in this, his own and unique art, in two of the short stories, "A Quiet Spot" and "First Love." In the first, the purely Turgenevian, tragic, poetic, and rural atmosphere reaches its maximum of concentration, and the richness of suggestion that conditions the characters surpasses all he ever wrote. It transcends mere fiction and rises into poetry, not by the beauty of the single word and parts, but by sheer force of suggestion and saturated significance. "First Love" stands somewhat apart from the rest of Turgenev's work. Its atmosphere is cooler and clearer, more reminiscent of the rarified air of Lermontov. The heroes—Zinaida and the narrator's father (who is traditionally supposed to portray the author's own father)—are more *animal* and vital than Turgenev usually allows his heroes to be. Their passions are tense and clear-cut, free from vagueness and idealized haze, selfish, but with a selfishness that is redeemed by self-justifying vitality. Unique in the whole of his work, "First Love" is the least relaxing of Turgenev's stories. But, characteristically, the story is told from the point of view of the boy admirer of Zinaida and of his pangs of adolescent jealousy for his rival and father.

At the height of his popularity, in 1860, Turgenev wrote a famous essay, "Hamlet and Don Quixote." He considered these characters as the two prototypes of the elect intellectual portion of mankind, which was divided into self-conscious, introspective, and consequently ineffective, Hamlets, and enthusiastic, single-minded, courageous at the risk of seeming ridiculous, Don Quixotes. He himself and the great majority of his heroes were Hamlets. But he had always wanted to create Quixotes, whose freedom from reflection and questioning would make them efficient, while their possession of higher values would raise them above the Philistines. In the later forties the critics, who had taken note of the consistent inefficiency of Turgenev's heroes, clamored for him to produce a more active and effective hero. This he attempted in *On the Eve*. But the attempt was a failure. He made his hero a Bulgarian patriot, Insarov. But he failed to breathe into him the spirit of life. Insarov is merely a strong, silent puppet, at times almost ludicrous. In conjunction with the stilted and vapid

Elena, Insarov makes *On the Eve* distinctly the worst of all Turgenev's mature work.

The best of the novels and ultimately the most important of Turgenev's works is *Fathers and Sons,* one of the greatest novels of the nineteenth century. Here Turgenev triumphantly solved two tasks that he had been attempting to solve: to create a living masculine character not based on introspection, and to overcome the contradiction between the imaginative and the social theme. *Fathers and Sons* is Turgenev's only novel where the social problem is distilled without residue into art, and leaves no bits of undigested journalist sticking out. Here the delicate and poetic narrative art of Turgenev reaches its perfection, and Bazarov is the only one of Turgenev's men who is worthy to stand by the side of his women. But nowhere perhaps does the essential debility and feminineness of his genius come out more clearly than in this, the best of his novels. Bazarov is a strong man, but he is painted with admiration and wonder by one to whom a strong man is something abnormal. Turgenev is incapable of making his hero triumph, and to spare him the inadequate treatment that would have been his lot in the case of success, he lets him die, not from any natural development of the nature of the subject, but by the blind decree of fate. For fate, blind chance, crass cruelty, presides over Turgenev's universe as it does with Hardy's, but Turgenev's people submit to it with passive resignation. Even the heroic Bazarov dies as resigned as a flower in the field, with silent courage but without protest.

It would be wrong to affirm that after *Fathers and Sons* Turgenev's genius began to decline, but at any rate it ceased to grow. What was more important for his contemporaries, he lost touch with Russian life and thus ceased to count as a *contemporary* writer, though he remained a permanent classic. His attempts again to tackle the problems of the day in *Smoke* (1867) and in *Virgin Soil* (1877) only emphasized his loss of touch with the new age. *Smoke* is the worst-constructed of his novels: it contains a beautiful love story, which is interrupted and interlarded with conversations that have no relation to the characters and are just dialogued journalism on the thesis that all intellectual and educated Russia was nothing but smoke. *Virgin Soil* is a complete failure, and was immediately recognized as such. Though it contains much that is in the best manner of Turgenev (the characters of the bureaucratic-aristocratic Sipyagin family are among his best satirical drawings), the whole novel is disqualified by an entirely uninformed and necessarily false conception of what he was writing about. His presentation of the revolutionaries of the seventies is like an account of a foreign country by one who had never seen it.

But while Turgenev had lost the power of writing for the times, he had not lost the genius of creating those wonderful love stories which are his most personal contribution to the world's literature. Pruned of its conversations, *Smoke* is a beautiful *nouvelle,* comparable to the best he wrote in the fifties, and so is "The Torrents of Spring" (1872). Both are on the same subject: a young man loves a pure and sweet young girl but forsakes her for a mature and lascivious woman of thirty, who is loved by many and for whom he is the plaything of a fleeting passion. The characters of Irina, the older woman in *Smoke,* and of Gemma, the Italian girl in "The Torrents of Spring," are among the most beautiful in the whole of his gallery. "The Torrents of Spring" is given a retrospective setting, and in most of the other stories of this last period the scene is set in the old times of pre-Reform Russia. Some of these stories are purely objective little tragedies (one of the best is "A Lear of the Steppes," 1870); others are non-narrative fragments from reminiscences, partly continuing the manner and theme of *A Sportsman's Sketches.* There are also the purely biographical reminiscences, including interesting accounts of the author's acquaintance with Pushkin and Belinsky and the remarkable account "The Execution of Troppmann" (1870), which in its fascinated objectivity is one of the most terrible descriptions ever made of an execution.

There had always been in Turgenev a poetic or romantic vein, as opposed to the prevailing realistic atmosphere of his principal work. His attitude to nature had always been lyrical, and he had always had a lurking desire to transcend the limits imposed on the Russian novelist by the dogma of realism. Not only did he begin his career as a lyrical poet and end it with his *Poems in Prose,* but even in his most realistic and civic novels the construction and atmosphere are mainly lyrical. *A Sportsman's Sketches* includes many purely lyical pages of natural description, and to the period of his highest maturity belongs that remarkable piece "A Tour in the Forest" (1857), where for the first time Turgenev's conception of indifferent and eternal nature opposed to transient man found expression in a sober and simple prose that attains poetry by the simplest means of unaided suggestion. His last period begins with the purely lyrical prose poem "Enough" and culminates in the *Poems in Prose.* At the same time the fantastic element asserts itself. In some stories ("The Dog," "Knock, Knock, Knock," and "Father Alexey's Story") it appears only in the form of a suggestion of mysterious presences in an ordinary realistic setting. The most important of these stories is his last, "Klara Milich" (1883), written under the influence of spiritualistic readings and musings. It is as good as most of his stories of purely human love, but the mysterious element is somewhat difficult to appreciate quite whole-heartedly today. It has all the inevitable flatness of Victorian spiritualism. In a few stories Turgenev freed himself from the conventions of realistic form and wrote such things as the purely visionary "Phantoms" (1864) and "The Song of Triumphant Love" (1881), written in the style of an Italian *novella* of the sixteenth century. There can be no greater contrast than between these and such stories of Dostoevsky as "The Double" or "Mr. Prokharchin." Dostoevsky, with the material of sordid reality, succeeds in building fabrics of weird fantasy. Turgenev, in spite of all the paraphernalia introduced, never succeeded in freeing himself from the second-rate atmosphere of the medium's consulting room. "The Song of Triumphant Love" shows up his limitation of another kind—the inadequacy of his language for treating subjects of insufficient reality. This limitation Turgenev shared with all his contemporaries (except Tolstoy and Leskov). They did not have a sufficient feeling of words, of language as language (as Pushkin and Gogol had had), to make it serve them in unfamiliar fields. Words for them were only signs of familiar things and familiar feelings. Language had entered with them on a strictly limited engagement—it would serve only in so far as it had not to leave the everyday realities of the nineteenth century.

The same stylistic limitation is apparent in Turgenev's last and most purely lyrical work, *Poems in Prose* (1879–83). (Turgenev originally entitled them *Senilia;* the present title was given them with the author's silent approval by the editor of the *Messenger of Europe,* where they first appeared.) They are a series of short prose fragments, most of them gathered round some more or less narrative kernel. They are comparable in construction to the objectivated lyrics of the French Parnassians, who used visual symbols to express their subjective experience. Sometimes they verge on the fable and the apologue. In these "poems" is to be found the final and most hopeless expression of Turgenev's agnostic pessimism, of his awe of unresponsive nature and necessity, and of his pitying contempt for human futility. The best of the "poems" are those where these feelings are given in ironic garb. The more purely poetical ones have suffered from time, and date too distinctly from about 1880—a date that can hardly add beauty to anything connected with it. The one that closes the series, "The Russian Language," has suffered particularly—not from time only, but from excessive handling. It displays in a condensed form all the weakness and ineffectiveness of Turgenev's style when it was divorced from concrete and familiar *things.* The art of eloquence has been lost.

Turgenev was the first Russian writer to charm the Western reader. There are still retarded Victorians who consider him the only Russian writer who is not disgusting. But for most lovers of Russian he has been replaced by spicier food. Turgenev was very nineteenth century, perhaps the most representative man of its latter part, whether in Russia or west of it. He was a Victorian, a man of compromise, more Victorian than any of his Russian contemporaries. This made him so acceptable to Europe, and this has now made him lose so much of his reputation there. Turgenev struck the West at first as something new, something typically Russian. But it is hardly necessary to insist today on the fact that he is not in any sense representative of Russia as a whole. He was representative only of his class—the idealistically educated middle gentry, tending already to become a non-class intelligentsia—and of his generation, which failed to gain real touch with Russian realities,[2] which failed to find itself a place in life and which, ineffective in the sphere of action, produced one of the most beautiful literary growths of the nineteenth century. In his day Turgenev was regarded as a leader of opinion on social problems; now this seems strange and unintelligible. Long since, the issues that he fought out have ceased to be of any actual interest. Unlike Tolstoy or Dostoevsky, unlike Griboedov, Pushkin, Lermontov, and Gogol, unlike Chaadaev, Grigoriev, and Herzen—Turgenev is no longer a teacher or even a ferment. His work has become pure art—and perhaps it has won more from this transformation than it has lost. It has taken a permanent place in the Russian tradition, a place that stands above the changes of taste or the revolutions of time. We do not seek for wisdom or guidance in it, but it is impossible to imagine a time when "The Singers," "A Quiet Spot," "First Love," or *Fathers and Sons* will cease to be among the most cherished of joys to Russian readers.

Notes

1. It is interesting to note that these pieces are precisely those Henry James singles out for particular praise.

2. What Turgenev was in touch with were not the raw realities of Russian life, but only their reflection in the minds of his generation of intellectuals.

Story and Novel in Turgenev's Work
Vladimir Fisher°

THE AUTOBIOGRAPHICAL ELEMENT

Turgenev's novels have overshadowed his stories. And in general, the latter were somehow unlucky. The critics, in the person of Belinsky,

° Excerpted from *Tvorchestvo Turgeneva*, ed. I. N. Rozanov and Yu. M. Sokolov (Moscow: Raduga, 1920), 3–39. Translated from the Russian for this volume by the editor.

met the first story[1] rather coldly. The success of *Notes of a Hunter* at the end of the 1840s and the beginning of the 1850s prevented the public and the critics from appreciating the great merits of the stories. The reflected light of the fame of *Notes of a Hunter* fell on two of the stories—"Mumu" and "The Inn." But after that began the era of the novels, which happened to coincide with the blossoming of the Turgenev story. But the vivid social significance of the novels crowded the stories out of the foreground. True, our socially minded critics noted some stories, but more was said apropos of them than about them (Chernyshevsky's article about "Asya"[2]); some stories provoked bewilderment ("Phantoms," "Enough," "The Dog"); others enjoyed success among the public as entertaining reading ("The Song of Triumphant Love"); they were always published enthusiastically in journals, they were translated, but they were little studied.

In the scholarly literature that has arisen recently, the stories have been addressed in order to treat questions of one sort or another that occur in connection with the study of the writer's worldview (Ovsyaniko-Kulikovsky)[3] or of his "manner" (Istomin).[4]

But the Turgenev story has its special interest if only because it is the product of the writer's pure inspiration, which does not lay claim here to the solution of any social questions, for which solution, in the opinion of certain people, Turgenev had no gift.

The autobiographical significance of Turgenev's stories, however, has been established, although hardly studied thoroughly. The writer's declaration that his entire biography is in his works relates primarily and especially to his stories. He himself pointed especially to the story "First Love." But that does not mean that the Turgenev story is of purely subjective origin. On the contrary, its interest is more objective, and the subjective image in the story stands not in the foreground, but, for the most part, at a double or triple remove: the person in whom we recognize the author is often the witness in a story, the observer, the narrator, but not the hero. The author draws not so much on experiences from his own life as on observations.

If one looks at Turgenev's stories from the biographical point of view, one will have to single out, in the first place, those that treat family legends and the author's family recollections; the first such story in time is "Three Portraits," which treats the author's ancestors on his maternal side; the figure of his mother is encountered, as is well known, in the stories "Mumu," "A King Lear of the Steppe," and "Punin and Baburin"; that of his father, in the story "First Love."

Other stories shed light on the author's school years: the narrator or hero is a university student or preparing to be one, and, moreover, at Moscow University; the author's brief stay at the latter left an incomparably greater mark on his artistic memory than did his stay at Saint Petersburg University, about which so much is said in "Memoirs of Literature and Life." But a Moscow coloration prevails in a great number of Turgenev's stories, beginning with "Andrey Kolosov"and ending with "Klara Milich," and also forms an organic part of the majority of his novels.

The stories in a third category cover the "years of wandering": the narrator or hero travels abroad, as Turgenev himself travelled after finishing his education; these are "Three Meetings," "Asya," and "Spring Freshets," the autobiographical nature of which has been established.

The other stories are probably also autobiographical to a certain degree, although that is more difficult to establish, so varied is their coloration.

Establishing the autobiographical element in Turgenev's stories is extraordinarily important for elucidating the process of their creation, but not for elucidating their essence: Turgenev's stories do not give a sequential history of the author's inner life, as do Tolstoy's works. Personal recollections, meetings, and observations only gave Turgenev the material out of which there arose something, but in its essence something different from poetic autobiography.

Even more insignificant and incidental is the autobiographical element in the novels. Certain features of Lavretsky's joyless childhood ("Woe to a heart that has not loved in youth!"), the student life of Lezhnev, who had written "an entire drama in imitation of *Manfred*" (Turgenev's *Steno*), the character Shubin, which reproduces in part Turgenev in his youth, with his eccentricity, self-analysis, and childish playfulness—that is approximately all of the autobiographical details that the existing evidence about Turgenev allows one to establish in the novels.

THE NARRATORS OF THE STORIES

The autobiographical origin of the majority of Turgenev's stories affects their form noticeably: the majority of them (twenty-five out of thirty-four) are narrated in the first person, while in the novels, whose plots are for the most part invented, that form of narration is not encountered. At the same time, the first person in the story is not the main person, and often is quite peripheral. But the author needs him for the form, and he, the author, expends considerable energy to create him, and in such a way that the reader does not confuse him with the author. . . .

Thus, Turgenev, while needing the fiction of narrators, is anxious in every way to leave him in the shade, not to introduce him into the plot if at all possible, and not to restrict himself with his manner. In fact only in a few stories is the narrator the main person, for instance, "Asya"; in the majority of instances he plays a secondary role, as in the story "Yakov Pasynkov," or he plays no role at all other than that of a viewer, observer, witness, for instance, "The Brigadier."

And nonetheless in the corpus of Turgenev's stories autobiographical or subjective traits appear every now and then; now we see a young master, the son of a female estate owner, then a young university student, now a traveller, then a hunter, now simply an elderly tall gentleman with graying hair. From time to time the narrator is a mouthpiece for the author's worldview or the author's artistic credo.

But there are quite objective narrator characters too: such is the Kaluga estate owner Porfiry Kapitonych ("The Dog"), the priest ("Father Alexey's Story"), and the old man ("The Watch"). There are absolutely undistinguished, fictional narrators, for instance, Mr. X ("A Strange Story").

Turgenev's lack of desire to imitate a narrator's manner does not come, of course, from an inability to create experiments such as Karl Ivanovich's story in Tolstoy.[5] A superb authority on mores, Turgenev has a masterful command of other people's speech and knows how to convey its slightest nuances, including pronunciation.[6]

But poetic autobiography is present in Turgenev's stories only as an element and does not comprise their essence. Cultural realia,[7] which saturate many of Turgenev's stories, are an element and a material, too, but cultural realia do not comprise their essence either. . . .

THE HISTORICAL BACKGROUND OF THE STORIES

One additional surface aspect of Turgenev's stories that ought to be recognized as such is the socio-historical element. In telling about Sanin and Gemma's love ("Spring Freshets"), the writer notes the awkwardness that Sanin feels when the prospect of selling his peasants presents itself to him. It is clear that this has very slight relation to the story's plot. But it is remarkable that Turgenev always dates his narratives precisely and indicates the place of action precisely. In general, that is the accepted practice in historical novels; it is also understandable that Turgenev indicates the years in his novels, which depict a specific moment in the history of educated Russian society. But what need have we to know that the action of the story "Klara Milich" transpires precisely in 1878?

In Turgenev the reader almost always learns in what year, or at least in what decade the action transpires. We learn that the action of "The Desperado" takes place in 1829, that of "First Love" in 1833, that of "A Misfortunate Girl" in 1835, that Sanin meets Gemma in 1840, and that he is 22 then, that "A Correspondence" relates to the years 1840–42, the action of "Faust" to 1850. The separate parts of the story "Punin and Baburin" are headed with figures: "1836," "1837," "1849," and "1861." Moreover, the time is marked by historical and historico-literary information. The story "The Jew" coincides with the forays abroad after the War of 1812; "The Watch," with Alexander I's ascension to the throne; Baburin's exile, with the arrests that raged in 1849. The action of "First Love" occurs right "at the height of romanticism"; that of "A Misfortunate Girl," at the time when Pushkin's Onegin is fresh in everyone's memory; "Knock—Knock—Knock" relates to the time of Marlinsky's great renown; Gemma reads Malss, a Frankfurt writer of the 1840s; the reader always knows what the heroes of a story read and what their literary tastes are: that characterizes them and the time. But, of course, only in part. So be it that Sanin was born in 1818, loves Gemma in 1840, reads Malss with her and contemplates selling his peasants. But if he had been born in 1848 and in 1870 loved a Gemma who was born later, the essence of their love would remain the same: the only difference would be that they would read someone other than Malss, and Sanin would have had to sell his estate instead of live people. Why does Turgenev need this chronology and illusion?

It is an almost unprecedented phenomenon. . . . This "historicity" of Turgenev's stories is only a surface aspect, an element, material, like autobiography and cultural realia. It is not an artistic necessity, but it is, for Turgenev, a psychological one.

In order to understand this, one must turn to those stories that happen to lack this chronology.

PESSIMISM

These are primarily those stories that are the almost unmediated expression of the author's worldview—"Phantoms," "Enough," and "A Dream." Here Turgenev's creativity is bared; here those "surface aspects" that were mentioned earlier do not turn up.

First, there is nothing autobiographical here: the author conveys his own attitude and worldview, true, but a general one that is not linked to any particular moment in his personal life.

Second, there are no conditions of place here, that is, cultural realia. In this regard, an especially interesting example is the story "A Dream," where there is not even a single name, but human relations are shown in their essence.

Third, there are no conditions of time here: no dates, no historical or historico-literary information.

And in order to understand the Turgenev story at all, one has to disengage oneself from the autobiographical element, from cultural realia, from the historical background, because none of these things is of the essence; it is essential to contemplate human relations presented by Turgenev in the purity in which they are shown in the story "A Dream."

Thus, a Turgenev story's main interest is psychological and philosophical, although only in a few cases are the philosophy and psychology not made up in the colors of place and time.

In the story "Phantoms" precisely the absolute freedom from the fetters of time and space is observed. Ellis carries the hero off to distant places and distant eras. The result is horror, melancholy, despair. . . .

Of course the essence of Sanin and Gemma's relations would remain the same in another era as well, but Turgenev wants to see them alive; and for that he needs specifically Frankfurt, specifically 1840, Gemma's Italian gestures, and the reading of Malss, specifically Malss, not of Sudermann.

Nature as an elemental force, as a substance, is horrible. And life in its essence is petty, boring, flat, and terrifying in that there is nothing terrifying in it. But

> Look around—and the everyday world
> Is multicolored and marvellous

And so, fettering a person to a place, fixing him in the framework of chronological dates, and observing him in that little corner, after forgetting about the infinity that surrounds him—that is Turgenev's artistic mission.

"Stay!" he exclaims in the *Poems in Prose,* "remain forever in my memory as I now see you!"

FATALISM

Another feature of Turgenev's worldview that influences the concepts of his stories in a specific way is a distinctive fatalism. While seeing only a phenomenon in the individual human, Turgenev sees a substance in human life, in the life of the masses. The aggregate life of people is such a complex combination of individual wills, such an interweaving of intersecting aspirations, that it is ruled by chance, which is not envisioned by any individual consciousness and for which no individual principle can establish norms. An individual thrown into the mass is powerless, like a straw in the wind, like a raindrop in a current: the drops create the current, but each individual drop is completely in the power of the current. Turgenev's most powerful poem, "The Crowd," expresses this sad capitulation of the individual to the mass.

An individual in an elemental mass of other individuals is given up to chance. The story "Three Meetings" is built on the play of chance. But in portraying life in general, Turgenev often ponders *"the mysterious play of fate* that we blind ones call blind chance" ("Faust"). "Neither can one alter one's *fate,* nor does anyone know himself, and besides, it's also impossible to foresee the future. In reality, nothing else happens in life except the *unexpected,* and we spend our whole lives doing nothing but accommodating ourselves to events" ("A Correspondence").

Chance rules in life. Chance sends Vyazovnin to Paris, where he so stupidly runs up against a sword; chance brings Alexey Petrovich ("A Correspondence") to the ballet, where he falls in love with a ballerina; chance brings N. N. together with Asya, Sanin with Gemma; chance turns Ridel's joke into the fatal reason for Teglev's suicide ("Knock—Knock—Knock"); chance governs the watch that invades the lives of the boys ("The Watch"); but fate often peeps out from behind chance. . . .

Therefore the life of an individual is not defined by his character. By virtue of his position an individual is inevitably passive; the active principle is the reality surrounding him. The perceived opinion about a weakness of will as the main trait of Turgenev's heroes has begun to waver recently. It is not weakness of will that makes many of Turgenev's heroes impotent in life and "superfluous," but something else, located outsides themselves—fate.

In the story "The Watch," the narrator's father, a minor business agent, after quarreling with his friend Latkin, curses him. "Fate itself seemed intent upon discharging my father's last wish. Soon after the rupture . . . Latkin's wife, who, true, had been ill a long while, died; his second daughter, a three-year-old child, went deaf and dumb from terror in a single day: a beehive had gotten stuck around her head; Latkin himself had an apoplectic stroke and fell into extreme poverty." No matter how Lavretsky's break with his wife may be motivated psychologically, one should not forget his Aunt Glafira's curse: "You won't make a nest for yourself anywhere!" In the story "The Inn" there is also the fickle finger of fate: Naum, who gets the inn through deceit, keeps being lucky; but "after being a successful manager for some fifteen years, he arranged to sell his inn at a profit to another petty bourgeois. He would never have parted with his fortune if the following apparently insignificant circumstance had not occurred: for two mornings in a row his dog, sitting in front of the windows, howled long and plaintively; he went out onto the street for the second time, took a good look at the howling dog, shook his head, set off for town, and on that very day agreed on a price with the petit bourgeois who had long wanted to buy the inn. A week later he left for somewhere far away—outside the province; the new owner moved in, and what do you think? That same evening the inn burned down, not a single closet survived, and Naum's successor was left a beggar." Fate sends Porfiry Kapitonych, a Kaluga estate owner with a bald spot and a belly, a dog who perishes after playing a definite role in his life ("The Dog"). The same fate sends Lukeria ("Living Relics") a disease and turns her from a "giggler, singer, dancer" into a saint.

Lukeria believes that that is God; but it is an unjust god who at the same time has a beehive get stuck to an innocent child's head; it is a god who gives Naum success in unfair business practices but punishes the innocent petty bourgeois who buys the inn from him; it is a god who manifests incomprehensible sympathy for Porfiry Kapitonych; it is a god who listens attentively to the curses of evil people, not the prayers of the good. His whims resemble those of the crotchety old woman who causes the mute Gerasim suffering ("Mumu").

In Turgenev there are no people who forge their own happiness: all are blamelessly guilty, lucky without reason. All are doomed.

THE COMPOSITION OF A STORY

That is precisely what a Turgenev story tells about. Generally speaking, it tells about how an outside force irrupts into a person's life, takes him into its universe, throws him here and there according to its arbitrary rule, and, finally, casts the shipwrecked person up unto his bank as a pathetic piece of debris. Moreover, fate does not reckon with a given person's predisposition toward one thing or another, but imposes a role upon him that is often beyond his strength. You would think him a Gogolian hero, but an adventure in the spirit of Pechorin[8] happens to him.

So, Lieutenant Yergunov, a blood brother of Gogol's Zhevakin, has an adventure reminiscent of Lermontov's story "Taman."

Aratov, a relative of Podkolyosin,[9] experiences a mysterious poem of love with a mystical ending ("Klara Milich").

Porfiry Kapitonych, the Kaluga estate owner, "a middle-aged man of average height, with a belly and a bald spot," experiences "something supernatural," before which "common sense" completely retreats.

Turgenev portrays the contact of tawdry people with the romance of life, of shallow and weak people with the mystery of love, and of sober people with the mysteries of nature.

In accordance with this, three moments are distinguishable in a Turgenev story:

(1) The norm. The depiction of an individual in the ordinary conditions of life in which another writer would in fact leave that person, for instance, Goncharov.

(2) The catastrophe. The violation of the norm thanks to the incursion of unforeseen circumstances that do not arise from the given situation.

(3) The finale. The end of the catastrophe and its psychological consequences.

The moments are laid out in just such a sequence in, for instance, the story "Asya," where N. N.'s trip is the norm; the catastrophe, his love for Asya; and the finale, N. N.'s lonely old age.

But these moments may follow in reverse sequence: the finale, that is, the depiction of the consequence of the catastrophe, may be at the beginning; then follows the story of the norm and of the catastrophe that came after it. The story "A Correspondence," for instance, is composed in that way, where the hero's death is told at the beginning, and then the norm unfolds from his correspondence—his relations with Marya Alexandrovna; and the catastrophe—his affair with the French singer.

The repetition of similar moments sometimes occurs in one and the same story: a finale turns into a norm which, in turn, is violated by a second recurrent catastrophe, which leads to a new finale.

That is how the story "A Dream" is constructed. The first norm here is the narrator's parents' happy, easygoing trip, about which his mother tells him later (chapter 9); the catastrophe is the appearance of the stranger, who becomes the narrator's father; the finale is the ruined life described at the beginning of the story, in the first chapter. That finale has turned into a norm. The new appearance of the stranger and his death comprise the second catastrophe in the story, which brings with it a new finale that comprises the contents of the last fragment of the story (beginning with the words "My mother and I never spoke of him").

It remains to make a separate analysis of each of these moments.

THE NORM

The moment in a Turgenev story that I have called the norm consists of a realistic depiction of the hero's circumstances of life. These norms can be reduced to several types. The main ones are the following:

(1) The narrator of the hero of the story is a student or preparing to be one; he lives in Moscow more or less independently, more or less sociably.

(2) The narrator or hero of the story travels abroad, without definite aims.

(3) The narrator or the hero of the story arrives in his village on business or as a consequence of the absence of business.

The transition from the norm to the catastrophe is accomplished by Turgenev with the help of a plot that provides the story's surface interest. The appearance of a female character usually serves to put the plot in motion. The moment of the appearance by the woman—usually the one who enters the room—is a very important turning point in the story. If the norm is portrayed for the most part realistically, then the plot intrigue is distinguished by its romantic character. The female character who appears in Turgenev is almost always full of enigmatic, mysterious, enticing beauty. Moreover, she stands in contradiction to the surrounding milieu. . . . The question of how that creature could turn up in this milieu arises; interest is aroused, the story's tempo increases. This tension is already felt in the conveying of the impression made by the heroine's appearance: it stuns, amazes, strikes, and rivets the narrator to the spot. The center of attention from that moment on is the female character, and the narrator's role is unimportant: he may be the hero of the story, like Sanin, or the hero of "Asya," or he may remain an accomplice, a go-between, a witness, as in the stories "A Misfortunate Girl," "Punin and Baburin."

And so, the realistic exposition in a Turgenev story represents a sort of thesis; the romantic plot intrigue, which thanks to the realistic grounding, accounts for the whole effect of the story, an antithesis.

The further transition to the catastrophe forms the synthesis. The female character does not remain a romantic daydream: having surprised the reader, she gradually stands out in bolder and bolder relief, becoming persuasive and lifelike. The realistic writer comes into his own. Upon the hero or narrator's close acquaintance with the heroine, the realistic and almost always wretched, sometimes difficult conditions of her life come to light. At home Zinaida ("First Love") has decay, slovenly poverty, and a vulgar mother with an inclination to malicious litigation. Asya is the illegitimate daughter of an estate owner and has grown up in extremely abnormal conditions. It is depressing at the Zlotnitskys' home ("Yakov Pasynkov"): "The very furniture, the red wallpaper with yellow cracks in it in the living room, the multitude of wicker chairs in the dining room, the faded worsted pillows depicting maidens and dogs on the sofas, the horn lamps and gloomy portraits on the walls—everything instilled in one an involuntary melancholy. . . ." And girls who know how to love only once in life grow up in those surroundings. Finally, the enchanting Gemma ("Spring Freshets"), a representative of the petit bourgeoisie, the fiancée of the solid merchant Klyber, called upon to use her beauty to save her impoverished family's situation, and later—the wife of an American businessman. When her mother discusses quite practically the benefits of her marriage to Sanin, in the presence of the latter, Gemma feels extremely awkward.

However, a female character does not always initiate the intrigue in a Turgenev story; sometimes an animal (twice a dog, once a horse), sometimes things ("The Watch") are the instrument of fate that brings on the catastrophe. But no matter what, the plot intrigue is always romantically unexpected; as is well known, Turgenev took special pains with it, finding that the absence of "invention" was the weak side of Russian writers. As Gutyar notes quite justly, the outline of a Turgenev work "is suggested only in part by the fate of those people who served as the protoypes of the story's protagonists."

THE CATASTROPHE

As applied to a Turgenev story, the term "catastrophe" does not have quite the same meaning as in a tragedy.

There is little of the tragedic in Turgenev, or the tragic in his works consists of the absence of tragedy where it ought to be, of the fact that the most terrible thing in life is that there is nothing terrible. But the term "catastrophe" is applicable here because what happens to Turgenev's protagonists bears the imprint of fate: both good fortune, which they are incapable of apprehending adequately, and misfortune, which turns out to be beyond their powers. The mother's story in "The Dream" is characteristic in this regard.

She is alone in a hotel room—her husband has gone to the club; she goes to bed. "And suddenly she felt so awful that she even turned cold all over and began to shiver. She thought she heard a light knocking behind the wall—the way a dog scratches—and she began watching that wall. An icon camp burned in the corner; the room was hung all around with damask. Suddenly something moved over there, rose a bit, opened up. And all black, long, that horrible man with the evil eyes came right out of the wall! She wanted to cry out and could not. She froze in fear. He came up to her quickly, like a beast of prey, threw something over her head, something stifling, heavy, white."

And so, that is how fate functions. Its emissaries penetrate walls covered with damask in which unclean doors are revealed. The turning point in the story is quite unreal. But Turgenev's devices are bared in general in "A Dream," and if one ponders the essence of life's phenomena, the stranger's emergence from the wall is not the least bit any stranger than the appearance first of Gemma in Sanin's life, and then of Marya Nikolaevna; it is just that in the latter instance a realistic motivation is given such as is lacking in the first.

It has already been noted more than once that for Turgenev the supreme confirmation of the individual is love, and that at the same time love is a pernicious, destructive, and dangerous force. Fate lures Turgenev's heroes into a whirlwind of passion, and whether they want that or not, it leaves them no choice: if they meet it head on, ruin and devastation threaten them; if they lack courage, they will be punished—by the misery of later regrets, like the hero of "Asya," by the horror of emptiness and the fear of death, like Sanin, or a rejected love will make its claims on them from beyond the grave, as happens to the hero of "Klara Milich."

However, there are people on whom fate does not bestow its attention. There is a certain level of life, a fullness of sensations, to which not everyone is capable of rising. Only a person who rises to that point will experience life in full measure, but he will also drink the bitter cup of suffering; only with the level of passion do life and beauty begin. The idyll that Turgenev paints in the story "Old Portraits," an idyll of old-world land owners, does not move him; Malanya Pavlovna's impenetrable stupidity, which her loving husband is also aware of, does not increase the delight of the idyll; and the fact with which the story ends destroys the idyll. In the story "Two Friends" that tranquil life is established in the finale: good Verochka, with her phlegmatic right, remains deaf to the language of passion, marries a husband once "without rapture," then marries a second time, to a person more comprehensible to her. "Pyotr Vasilievich, his wife, and all their domestics spend the time very monotonously— peacefully and quietly; they enjoy their happiness, *because on earth there is no other happiness.*" A specter of life, however, arises above theirs, and that is the memory of Vyazovnin; but he, himself incapable of rising to the level of passion, has flashed by in their life like a shadow, and they remain on the bottom. No catastrophe has occurred.

A catastrophe is possible only for those people who have the attributes necessary for reaching life in its fullness, even though they may have no desire to do so: passion nevertheless will pull them into the whirlpool. In the story "Faust," Vera, thanks to her mother's efforts, has been seemingly insured against the element of passion since childhood. Its most powerful conductor, art, was removed. Vera leaves for the canopy of a marriage "without rapture," like Verochka; but a person from another world, with a copy of Goethe's *Faust* in his hands, turns up and "ploughed up raging voices" in the young woman. . . .

Real life prudently creates one marriage; fate, the romance of life, erects above it its own mighty superstructure, which crushes that marriage.[10]

But the topic here has been individuals unwillingly carried away by passion, who shun it out of "fear" or good sense. There are those who play with fire, who set out into the ocean of passion without worrying about an anchor. Such is Zinaida ("First Love"). But the highest degree is to accept the cup of life without faint-hearted fear, but to limit oneself to the lofty commands of duty. Such is Yakov Pasynkov, who has made denial his principle. Those who have not stood at the necessary height also come to this conclusion. "Life is hard work. Denial, constant denial—that is its secret meaning, its unriddling: not the fulfilling of favorite ideas and dreams, no matter how elevated they might be, but the fulfilling of duty—that is what a person should worry about; without putting chains on himself, the iron chains of duty, he cannot reach the end of his days without falling." Only if a person is anchored to duty will he not be swept away by a catastrophe.

That is the meaning of Liza Kalitina's ideal.[11]

THE FINALE

The catastrophic nature of events in Turgenev's stories is often overshadowed by descriptions of storms; they are rather frequent ("A Quiet Spot," "Faust," "Spring Freshets," "A Dream"). And where there is no storm or tempest, it is overshadowed with the help of similes and metaphors. . . .

The storm of life, the storm of passion does its work and leaves debris. The debris of life's storm includes Chulkaturin, the heroine of "Three Meetings," Alexey Petrovich of "A Correspondence," the hero of "Faust," Zinaida of "First Love," the Brigadier, King Lear of the Steppe, and Sanin. Others perish, like the baron in the story "A Dream," or Vera ("Faust"), or the hero of the story "Klara Milich." Others remain debris; moreover, something from the past remains in their hands, a romantic recollection. . . .

FROM STORY TO NOVEL

Turgenev began his literary activity in the era of romanticism's decline. . . . Turgenev himself was profoundly imbued with romanticism, enthusiastic about its very important representatives Goethe and Byron. But in the 1840s Turgenev surrendered his romantic individualism. That capitulation can be heard in his first narrative poems, *Parasha* and *A Conversation,* and especially in the poem "The Crowd," which has a greater significance for Russian literature than is usually imagined. It is a sad rejection of Byronism. The individual who has proudly torn himself away from the crowd cannot hold out in his solitary position, becomes conscious of his weakness, and recognizes the victory of the crowd. It was not easy for Turgenev to accomplish that rejection. The poem echoes with sadness and resignation. The young Turgenev, himself broken inside, given to excessive analysis, lacking in will, began his search for a strong, integrated, beautiful person. But how and where to look? The Byronic method had been rejected. The Byronic heroes married their Parashas and began living happily on their estates. The romantic phantasmagoria had been dispelled. . . .

In his early stories, too, he angrily condemns romanticism. It is enough to read "Andrey Kolosov" and "The Diary of a Superfluous Man" to get an idea of that anger.

The poet feels that there is no room for him in the crowd, but neither is there room outside it. And he escapes to simple people, to nature, to the heroes of *Notes of a Hunter,* who have extracted wholeness and simplicity from the innermost depths of mother nature. But here too he remained an outside observer: there was no point even in talking of a return to nature for Turgenev, of taking to plain living—it was not for nothing that he had broken with romanticism. He will return to a higher arena of life; he needs to determine the relationship of the individual to society, to the people, to humanity. After all, romanticism was a temporary cutting away of the individual; he has to be reunited with the society around him, because it is impossible to live outside it. So that the individual personality will not be swallowed up, like a speck of dust, in infinity, Turgenev will try to attach it more firmly to the moment, to tie it to societal evolution, and only then to raise the question of what to do. Because the individual, torn away from the conditions of time and place, seemed to Turgenev to be so horrifyingly impotent that in reply to the question of what to do, he said: "After crossing one's useless arms on one's empty chest, preserve the last and only virtue accessible to him [to man], that of the recognition of one's own insignificance" ("Enough").

It was from that state that Turgenev in fact fled to the world of his novels, where the broadly understood feeling of duty was, on the one hand, to persuade a person that "his arms" were not "useless," but that, on the contrary, mankind needs their work; on the other hand, that very feeling of duty was to safeguard a person against the storms of the universe of passion threatening him on all sides.

That is how the novel grew out of Turgenev's story. And in the majority of those novels one can distinguish with greater or lesser clarity the layerings that turned the story into a novel.

At the same time as Natalya's love for Rudin arises, develops, and is concluded on Lasunskaya's estate, conversations about Rudin are being held on a neighboring estate, the story of his youth is being told, about the milieu that produced him. The first element is a typical Turgenev story; the second gives this story a sociohistorical background; a third element—Rudin's story about his activity—deepens the sociohistorical aspect of the novel.

In *A Nest of Gentlefolk* two stories can be found: the heroine of the first is Varvara Pavlovna; the heroine of the second, Liza.

Lavretsky's genealogy, his conversations with Panshin and Mikhal-evich, and his life in the countryside create a social novel.

The novel *Fathers and Sons* consists of three episodes: (1) Bazarov at the Kirsanovs', (2) Bazarov at Odintsova's, (3) Bazarov at his parents'; the first episode has sociohistorical interest; the two others, universally human.

Smoke includes the story of Litvinov's student love for Irina; the episode in Baden makes up the sociohistorical aspect of the novel.

Hence the inserted episodes, biographical digressions, genealogies that are so typical for Turgenev. There he is unburdening his heart, talking about the universal while creating a novel; on the other hand—the chronological dates and historical background.

However, while depicting the personal side of his heroes' lives in his novels, Turgenev feels at home, but he seems to avoid portraying them on a wide arena of activity, although that apparently was in fact supposed to provide the basis of the novel's design. Rudin at Lasunskaya's estate is drawn graphically and vividly; we hear only a fleeting account of his years of study and activity. Lavretsky's love for and life with his wife, Lavretsky and Liza's love are drawn vividly; but the fact that Lavretsky realizes his goal of "plowing the soil" and what he does for the peasants are related in a general way, casually. The author is passionately interested in how Yelena comes to love Insarov and how she leaves with him; but Insarov's preparation for future activity is spoken of in passing, and the author decides not to depict that activity and kills off the hero. And Bazarov is depicted not where he developed, not in the milieu of which he is a representative, but on gentry estates, where he argues, loves, and dies. The same goes for Litvinov.[12] Only in *Virgin Soil* is an attempt made to depict the activity itself, but here too the arena of the novel's action is a gentry estate, and moreover, the depiction of the activity itself does not belong to Turgenev's best pages.

How Tolstoy's Nekhlyudov,[13] Levin, and Vronsky[14] manage their estates—that we know clearly and definitely; how Lezhnyov, La-vretsky, Litvinov[15] manage their estates—Lord only knows.

They simply manage them.

Obviously, Turgenev the artist needs his heroes' social activity only as an outside force that defines a human in a certain way. His attention is concentrated on individuals; everything else is kept at a distance. What is interesting is how an individual lives, loves, and dies; for the sake of fullness and expressiveness of image conditions of time and place that are in and of themselves perhaps not very important are taken into account. Such is the writer's unconscious worldview.

Consciously, Turgenev may have had claims to the solution or raising of questions of the day; that was precisely what the critics looked for in his novels. And all the misunderstandings that have arisen because of that have occurred because critics were unable to appreciate what Turgenev had to offer, and demanded what he could not offer, although he tried. Perhaps unaware of it himself, he transferred these questions to a completely different plane.[16] Recent criticism, not without grounds, has expressed doubt about Turgenev as a social writer. But the desire to be one cost Turgenev dearly; he had to seek new devices, more or less successful ones, in order to give the novel social significance; he had to write such a decidedly weak work as *Virgin Soil.*

DIALOGUE IN THE NOVEL

In the Turgenev novel, as compared to the story, dialogue plays a large role. Avoiding depicting his contemporary heroes in deed, the writer portrays them marvelously in word. It is no accident that the hero of the first novel is an orator; and all the succeeding heroes speak interestingly and expressively. Turgenev conveys the charm of Rudin's speech, who speaks out against scepticism and who by striking certain strings of the heart forces others to sound at the same time; Lavretsky's speech about Russia echoes with sober sense; Bazarov's speech echoes with sharp and casual expressiveness. And many interesting and sensible conversations are related on the pages of Turgenev's novels. And the subject of these conversations is always Russia, the current moment, the contemporary generation's view.

Of course, there are dialogues of a purely personal character, just as in the stories; in them Turgenev is an incomparable master, now conveying Liza's sometimes simply unclear but profound speech, now Homerically reproducing the speech of secondary characters— Marfa Timofeevna, N. A. Astakhov, or Bazarov's parents.

But the dialogues on contemporary topics that constitute a peculiarity of Turgenev's novels can be subdivided into the categories of debates and didactic dialogues. . . .

We shall call didactic dialogues those whose ideal nature can in no way be concealed: the speech of the author himself can be heard— what in the old days was called that of a spokesman for the author. The presence of such dialogues, interesting as they may be in and of themselves, cannot be considered a virtue in a novel: Turgenev falls back on them when he lacks power of invention. That can be especially felt in *Rudin,* where Lezhnyov provides an evaluation of Rudin on the reader's behalf. There is no concern for the style of the person speaking here; there is no debate here—the listeners offer only the necessary responses; the voice of the author can be heard distinctly.

This device, which subsides in Turgenev's best novels (*A Nest of Gentlefolk* and *Fathers and Sons*), is repeated in the others. In *On the Eve* we again here authorial speech in Shubin, when he talks to Yelena about Uvar Ivanovich. In *Smoke* Potugin speaks for the author; in *Virgin Soil* it is Nezhdanov, in his poem about Russia. . . .

DIDACTIC CHARACTERS

This Lezhnyov, who plays the role of a chorus in *Rudin,* has another importance as well. "Here's the sort of person we need more of," the writer seems to want to say. Indeed, Lezhnyov puts into practice ahead of time the activity that Turgenev, using Lavretsky as a mouthpiece, will later proclaim the most necessary and greatest one: he plows the soil and apparently does so as well as possible. For that Turgenev rewards him with personal happiness: the novel ends with Lezhnyov's idyll. . . .

In *On the Eve* a didactic character again appears, the one least successful in an artistic sense but most successful in a didactic one— Insarov. That character is put together mechanically from traits that Russians lack but that are desirable and are essential, the very first condition for any action, without which even the quality of genius will turn out to be barren. Turgenev deprives Insarov of everything human: the absence of any spiritual struggle when deciding to leave Yelena, on the grounds that she is a person who does not correspond to his goals, the examination for the rank of wife that he gives her— those things alienate one; and one refuses to believe that Insarov will accomplish something great, because greatness is also accomplished through passion and feeling—and Turgenev knows that perfectly well.

Litvinov is the new result of Turgenev's "search for a man." His goal is the same as Lezhnyov's and Lavretsky's. He is more alive than Lezhnyov because he is more subject to the effect of the passionate element; but he is deader than Lavretsky. His gesture when he indicates to Irina the place beside him in the train car is splendid, but it is didacticism. Turgenev seems to have sensed a certain betrayal of artistic truth here and wrote the story "Spring Freshets" after *Smoke;* Sanin experiences approximately the same thing as Litvinov, but he ends in a more Turgenevian fashion; he remains in the company of the temptress, enduring all the humiliation of his false position and, after the need has passed, breaks free. But what is allowable in a story of his is impermissible in a Turgenev novel.

Turgenev the didactic strives generously to award his businesslike "good" people with personal happiness, leads them solicitously to the family idyll with the beloved; sometimes he sets obstacles for them—passion, but he helps them overcome delusive temptations.

But where Turgenev remains a pure artist, in the stories, those temptations turn out to be insuperable. . . .

PSYCHOLOGY

Didacticism, satire, philosophizing—all these devices result from Turgenev's desire to make a social statement. But the eternal triumphs over that element, and the artist defeats the social critic. No matter what practical means the writer proposes, no matter how he calls for "small deeds," no matter how he rewards his "good people" with prosperity and happiness, he knows at the bottom of his heart that this is all "smoke"; that a lost life is lost, even though its experience was useful for the future generation; that the proud individual is threatened by the monster of death; that in life the individual is manipulated by fate; that man is insignificant. This profound consciousness of the individual's helplessness determines Turgenev's special manner of depicting individual psychology. That manner is absolutely contrary to Dostoevsky's. The latter extremely individualizes every psychological experience; Turgenev sadly makes it part of a general law, seemingly devaluing the personal in this way. He does this with the help of experienced aphorisms that he always seems to have ready. . . .

This basic view of Turgenev's gives rise to two peculiarities of his psychological manner: laconicism or negligence in the depiction of psychological experiences. Turgenev's laconicism is often distinguished by great power; he uses it when he has an especially solicitous attitude toward the person being portrayed, as though afraid of reducing him to a category, sparing him.

After receiving the news of the death of his wife, "Lavretsky dressed, went out into the garden, and walked up and down a single lane until morning."

After Varvara Pavlovna's arrival and Liza's meeting her, "Marfa Timofeevna sat up all night long at the head of Liza's bed."

Lavretsky's last meeting with Liza, at the monastery:

> Making her way from choir to choir, she walked past him close by, walked past in the even, hurryingly humble tread of a nun—and did not look at him; the lashes of the eye directed at him just trembled slightly, she just inclined her emaciated face even more— and the fingers of her compressed hands, wrapped round with rosaries, pressed against each other even more tightly. What did they both think, what did they feel? Who can know? Who can say? There are certain moments in life, certain feelings. One can only point at them—and pass on by.

Here is supreme economy of means, supreme solicitude for feeling. And along with that extreme negligence of human psychology turns up in Turgenev. . . . Hence the total ignoring of individual psychology in many characters unattractive to Turgenev. . . .

THE ELEGY

The pessimism of Turgenev's consciousness, which manifests itself in the conclusions of his novels and in his psychological manner, finds, however, a distinctive antidote in his creative intuition. There are forces that he counterposes to the individual's helplessness and insignificance in the face of death. Those forces are love and simplicity. This surmounting of pessimism is expressed in Turgenev lyrically, and his best novels conclude with solemn lyric chords.

If, as has been pointed out, Turgenev flees the horror of eternity by escaping to the temporal, then the dissatisfaction with the temporal and the limited awaken in him, on the other hand, an elevated longing for the eternal, the nontransitory. Although Rudin has not accomplished anything, he has left in young souls some sparks of enthusiasm, love, and truth, and those sparks will live; Rudin's temporal existence stretches into eternity, and he is spoken of in Lezhnyov's cozy home. Although Lavretsky and Liza have left the walk of life without touching "the cherished goblet in which the golden wine of enjoyment bubbles and plays," in the words he addresses to the young generation there is no bitterness: he gives them a blessing, and there is something Pushkinian in these reconciling chords of his speech.

Although Bazarov has died, and his mighty, proud powers turned out to be fruitless, he is silently present at the festival of life in the Kirsanovs' home, he lives in their memories and in his parents' tears. "Can it really be that their prayers, their tears are fruitless? Can it really be that love, sacred, devoted love is not all-powerful?" Turgenev asks. As a thinker, he should have answered: "Yes, fruitless and powerless." But the lyric poet answers: "Oh, no! No matter how passionate, sinful, and rebellious a heart is hidden in the grave, the flowers growing on it look at us serenely with their innocent eyes; they speak to us not only of eternal peace, that great peace of 'indifferent' nature; they also speak of eternal reconciliation and of life eternal."

Turgenev's creative thought has made its circle from the horror of infinity to the framework of the temporal; from the temporal it stretches its wings toward the infinite.

The result is an elegy in the form of a novel.

THE PICTORIAL AND MUSICAL ASPECT
OF THE TURGENEV NOVEL

One of the means of overcoming Turgenev's elegiac longing that is developed in his novels is beauty. He needs colors and sounds in order to justify life, and he generously scatters moonbeams and the sounds of the piano throughout his novels. The action of his novels always occurs in the spring or summertime, the sun shines brightly during the day, at night the moon and stars come out, and in the gentry manors pianos are heard. . . .

The sounds of the piano and the cello that are always heard in Turgenev's manor houses give a musical charm to his images. But *A Nest of Gentlefolk* is especially noteworthy in this regard. Here music sets off the contents of the novel. When his unrecognized love for Liza begins in Lavretsky, the old man Lemm dreams of composing a cantata about the stars. On that wonderful night when Lavretsky's mouth brushes against Liza's pale lips, the old musician's dream is fulfilled; inspired, he plays his piece for Lavretsky, a "song a triumphant love." But on the following days these sounds die down in order to give way to the more bravura melodies played by Varvara Pavlovna and Panshin. The years pass. Lavrestky's visits the Kalinin estate, where everything has changed, where a new generation is having a good time. He goes up to the piano, plays a chord—it is the first chord of the piece by the deceased Lemm. It rings out like a memory, and then falls silent.

That chord of recollection can be heard in all of Turgenev's stories. Past experience is dear to him. Like shadows, like smoke, everything temporal passes, but the eternal is left—and we are allowed to feel that eternal by the poet, who, like Lavretsky, goes up to the piano in a gentry manor and plays a memorable chord.

Notes

[1. "Story" as used in the title seems the best rendering of the Russian *povest* in this context. Readers unfamiliar with Russian, however, should be aware that in the final analysis, *povest* lacks an adequate English equivalent, primarily because the Russian term is a very slippery one. In the twentieth century it has come to indicate a work of prose fiction longer than a short story and shorter than a novel, but in many cases a writer's choice between *povest* and *roman* (novel) can only strike one as subjective and even arbitrary. Moreover, in the nineteenth century the term was applied to such disparate works as Pushkin's short stories and Dostoevsky's *Crime and Punishment*.]

[2. For information about Chernyshevsky and his article, see the introduction to this volume.]

[3. D. Ovsyaniko-Kulikovsky, "I. S. Turgenev," vol. 2, *Sobranie sochinenii* (St. Petersburg: Prometey, 1910–1911).]

[4. K. K. Istomin, " 'Staraya manera' Turgeneva (1834–1855). Opyt psikhologii tvorchestva," *Izvestia Otdelenia russkogo yazyka i slovesnosti Akademii nauk* 2 (1913):294–347; 3 (1913);120–194.]

[5. Reference to Tolstoy's *Childhood*.]

6. Yu. I. Aykhenvald reproaches Turgenev for mocking errors in French pronunciation. Turgenev does not mock, but, rather, conveys the errors in any pronunciation— the accent of Germans speaking Russian or French, the accent of Frenchmen pronouncing Russian names, the accent of an Italian speaking French. Turgenev hears his heroes' speech, he hears how the heroes of the novel *Fathers and Sons* pronounce the same word, "principle." Not to mention the speech of the masses, one can point out Bersenev's involved, academically meandering speech (*On the Eve*), the speech of Kollomeytsev, who pronounces "brrr" the French way, as remarkable masterpieces of this sort.

[7. The Russian word that Fisher uses here, *byt,* is notoriously difficult to render into English. In this context the word suggests the sorts of sociocultural details that anchor a literary work in a specific time and place.]

[8. Hero of Lermontov's novel *A Hero of Our Time* (1840).]

[9. Hero of Gogol's comedy *The Marriage* (1842).]

10. This motif is outlined sketchily in the narrative poem *The Priest*, published at the beginning of 1917.

[11. Reference to the heroine of *A Nest of Gentlefolk*.]

[12. The references in the paragraph are to *Rudin, A Nest of Gentlefolk, On the Eve*, and *Fathers and Sons*, in that order.]

[13. Hero of *Resurrection*.]

[14. Major protagonists in *Anna Karenina*.]

[15. Characters from Rudin, *A Nest of Gentlefolk*, and *Smoke*, respectively.]

16. A strange fact, it would seem: for a half-century Russian criticism has viewed Turgenev's novels as historical criticism of the Russian intelligentsia; over the course of the same half-century Western Europe has been interested in those novels and has been reading them avidly; it is not the fate of the Russian intelligentsia, after all, that interests Western Europe!

Turgenev's Early Genre   Leonid Grossman°

In spite of its distinguished recognition in Russian criticism, *Notes of a Hunter* has not yet been sufficiently studied as a literary work. Meanwhile, it presents great interest in the evolution of the genre of the *short story*, and with regard to Turgenev's works it represents one of the writer's favorite creations, one that he worked on over the course of nearly his whole life. The first sketch in the series is separated from the last one by a distance of nearly thirty years, and nearly all of Turgenev's literary activity, with his comedies, novellas,

° Excerpted from "Etyudy o Turgeneve," *Sobranie sochinenii v 5–i tomakh* (Moscow: Kn-vo "Sovremennye problemy," 1928), III, 38–63. Translated from the Russian for this volume by the editor.

stories, and novels, transpired between "Khor and Kalinych" (1847) and "There's a Knocking" (1875). This circumstance gives the book a special interest and obliges us to take a more attentive look at the series of short sketches that constituted Turgenev's first acclaim and evoked new artistic echoes in him to the end.

The complex, difficult, and diverse questions that consumed Turgenev's thought in the 1830s retreated from him somewhat toward the end of the 1840s. At least in the artistic sphere, philosophical questions about God and the individual, about the superman and the crowd, and about the mystery of the universe and the metaphysical laws of individual existence gave way to other inquiries and thoughts. The lofty enthusiasm of *Steno, A Conversation,* and a whole series of his lyric poems was replaced by a new direction. Turgenev seems to have tired of the philosophy, religious questions, literary refinement, or delicate aestheticism of his early sketches. He seems to have begun to long for greater spontaneity, freshness, and ingenuousness, for naive, unaffected art. His broad learning, which nourished his early narrative poems and dramas, and the whole broad range of his youthful inquiries now seemed to him something strange, pretentious, and alien to genuine art. Turgenev seemed to set himself the goal of overcoming in himself the magister of philosophy, the Hegelian, the connoisseur of narrative art of the eighteenth century, in the name of an unconscious immersion in the whirl of life for its unmediated reflection. A completely new literary style that was first manifested in the hunting sketches corresponded to the new tone that had begun to sound in the artists's soul. . . . Originally it seemed to him that he could achieve that only at the cost of a great sacrifice— the renunciation of art. In order to accept simple life with its age-old laws and the charm of simple feelings experienced in profound peace, he was ready to burn the idol he had worshiped with fanatical devotion since his young years—all his artistic work.

The story of how *Notes of a Hunter* came about is well known. After Belinsky's cooling toward Turgenev's poetic works, Turgenev had formed the firm intention of giving up literature altogether; only as a consequence of I. I. Panaev's requests, Turgenev tells us, "who did not have anything with which to fill the 'Miscellaneous' section of the first issue of *The Contemporary,* I left him a sketch entitled 'Khor and Kalinych.' (The words 'from *Notes of a Hunter*' were thought up and added by the same I. I. Panaev, with the goal of earning the reader's indulgence.) The success of that sketch encouraged me to write others, and I returned to literature."

In this late account Turgenev's testimony about his decision to renounce art completely and his curious indication of the genesis of *Notes of a Hunter* are equally important.

It turns out that the title for the whole series was not thought up by Turgenev himself, and the book of famous sketches came into being quite by chance. That needs to be remembered for the proper appreciation of the meaning and theme of his hunting stories, as well as for the refutation of the successive legends that have grown up around them.

After deciding to continue his series of sketches, Turgenev definitely laid out for himself a completely new artistic manner, one responding both to his own spiritual need to take to the simple life and to the literary style that had come into being. *Notes of a Hunter* would be written in the spirit of a fashionable trend and wholly attach itself to the predominant narrative genre—the unpretentious and ingenuous "peasant story."

Such are the origin and the tone laid out for the future sketches. It is important to note the purely aesthetic nature of Turgenev's crisis: having recognized the weakness of his narrative poems and lyric poetry, he considered it essential either to renounce art entirely or to take a completely new road. The topic, intention, and style of the forthcoming sketches appeared before him as a distinct artistic task, as a new literary device that could renew and perhaps even save the artist in him. He burned the objects of recent worship—complicated philosophical problems, questions about the nature of the world, the daring individual's challenges—in order to plunge wholeheartedly into the fresh stream of a new poetic genre.

It is important to establish the profoundly *literary* nature of the history of the conception and writing of *Notes of a Hunter* so as to bid farewell forever to the long-prevailing legend about its main goal—the struggle with serfdom.

Turgenev entered European literature under that sign and long remained in the Western reader's consciousness first of all as a fighter for the fall of slavery in Russia. Over his open coffin the French writer Edmond About proposed that a simple pedestal decorated with a broken chain be erected to him. That is a very indicative image, and one to which the reading public—and until recently critical tradition as well—readily reduced the significance of the author of *Notes of a Hunter.*

Itis well known that the legend of the emancipationist tendency of the *Notes* arose at the time of its appearance and was later supported by Turgenev himself. . . . Turgenev himself later strengthened this honorable legend with the famous declaration about his Hannibalic oath, the vow he made early on to struggle mercilessly against his fiercest enemy—serfdom.

Illusions are pardonable, even if one deliberately takes comfort in them. At a distance of two decades Turgenev could imagine that moment in that sort of altered and somewhat stylized light. It could seem to him now that he "even left for the West in order better to fulfill his oath" about the struggle with the enemy, "in order from afar to attack him more strongly."

The facts decisively refute that testimony.

At the end of the 1840s Turgenev left for abroad for a whole number of varied and complicated reasons: his love of Europe, and the desire to study, and the need he always had to be located in the major centers of intellectual and cultural life, and, finally, personal reasons—his love for Viardot—those are what primarily drew him to the West. There he gave himself up widely to the most diverse influences and impressions—artistic, scientific and scholarly, theatrical, and political. Even if one accepts his formula, one has to admit that Turgenev carried out that Hannibalic oath of his extraordinarily carelessly and by-the-by; in Paris he worked on his comedies as well as on his translated and literary pieces, and also on the study of Spanish playwrights; he read Calderón enthusiastically, translated Abbé Prévost, took a great interest in new music, even tested his own powers in musical composition. None of this corresponds at all to the notion of "a strong attack on the enemy." Finally, in his own work itself, in *Notes of a Hunter,* Turgenev is consumed with the resolution of the literary problems posed there and, as usual, absolutely free of socio-political commentary. "I do not have *den politischen Pathos,*" he declared in the summer of 1849, just at the height of his work on *Notes.*

He retained that characteristic until the end. Not for nothing did he leave us the following valuable observation: "I not only do not wish to, but I absolutely cannot, am absolutely unable to write anything with a preconceived idea or aim, so as to put forth one idea or another. For me a literary work comes about in the same way that grass grows." Such was the profoundly organic peculiarity of Turgenev's nature that was characteristic of him from the very beginning: *Notes of a Hunter* is just as free of an authorial need "to put forth one idea or another" as are Turgenev's other works, and like them, it was created organically, inevitably and simply, "the way that grass grows. . . ."[1] In truth, the author of "Forest and Steppe," in spite of his later avowals, in unfolding the pictures of his manorial steppe and forest Russia, thought very little about the propagandistic "flammability" of those refined watercolors.

The literary genre of the peasant story had been established and was very popular at that time. For Turgenev it meant a complete departure from the poetics of the 1830s that he had overcome. In his letters from the period when he was writing the first series of *Notes of a Hunter* he continually notes his disillusionment with the literary style of the era of *Steno* along with his profound admiration for a ripe, new, fresh, and very promising genre that seemed to bring deliverance to the young generation of artists from the outmoded forms of dying romanticism.

In the varied epistolary remarks is an entire new esthetics. In a work of art Turgenev especially values "a sober and subtle intelligence, a refined style, and simplicity." He is horrified by Gutzkow's *Uriel Acosta,* seeing it as a forced work filled to overflowing with political, religious, and philosophical observations, garish effects and theatrical surprises; he is revolted by works smelling of artifice, craft, convention, "which are the result of a literary itch, the prattle of egoism studying and admiring itself." He pronounces a severe sentence on Roman poetry for the fact that it is all "cold and artificial— real literature by a writer." Even in the Koran the oriental bombast and absurdity of the "prophetic language" give him pause.

But how the old Spaniards delight him! It seems to him that Calderón's works "grew up naturally out of the fertile and mighty soil; their taste and smell are simple; no literary dressing can be sensed here at all." With what energy he contrasts Homer's youth and freshness, "that life that seems eternally lit by a laughing sun," to Jean-Paul's artificial literary manner, his "half-sentimental, half-ironic fussing around with his own sick self."

George Sand's novella *François le Champi,* written simply, truthfully, grippingly, delights him. "And most important, one senses that the writer is fed up beyond measure with theoreticians and philosophers, that she has been tormented to death by them and is enjoying plunging into the fountain of youth of a naive art that does not draw one away from the earth." And it is not surprising that a "remarkable story by a certain Grigorovich," written in the same spirit, is just as important an event for Turgenev.[2]

The history of this new literary genre that so captivated the young generation of writers of the 1840s is not our aim. We are interested only in Turgenev's attitude toward this latest word in European literature, toward this difficult kind of *peasant story,* scène rustique, fable champêtre, paysannerie, Dorfgeschichte. Turgenev himself subsequently called this genre "the rustic story."

But already at the end of the 1840s he contrasted the simple and serene contemplation of everyday reality in all the charm of its genuine relations and concrete details to the goals of religio-philosophical art with its abstract style, oracular mysteriousness, and attempt to resolve problems of universal and eternal significance. Not for nothing did he so value George Sand for her ability to "*rendre les impressions les plus subtiles et les plus fugitives d'une manière claire, ferme, comprehensive et dessiner jusqu'au parfums, jusqu'au moindres bruits.*"[3] Such is the sense of the new poetics providing the foundation for Turgenev's hunting sketches.

He gave an expressive formula for describing his new manner.

In his letters to Viardot about "The Singers," he says incidentally: "The contest took place in a tavern and there were many interesting personalities there, which I attempt to portray à la Teniers." The name of the Dutch painter here not only defines the usual subject for him—a scene in a tavern, peasants playing or singing, but also denotes a distinct artistic style. The name Teniers, which was especially popular in Russian literature from the 1820s to the 1840s, designated a low-keyed, everyday approach to theme and sort of served as a demonstrative term for a new narrative genre.[4]

Such are the genesis and artistic principle of *Notes of a Hunter*. At the end of the 1840s Turgenev set himself a specific compositional goal—to produce a series of works in the style of the new rustic story.[5] Over the course of several years running, side by side with other writings, he also worked on the solution of this artistic task that had so caught his interest; it fascinated him so much that Turgenev came back to this type of sketch in his later years too. In his declining years, as we have seen, he accepted the legend suggested to him about the militant, emancipationist goal of *Notes*. But in the process of his early work on it he defined that much more correctly, profoundly, and truthfully. It is simply "sketches from the mores of the Russian people, the strangest and most surprising people in the whole world." The formula for the new literary genre obviously was mastered superbly well by the young writer. . . .

And nonetheless serfdom in and of itself, outside a tendency of struggle and attack, played a role in the creation of *Notes of a Hunter*. Let us note immediately what that role was: the meaning of serfdom for Turgenev was purely *compositional* here. Features, facts, episodes, and character types from the serf order served him as grateful material for the solution of a whole number of compositional difficulties.

The question of composition was in general one of the most difficult artistic problems for Turgenev. In old age he often admitted that "the construction of stories, their architectural aspect" was the most unpleasant part of literary work for him and that "he lacked the imagination for composing a novel with a complicated plot." In the early period that characteristic of Turgenev's nature as a writer produced especially noticeable results, and nowhere did it appear as distinctly as in *Notes of a Hunter*.

Here the sometimes excessive absence of plot, action, dramatic subject is felt. The creators of the genre, Auerbach and George Sand, never display such indifference to the question of plot formulation as Turgenev does. If we cast our gaze over the twenty-two original sketches of *Notes of a Hunter* (written in the years 1848–1852), we will frequently find in them the prevailing bare device of stringing together portraits and landscapes. Action is almost always absent in them; dynamism did not come easily to Turgenev; his characters and pictures are presented to us in a static state, and his sketch usually breaks off just where a story apparently ought in fact to start.

Notes of a Hunter is above all a series of portraits that are often arranged in pairs: "Khor and Kalinych," "Yermolay and the Miller's Wife," "Two Landowners," "Tatyana Borisovna and Her Nephew," "Chertopkhanov and Nedopyuskin"—all these are inscriptions for paired portraits. Frequently, however, the title announces a single person—"My Neighbor Radilov," "The Freeholder Ovsyannikov," "Pyotr Petrovich Karataev," although often, of course, several portraits are gathered in the sketch itself. But the absence of action should be recognized as an almost general rule for all the sketches. Almost nothing happens in them, and the portraiture calmly alternates with landscapes, without producing any human motion, struggle, or action on its background. . . .

Not until 1872 did Turgenev, by then an experienced narrator, in spite of his ancient antipathy to the "construction" of tales, impart to these marvelously drawn figures purely tragic action. A friend and interlocutor of Flaubert's, he now created what is undoubtedly one of his masterpieces (not recognized as such even now, however), "The End of Chertopkhanov," which is truly worthy of the pen of the author of *Coeur simple.* . . . Turgenev now knew the secret of an interesting and exciting plot; and how significant that for the working out of the dramatic plot that has arisen he turned to the rich storehouse of his own sort of unused early heroes—to the old *Notes of a Hunter.* Precisely now the master of the short story developed and finished a story for which in his youth he had sketched out only an artistic list of characters, a certain graphic rubric of "dramatis personae."

The whole composition of the story is built now on a chain of disasters. Masha's departure, the death of Nedopyuskin, the theft of the amazing horse Makel-Adel, the maddened Chertopkhanov's despair, the passionate search for the horse, the new gloomy and slow drama upon the appearance of the false Malek-Adel, the scene of the murder of the unfortunate horse, which had blamelessly deceived its master's illusions but which until the end had trustingly snuggled up against the master with its muzzle, lastly, the death of Chertopkhanov himself, with his hunting whip in one hand, the tobacco pouch sewn by Masha in the other—all of this is full of action, movement, events, episodes, draws into its current new characters who are quickly and sharply sketched (Leyba, the deacon), and creates in the dimensions of a short story the conflicts of genuine tragedy.[6] So the aging Turgenev learned to construct a short story after the long experience of his novels and stories, after many years of great attention to the development of the European novella, after friendship, conversations, and correspondence with the "infallible" Flaubert. . . .

But in his youth that gift of building a story on a chain of events, that dynamism of narrative technique were profoundly alien to him. He himself doubtless must have sensed this major shortcoming in his narrative manner. By as early as 1853 *The Notes of a Hunter* no longer satisfied Turgenev. In setting to work on his first novel, testing his powers on novellas and long stories, he now realized all the difficulty and all the artistic value of the correct structure and the successful architectonics of a work of literature. Hence his censure of his earlier attempts, which lacked these compositional qualities: "My *Notes* [*of a Hunter*] now seems to me to be an immature work. . . . I hope that I have moved ahead and will still do so— and that I'll do something more solid."[7]

Doubtless even somewhat earlier in the process of working on his *Notes* Turgenev was already pondering a way of correcting his shortcomings in composition. The question arose before him of whether a series of such portrait and landscape studies without a plot and dramatism is not too monotonous and tiring for the reader; whether he did not need to introduce the uusual elements of movement and struggle into the peaceful canvas.

Turgenev, of course, answered these questions in the affirmative and made a series of attempts in the charted direction. One device used by him for the goal of resolving compositional difficulties was the plot element of the love drama, which imparts a certain dramatic movement to such sketches as "The District Doctor," "My Neighbor Radilov," and "A Meeting." But love themes turned out to be insufficient for giving the sketches the needed dynamism. And Turgenev adopted the phenomenon of serfdom as a new active enzyme of dramatism for his hunting stories.

That was an intelligent technical move and a quite proper artistic device. The landscape and portrait sketches immediately became more lively and pointed thanks to the topic of struggle, were made stronger by the motif of cruelty, and became colored with all the emotional hues of suffering, indignity, despotism, quiet grief, and the shameless wielding of power—in a word, all the means that give movement, excitement, and heightened interest to fixedly contemplative sketches.

And serfdom really did provide Turgenev with vast and grateful material for the dramatization of his narrative manner. The prohibition against serfs marrying, the count's "maîtresse" who shaves a servant's forehead for spilling hot chocolate, the birching of the butler for insufficiently warmed wine, the exile of the serf girl who had not submitted to the clerk's advances, the systematic financial ruin of the peasants by crafty stewards and so on and so forth—how many powerful moments, how many indignant or touching emotions, what agitated movement they imparted to Turgenev's original calm narrative manner!

It is not surprising that the young author highly valued that compositional lever, which imparted so much force and life to his "stationary" descriptive experiments. It was not as a journalist and a satirist that he made himself at home with this fruitful theme, but as an artist and belletrist. The powerful potential dramatism of slave-owning, even within the narrow confines permitted by censorship, injected so much movement into this series of sketches that for their author the chance to successfully solve the difficult problem of construction of his rustic story was immediately revealed.[8]

This newly discovered law of composition suited Turgenev forever. It is worth noting that while working on the compositional difficulties of his rustic stories in the early period, Turgenev discovered secrets of narrative construction that would serve him to the end. He would be able to apply them later even in the construction of his long stories and novels. We know that there the portraits of heroes grew into entire artistic genealogies, the early studies and sketches give full-size figures who appear against a background of other masterful depictions of ancestors and contemporaries—and the marvelous artistry of Turgenev the portraitist allowed itself full play in those model genealogies of the Lavretskys and Kirsanovs. . . .

After discovering for himself these laws of a story's dynamics, Turgenev was never unfaithful to them. He retained the compositional elements of his early sketches in his stories and novels. And in the same way that separate portraits grew into broad galleries there, and separate landscapes into rich panoramas, so the timid love plots of his rustic stories developed into profound dramas of love, and the obscured serf theme of *Notes of a Hunter* then grew into complex social conceptions under the sign of which his "social" novels received noisy recognition.

So, from the purely design aspect, *A Nest of Gentlefolk, Fathers and Sons,* or *Virgin Soil* strike one as a greatly extended *Notes of a Hunter,* where the basic elements of early Turgenev constructions—portrait and landscape; love drama and social idea—are developed in diverse new combinations, the former as the statics of the novel, the latter as its dynamics.

But there the novelistic and social aspects often overshadow those purely pictorial values that remained the highest artistic absolutes for Turgenev. The only book in which the still inexperienced author allowed himself the luxury of indulging most fully his artistic inclinations, complicating them least of all with attendant "dynamic" plot elements, remains his first book of hunting sketches, superb in its compositional naiveté and spontaneity. Therefore, the bases of Turgenev's style are revealed most clearly in it, and the principles of construction of his later works are disclosed with the greatest sharpness. We are present here at the artist's first shy attempts to construct his story according to the canonical laws of motion, action, and struggle, that is, according to laws still profoundly alien to his artistic nature.

So the composition of *Notes of a Hunter* heralds the architectonic devices of the mature Turgenev. His novel remains in its subsoil and first principle a remarkable collection of profoundly self-valued portraits and landscapes set in motion by the colliding aspirations of love and social conflicts.

Notes

1. In the interesting "Reminiscences of Ye. M. Feoktistov," who was especially close to Turgenev at the beginning of the 1850s, we find much substantial evidence of the writer's fundamental apoliticism, together with a curious appraisal of *Notes of a Hunter:* "Knowing him [Turgenev] very well, I was able to notice that only heresies in the field of art, not political heresies, made him lose his composure." Turgenev said of Cicero: "He was born to be a writer, but *politics for a writer* is poison." Feoktistov considers Turgenev's declaration about the "Hannibalic oath" sworn by him "rather strange coming from the mouth of Ivan Sergeevich. Turgenev never set himself the task of fighting against serfdom." Having touched on a literary theme typical for that time in *Notes of a Hunter,* "Turgenev produced a greater impression on readers than anyone else, but that was because he was immeasurably more talented than the others: never, however, in spite of his Hannibalic oath, was he carried away by a tendency or did he sacrifice the demands of art for it, for he was exclusively an artist, and any sort of political aspirations and goals were absolutely alien to him. Among the select circle of that time I never met a person who, by his very nature, would have been less inclined to occupy himself with politics than Turgenev, and he admitted that himself. 'For me what is most interesting is not *the what, but the how and the who'* —that is the phrase that the people close to him and others had to hear incessantly."

[2. Reference to D. V. Grigorovich's *The Village* (1846).]

3. Letter to Pauline Viardot of 5/17 January 1848.

4. As the author of the short excursus "Teniers in Russian literature" notes, that name was used by us in the first half of the nineteenth century for decribing the character of a writer "realistic in tendency, drawing from everyday life for content." As early a writer as Narezhny received the appellation "the Russian Teniers"; later, N. Kovalevsky, in his story "Gogol in Little Russia" (1841), appealed to the Flemish master's name for characterizing his own theme, and Belinsky used Raphael's and Tenier's names to indicate the two opposite poles of artistic perception of life ("Answer to *The Muscovite'*). Peasant life was depicted in the spirit of Tenier's paintings by Grigorovich, Dahl, Slepushkin, F. N. Glinka, and even Koltsov. Teniers became a symbol of realism in Russian literature and in that sense his name survived into the 1840s.

5. In linking *Notes of a Hunter* to Auerbach's Schwarzwald stories, A. Ye. Gruzinsky notes here a certain closeness in literary manner, a similarity in devices of style. Thus, the beginning of the stories "Tatyana Borisovna and Her Nephew" or "Yermolay and the Miller's Wife," where the author enters into direct communication with the reader, inviting him to take part in joint observation, strongly reminds one of the beginning of Auerbach's story "Brosi and Moni," where the same device is used (A. Ye. Gruzinsky, *I. S. Turgenev* [Moscow: Gran, 1918], 87–88).

6. We have another example of such compositional development in the history of the text of "Two Friends." In the first edition (1853) Vyazovnin's death is portrayed in three lines: "His head suddenly began to spin and he fell into the sea. The ship was immediately stopped, boats were lowered, but Vyazovnin had disappeared forever." Sixteen years later, in the final edition of the story (1869), the death of the hero, essential for compositional aims, develops into an extensive dramatic episode with a whole series of new characters (Mlle Julie, Captain Leboeuf, Lieutenant Barbichon, Lecocq and Pinochet) against a background of Parisian boulevards, restaurants, the Chateau de Fleurs and the Vincennes Woods, where the fatal sword duel in fact transpires.

7. Letter to Dr. I. F. Minitsky.

8. The chronology of *Notes of a Hunter* thoroughly supports our conclusion: the series began with stories without movement and plot ("portrait and landscape sketches"). The most characteristic of them relate to the first period of publication of *Notes*. In issues 1, 2, and 5 of *The Contemporary* for 1847 "Khor and Kalinych," "Pyotr Petrovich Karataev," "The Freeholder Ovsyannikov," and "Yermolay and the Miller's Wife" were published. The "serfdom" stories "The Steward" and "The Office" did not appear until the end of 1847. The most dramatic sketches from *Notes of a Hunter* ("The End of Chertopkhanov," "Living Relics," "There's a Knocking") were published twenty-five years later—in the 1870s. That is how Turgenev's general path from static description to dynamic narration took shape. But, of course, a chronological line can not be drawn out with a geometrical rectilinearity that is altogether hardly characteristic of art and life. Turgenev's creative evolution knew returns and appeals to his former manner here as well. Portrait and landscape sketches could appear even in spite of the dominance of another artistic system ("Old Portraits," for instance, which return us to the early type of *Notes of a Hunter,* was written in 1881). We have aimed not at the fixing of mathematically immutable laws, but only at the demonstration of a general artistic tendency that is quite supported by the facts of chronology and Turgenev's literary history: from stationary descriptions he gradually moved toward the active dramatization of his works through diverse means and themes. A definite role in this direction at the end of the 1840s was played by serfdom as well.

A Gallery of Idealists and Realists

Walter Smyrniw*

Turgenev's artistic accomplishments, his formal innovations in *Notes of a Hunter* have for the most part failed to receive due recognition. This resulted primarily from the sociological and historical interpretations of the work. The dominance of this approach, which in fact has not abated to the present time, particularly in Soviet scholarship, has both muffled and obscured the new formalistic and thematic investigations of *Notes of a Hunter*. Moreover, the social and historical criticism has tended to distort the fact that in the beginning Turgenev did not intend to participate in the emancipation movement by way

* From *Turgenev's Early Works: From Character Sketches to a Novel* (Oakville, Ont.: Mosaic Press, 1980), 96–103. Reprinted with the permission of the author.

of his *Notes of a Hunter*. Initially, Turgenev was not prompted to take up the pen for the sake of an abolitionist ideology, as Harriet Beecher Stowe was. Turgenev's sketches emerged as part of his literary explorations of the potentials in the new literary developments in order to draw a portrait of a new hero, to create an image of a "natural man" who would be an antithesis to the romantic hero.

Although Turgenev persisted for several years in his attempts to create a new hero, the endeavors did not meet with success. The heroes whom Turgenev depicted by using some of the emerging realistic techniques were on the whole quite unattractive. In the main inadequately developed, these personages were not cast as typical representatives of man's nature or destiny and thus could not be associated with any ideology. Ultimately Turgenev found an ideology suitable for an integration with the artistic elements of physiological sketches. But he did not derive this ideology from the Russian emancipation movement. Rather he adopted it from Friedrich Schiller's treatise "On Naive and Sentimental Poetry."[1]

Schiller's treatise provided Turgenev with the notion that as a result of inevitable processes in nature men evolve either into idealists or realists. In his essay Schiller asserted: "Since the realist allows himself to be determined by the necessity of nature and the idealist by the necessity of reason, therefore, the same relationship must take place between them which can be found between the effects of nature and the actions of reason" (493). This thesis enabled Turgenev to come to the realization that it is not necessary to deprecate such idealists as the romantics. This may have prompted him to suspend his former detraction of romantic heroes and to assume a new attitude in the portrayal of both romantic and realistic characters. Starting with "Khor and Kalinych" Turgenev began to depict the idealists and romantics in accordance with Schiller's precepts.

Turgenev portrayed several peasant idealists in *Notes of a Hunter*. To this group belong not only Kalinych, but also Kasyan in "Kasyan from the Beautiful Lands" and Yermolay in "Yermolay and the Miller's Wife." These men have several common traits. All of them manifest a disregard for material wealth and worldly values. They ignore or even violate the existing norms of the social order. For instance, they avoid physical labor and develop a degree of independence in spite of the prevailing bondage of serfdom. These social nonconformists live, however, in complete harmony with their natural environment. These idealistic peasants are endowed with discerning mental faculties, and Kalinych and Kasyan even manage to acquire the skill of reading. Although capable of making astute observations, they are not engaged in the pursuit of ideas. Rather they respond spontaneously to emotional and mental impulses.

In these études Turgenev did not necessarily render an objective or typical tableau of the prevailing realities in the peasant milieu. These sketches represent a substantial departure from physiological accuracy. However, the delineation of the peasant idealists is in keeping with Schiller's assertion about the factors that govern the behavior of idealists. Schiller maintained that the actions of such men are effected by complete submission to an ideal, or to emotional impulses which result in what Schiller termed *"Willenshandlungen"* (acts of the will) (492–93).

Schiller's influence can also be discerned in the depiction of the realists in *Notes of a Hunter.* Not all of these personages manifest the rational view of life and the sound, practical administrative sense of Khor, the first realist. But nonetheless the actions of the other realists in Turgenev's sketches coincide with Schiller's conception of realistically oriented activities. Turgenev's peasant realists display the very outlook on life which Schiller designated as realistic. Without showing a blind obedience to the forces of nature, or a fatalistic frame of mind, Turgenev's realists appear reconciled to the unavoidable processes of life and stoically accept and endure all that they consider inevitable. Khor, for instance, valued freedom highly and hence preferred to live in the swamp rather than to be under the direct control of a social order. He had the necessary funds to purchase his freedom, but he knew that if he were to sever the bonds of serfdom, he would encounter another authority, the unofficial tyranny of the government administrators who could still control the free peasants.

Khor is not the only peasant in *Notes of a Hunter* who comes to terms with serfdom. In "The Spring of Malinovo" Turgenev introduces the reader to Mikhaylo Tuman, a former domestic serf who has been granted freedom. Tuman alludes to his former and to his present mode of life, but he neither rejoices in his freedom nor disdains his previous bondage. On replying to a question from the narrator, Tuman acknowledges that in recent times life has become less oppressive for the serfs. But Tuman refrains from complaining about previous conditions. In fact Tuman provides a rationale for the former cruelties by saying that it was fashionable in the preceding epoch to treat the serfs brutally. The changes in his own status and the existing plight of the serfs Tuman considers as an inevitable process of life. This very outlook is further emphasized by Tuman's attitude to the misfortunes encountered by a serf named Vlas. In the course of the conversation Tuman reveals merely a detached curiosity by way of the questions he puts to Vlas. He is not moved in the least on hearing the details about the death of Vlas' son, about the starvation endured by this family and about the serf owner who would not lower the quitrent for Vlas. Tuman does not even offer verbal sympathy to his fellow man. When Vlas ends the tale of his misfortunes, Tuman concludes: "How about that? Things look bad, Vlas, old man."[2] Vlas himself is not surprised by this attitude. He too accepts his plight as inevitable. Vlas spoke of his hard lot with a slight smile and with such an objective detachment that, Turgenev points out, it seemed as if he were speaking about another man rather than about himself.

The peasant realists accept thus the existence of serfdom. But Turgenev points out on several occasions that it is by no means an outright passive submission. Many peasants strive, and at times quite desperately, to improve their lot. For example, in "The Spring of Malinovo" Vlas goes on foot to Moscow in order to beseech his master to lower the quitrent. A more elaborate illustration of the peasants' attempt to alleviate their plight occurs in "The Bailiff." There Turgenev shows how the peasants appeal directly to their master, whom they implore to relieve them from the excessive burdens of serfdom and to curtail the personal abuses that they are enduring from the bailiff.

On more than one occasion Turgenev points out that the peasants are not resigned to passive acceptance of the abuses inherent in the prevailing social order. But during the writing of the sketches he was not concerned primarily with detailed expositions of the oppressions of serfdom, as some of his contemporaries were. The brevity of the references to the hardships which the serfs endure certainly indicates that Turgenev was not inclined to accentuate the plight of the peasants in *Notes of a Hunter,* as for instance Grigorovich had in "The Village" and "Anton Goremyka." Turgenev refrained from detailed expositions of the evils of serfdom in most of the works that comprise *Notes of a Hunter.* Furthermore, a large number, if not the majority, of these sketches contain merely oblique references, or are completely irrelevant to the problems of serfdom. Turgenev alludes to serfdom primarily in order to show the peasants' relationship to an unavoidable facet of their existence, to a feature of their reality which reveals either the realistic or idealist traits among the peasants. But Turgenev did not confine himself to this premise. He adopted other criteria, which he also employed as touchstones that reveal a character's view of life, such unavoidable phenomena of life as love and death.

Turgenev devoted an entire sketch to the delineation of a realistic outlook towards death. He noted this attitude among the peasants and declared in "Death": "The Russian peasant dies in an astonishing way. His frame of mind before death cannot be called either indifference or stupidity; he dies coldly and simply, as if he were performing a ritual" (216). Turgenev substantiates this statement with three illustrations from the lives of Russian peasants. In "Death" Maxim, the peasant who had been fatally crushed by a falling tree, was completely reconciled with the inevitability of his death, as was another peasant dying from the burns he received in a barn fire. In silence both men endured the pain from their injuries, and they awaited death stoically. By way of this example in "Death" Turgenev points out that the peasants do not manifest this attitude merely on the deathbed. On hearing about the imminence of his death Vasily Dmitrich calmly and resolutely returns from the hospital to put things in order at home prior to his departure.

Turgenev did not confine himself to illustrations of death among the peasants. In "Death" he also described the illness and death of an impoverished student, Avenir Sorokoumov. Turgenev emphasized the student's realistic frame of mind by stating that "Avenir, in contrast to all other consumptives, did not delude himself in the least about his illness. And what of it? He did not sigh, was not distressed, and did not even once hint of his condition" (222). Yet Avenir did not display a romantic longing for death (a *Todessehnsucht*). He had a keen interest in many facets of life in spite of the knowledge of his forthcoming death. And Avenir maintained a stoic composure till the very end: "Your friend passed away with full control of his senses, and, one may say, with a similar dispassion, without showing any regrets even when the entire family was saying good-bye to him" (223).

"The Country Doctor" is a further sketch devoted to the theme of death. A young woman, Alexandra Andreevna, is striken with an incurable illness. The heroine knows that she is a terminal patient. Aware but unafraid of death, Alexandra Andreevna declares: "Death does not in the least frighten me" (50). She faces the prospect of dying, indeed, more calmly and realistically than the physician attending her. Yet Alexandra clings tenaciously to life, without complaining either about the physical pain or the prospect of parting forever from her physician, the first love in her life.

The theme of death in *Notes of a Hunter* is completely irrelevant to the problems of serfdom. Moreover, the illustrations of the realistic mode of behavior at the time of death are not confined to examples from peasant life. On the contrary, Turgenev shows that in various social strata one can encounter Russians capable of facing death resolutely and realistically. It is noteworthy, moreover, that all such personages display the very aptitude that Schiller cited as a realistic trait of human nature.

Love is a further criterion which Turgenev employs in *Notes of a Hunter* to delineate the realists' ability to accept the inevitable in life *(die Notwendigkeit)* without succumbing to an outright submission to what Schiller termed "blind necessity" *(die blinde Nötigung)*. Turgenev describes how both the serfs and members of the gentry can accept the reality of love. Maintaining a complete fidelity to their emotions, they are capable of transgressing both social and religious norms. Arina in "Yermolay and the Miller's Wife" abides by her feelings and has an affair with a servant in spite of the knowledge that her mistress would never approve her marriage. A similar event occurs in "My Neighbor Radilov." A member of the gentry, Radilov ultimately decides to break the laws of the Orthodox Church by eloping with his sister-in-law. "Pyotr Petrovich Karataev" is another sketch in which the hero, acting in accordance with the nature of his emotions, violates the laws of his society and the mores of his class by living secretly with a serf girl whom he has abducted from a neighbor.

A realistic attitude towards love entails not merely a resignation to the inevitability of emotions, but at times also a stoic reconciliation with one's fate when it becomes necessary to part from the loved one. Turgenev illustrates this in such sketches as "The Country Doctor," "Pyotr Petrovich Karataev," and "The Meeting." In these works it is particularly evident that Turgenev emphasizes the realistic attitude of women at the time they part from their beloved. As a result of this stoic reconciliation, the realistic heroine becomes essentially a "strong heroine."

Many of the personages from *Notes of a Hunter* correspond closely to the idealistic and realistic traits which Schiller outlined in his treatise "On Naive and Sentimental Poetry." But this dichotomy does not extend to all of the characters in Turgenev's work. Turgenev found Schiller's thesis on human nature expedient for the composition of his poetic sketches. It provided the concept of a "natural man," a *raison d'être* for both the romantics and realists. Turgenev composed many variations on this theme, but evidently he also came to the realization that Schiller's thesis is not applicable to all Russians. As a result Turgenev depicted in *Notes of a Hunter* a further group of character who belong neither to the category of realists nor idealists.

In Russian literary criticism *Notes of a Hunter* has been predominately regarded as Turgenev's "reserved" and "objective" protest against serfdom. Turgenev did not object to this interpretation. On the contrary, in his "Literary Reminiscences" he proudly alluded to the alleged statement by Alexander II about the influence of the *Notes of a Hunter* on the Emancipation. But in spite of the significance and influence that such intepretations may have had on the ideological and social changes in Russia they are not revelant to the literary origin of Turgenev's *Notes of a Hunter.*

When Turgenev began the writing of *Notes of a Hunter* he did not conceive them as a means to protest against the institution of serfdom. His objectives were essentially literary. He endeavored to modify the prevalent version of physiological sketches so that they would reflect not merely the peculiarities of certain individuals, but also typical character traits. At the same time Turgenev sought to develop an appropriate technique of depicting the character types of "natural man." Thanks to Schiller's thesis on character typology, Turgenev was able to attain both goals simultaneously.

Turgenev applied Schiller's dichotomy principle to Russian reality and discerned idealists and realists in all walks of life: among the gentry, among doctors, students, servants and artisans, as well as among the peasants. He perceived these character types not only among the adults, but also among children, for he devoted an entire sketch, "Bezhin Lea," to the delineation of realists and idealists among young peasant boys.

The typology certainly enabled Turgenev to realize his literary objectives. Had he not adopted Schiller's typology and depicted such peasants as Khor and Kalinych merely in the vein of physiological sketches, he would have provided posterity with a more detailed, a more graphic account of the peasants' life under serfdom, but he would not have contributed anything new to Russian literature. Moreover, the successful adaptation of Schiller's thesis on the dichotomy in man's nature encouraged Turgenev to continue the development of his character typology.

Notes

1. Schiller equated the terms "naive" and "sentimental" with realism and idealism; see his "Über naive und sentimentalische Dichtung," *Schillers Werke: Nationalausgabe*, XX (Weimar: Volksverlag, 1962, 492); hereafter cited in the text.

2. I. S. Turgenev, *Polnoe sobranie sochinenii i pisem v 28—i tomakh: sochineniia v 15–i tomakh,* (Moscow-Leningrad: AN SSR, (1962), IV, 42; hereafter cited in the text.

Theme and Symbol in "First Love"

Judith Oloskey Mills°

"First Love" has long been acclaimed as one of Turgenev's major artistic achievements. Despite the agreed-upon excellence of the work, however, the attention which it has received in the critical literature, Russian and Western, has been cursory. Typical of the statements acknowledging its quality is Freeborn's remark that in the years 1860–62 Turgenev brought the forms of the novel and the short story to perfection and that "First Love" is the most brilliant and

° From *Slavic and East European Journal* 15, no. 4 (1971);433–440. Reprinted by permission of AATSEEL of the U.S., Inc. Quotations originally in Russian have been translated by the editor.

enchanting of his stories.[1] Other critical references to the story, similarly brief, usually concern the scantiness of plot or the story's biographical origins, especially in the depiction of the mother and the father. J. A. T. Lloyd observes, "of plot there is scarcely any,"[2] and notes that Turgenev's recall of youthful impressions is especially intense. Magarshack makes the same observations about the factual material in his biography of the author.[3] André Mazon treats the story in terms of its factual correspondence to Turgenev's life, noting the departures made in the interests of realism.[4]

The most extensive study of "First Love" in Russia is Ovsyaniko-Kulikovsky's thorough analysis of the heroine, Zinaida. A powerful force within the story, she fits, within broad limits, into the category of Turgenev's strong women. As such, she is often the focus of critical attention. Ovsyaniko-Kulikovsky considers her a personality formed on contradiction, loving power and freedom but herself becoming a slave to passion.[5] Nina Brodiansky calls her the most enchanting of Turgenev's heroines.[6] Both critics are concerned with a character analysis of Zinaida, attempting to define her personality and comparing her with other of Turgenev's women.

The one effort known to me to treat "First Love" as a whole has been made by Charles Morgan.[7] He sees the chief virtue of this work in the achievement of the harmony which Turgenev constantly sought in his work. This harmony, in Morgan's opinion, resulted from Turgenev's innate sense of balance and of the civilized, which formed his point of view as a writer. It permitted him to see love and passion objectively, without condemnation and without employing the ugly naturalistic terms of sadism and masochism. Morgan's apology for Turgenev's objectivity, aimed at making him acceptable to the reader and critic more accustomed to contemporary naturalistic descriptions, should not be permitted to obscure other aspects of Turgenev's harmony. With equal justification we may posit of this work a structural harmony, resulting from Turgenev's skillful use of symbols and images. This concept of harmony is not negated by the role played in the story by passion. And although Turgenev does not use vivid naturalistic descriptions, neither does he hide the sado-masochistic elements in the love he treats. The torments of love in Turgenev's works have often been cited. Indeed, Irving Howe goes so far as to call him "a man, and, in some sense, a writer of disarranged sexuality."[8]

Morgan identifies the two dominant themes of "First Love" as youth and love. Zinaida, the pivot of passionate exchanges, is young and experiencing her first passionate involvement. There is, however, another "first love," and Zinaida's pivotal position should not obscure the role of the youthful narrator, Volodya. This second young victim of first love has not received adequate consideration.

The narrator of "First Love" is another "superfluous man" of nineteenth-century Russian literature, a direct descendant of the narrators of "Andrey Kolosov," "The Diary of a Superfluous Man," and "Asya." Although the notion of the superfluous man had for Turgenev primarily political and social implications, the term is intentionally applied here to a psychological phenomenon. For it is the contention of this paper that in "First Love' " Turgenev has supplemented the theme of passion with a study of the psychological causes of the superfluous man. The story presents at least a rudimentary analysis of the adolescent personality which is arrested in its development and remains permanently ineffectual. The causes of a psychological problem are delved into in a way which is not characteristic of Turgenev. That Turgenev intended this second theme to be an important and integral part of the story is, as I shall attempt to show, evident from his use of image and symbol.

The concept of the superfluous man with origins in an undeveloped adolescent psyche was not a theme totally new to Turgenev. It occurs also in his first story, "Andrey Kolosov," although in a rather primitive form when compared to the later work. The two stories are similar in overall structure. They share the "framework" technique and the first-person narration of past events, which forces a certain objectivity about the experiences narrated. Both stories juxtapose an adolescent with a more mature man. The juxtaposition provides contrast, but it also serves to stifle the younger man's development.

In "Andrey Kolosov" Turgenev describes the unsuccessful attempts of the young narrator to emulate his ideal, Kolosov. Kolosov is the hero of the story, and the strength of his personality precipitates whatever action occurs. The attraction for him of the student group in which he moves rests on his ability to act decisively and spontaneously without introspection and without regret, a rare ability in that reflective age. He is a new "natural man" who responds immediately to his emotions without dissection or self-laceration. He has attained that knowledge of life to which the young romantics aspire but which constantly eludes them. His friend Shchitov is a less well developed variation on the same theme. The contrasting types are described in terms of maturity versus immaturity and also as "sensible" and its opposite. The opposition is reinforced throughout the story by Turgenev's choice of vocabulary. Kolosov and Shchitov, who are so much admired, are characterized as "sensible" and "to the point." Kolosov's presence among the students results in a "sensible conversation."[9] Shchitov is able to calm the agitated group by a "sensible word" (V, 21).

The narrator is quite different. He is a product of the romantic thirties, representative of the contemplative generation. He is one of those young men who dream but the content of whose dream is illusory: "I wanted something, strove for something, and dreamed of something; I confess that even then I did not know very well what precisely I was dreaming of" (V, 9–10). As a substitute for activity, he becomes infatuated with Kolosov and tries to imitate him, seeking a pattern for proper activity. He would like to emulate Kolosov's "sensibility." He rejects an abstract discussion of what constitutes an "unusual man" in favor of a story on grounds that a story would be "more the point" (V, 8). However, in telling the story he continually slips into extensive description, reverting to his contemplative nature. His audience on two occasions demands that he get down "to business" (V, 9, 10).

Although the narrator is chronologically young (eighteen) at the time of the events of the story, he is made to seem even more immature. He is called the "small man" (V, 7). Throughout the story he is connected with child imagery, with the implications of purity and innocence which stand in sharp contrast to Kolosov and Shchitov. He is one of the students whose "half-childish melancholy" (V, 11) is dissolved by Kolosov's sensible conversation. When the narrator first becomes infatuated with Kolosov, he venerates him "childishly" (V, 13). When the narrator postpones his talk with the girl's father, he says that the word "tomorrow" was invented for indecisive people and for children, and that he, like a child, was consoling himself with this magic word (V, 34). The narrator thus defines himself not as an indecisive adult but as a child. The contemplative thirties pass, but the young man is arrested in his immature state: ten years later when he relates the story he has not changed. His permanent superfluous state results not from indecision but rather from arrested development.

The love story, which involves Kolosov and the narrator with the same girl, Varya, is less important for itself than for the light it sheds on those two personalities. Kolosov loves Varya but leaves her when he becomes bored. The narrator thinks he loves her and declares his love, but he takes flight at the thought of marriage. Varya transfers her love from Kolosov to the narrator with minimal effort. Insignificant to the action, she is merely the necessary female component of the triangle. She is certainly not the prototype for Zinaida.

Whereas in "Andrey Kolosov" Turgenev merely recorded the thwarted development of the superfluous man, in "First Love" he shows the process which actually stifles maturation. In the first story the theme was reinforced by the repetition of pertinent concepts. In the later story the same concepts are embellished by a system of symbols and images which give the theme a more definite structural pattern.

The contrasting male pair is the narrator Volodya and his father Pyotr Vasilich. Each is in love with Zinaida. The love theme is better developed in this story for it touches the three characters in depth and, with the exception of Zinaida's mother, extends to all the other characters in the story. Volodya would like to pattern himself after his father, but he is not so totally imitative as the narrator of "Andrey Kolosov." He aspires to Zinaida's love and is quite willing to act on his own. His spontaneous action, however, is curtailed by the other two principles. Volodya is trapped by his own lack of strength and by those who will in no way help him. The world in which adults live and act is always just beyond his reach.

The love to which Volodya aspires is for the exceptionally strong; it is never free of sado-masochistic elements. It means pain for all involved, yet it is for this reason all the more attractive. When Zinaida is first seen by the narrator, she is striking her admirers on the forehead with a small globular flower. This is symbolic of the pain awaiting those who become involved with her. Throughout the story she intentionally inflicts pain. She sticks a pin into Lushin's hand and commands him to laugh. Volodya is drawn into emotional involvement by brief but painful physical contacts. She slaps him while he holds her yarn. When he kisses her hand, her nail scratches his nose. His yawn draws a sharp slap, and in the hope of a similar reward he simulates another. She twists his hair around her finger until she pulls it out. She flirts with him on one occasion by slapping him with her glove. On another occasion he jumps from a wall and falls unconscious at her feet.

Zinaida is imperious and totally in control. Not one of her suitors can make an impression on her, but each is used to her own advantage. Zinaida does not find her equal until she meets Volodya's father, who although he seems to be the least well developed main character in the story is the motivating force to the action and the definitive influence on both Volodya and Zinaida. With Pyotr Vasilich Zinaida learns that self-sacrifice can be as pleasurable as tormenting others, and with a recklessness that is rare even among Turgenev's heroines, she sacrifices herself for a moment of satisfaction. Ultimately he controls her, and the physical sign of this psychic power is the final whiplash on her hand. There is no place in the domain of Zinaida and Pyotr Vasilich for any of the others, least of all for Volodya. Volodya suffers pain, but his pain never reaches the intensity of that experienced by Zinaida and his father. Nor will he fully experience love.

Her daydream is another indication of Zinaida's unique position. In it Zinaida is a princess whose guests love her but receive no response from her. She is the feminine egotist whose world revolves around her. None but her equal should dare approach her. Volodya would try, but as he crosses the boundary, his destruction begins. Zinaida refuses to accept him and in the process forces him to remain a child. The image of the child pervades the story and has the same function as it did in "Andrey Kolosov." In their first conversation Zinaida defines the difference between them. "What a strange habit children have—she corrected herself—young people have not to speak openly about their feelings" (IX, 16). Volodya is anxious to show her that she is not dealing with a boy, but when he falls unconscious from the wall, she calls him "my dear boy" (IX, 45). He does not respond to her kisses as an adult, realizing that he is still a "child" (IX, 45). When she sends him off to play with her younger brother, she delivers another blow: "The arrival of this boy turned me into a boy as well" (IX, 62).

Volodya's total enslavement is expressed in terms of animal imagery, in each case helpless and insignificant animals. Zinaida plays with him like a cat with a mouse (IX, 35). Volodya hangs around her house like "a beetle tied by the foot" (IX, 35). The perceptive Lushin, who warns him that he is involved in something which is beyond his capacities, sees him as a rabbit deprived of half of his brain ("Why are you looking like a rabbit that has had half its brain removed?" IX, 61).

The impossibility of Volodya's even achieving equal status in love is evident in the changes which are made in the conventional symbol for the onset of love, the storm. Looking at it, Volodya can see lightning, but it is so far in the distance that the thunder is inaudible. The lightning itself is not especially vigorous. It flickers and trembles "like the wing of a dying bird" (IX, 28). The storm's distance symbolizes the first timid intimations of love. Volodya will not experience its full force just as he does not feel the full force of the storm. The end is already in sight; the bird is dying. The use of a natural phenomenon to symbolize the development of love is a standard device in Turgenev. The storm here reinforces the impotence already present in the child motif.

Turgenev uses a set of symbols which well suits the psychological make-up of the characters and at the same time is part of the external action of the story. Zinaida imagines herself a princess. Volodya, when he is first introduced into the story, presents himself as a horseman and imagines himself a knight in a tournament (IX, 9). Before the action of the story begins, he thinks of himself as a figure equal to Zinaida. This image is intensified in the scene where he takes his rifle and goes out hunting. (Ironically his game is crows.) On first sight of Zinaida in the garden with her suitors he drops the rifle. This lack of presence is a portent of the relationship which will develop. It also puts him in sharp contrast to his father, who immediately prior to this action has been described as a man totally "self-assured and self-possessed" (IX, 9).

Volodya's hopes are dashed the first time he sees her follow the figure of his father with her eyes. He wanted to go over to her, but his father's image had interposed and he could see that she no longer noticed him. To this point Volodya's only competition has been the circle of admirers to which he had been readily admitted. Zinaida is willing to grant him as much attention as she grants any of the others. But none of them will be able to compete with Pyotr Vasilich.

Volodya's father is not unkind to him but distant and unemotional ("My father treated me with indifferent affection"; IX, 8). Like Zinaida, he is inclined to treat Volodya as a child and to dominate him in a way which is inoffensive, yet harmful to him. The well-maintained distance between father and son is broken only to serve the father's purpose. He takes Volodya by the hand (like a child) into the garden to question him about the previous evening at Zinaida's. The scene is parallel to the one in which Zinaida demands truthfulness from him because he is still a "child." Except for an occasional distracted caress Pyotr Vasilich lets Volodya go his own way. Volodya resents this and seeks a relationship, sought also by the narrator of "Andrey Kolosov," which would give him a pattern upon which to fashion his own maturity and masculinity. His father could if he wished with one word awaken the boy's confidence and trust ("with a single word, a single motion, arouse my unlimited confidence in myself"; IX, 30). But these words of encouragement are infrequent.

Zinaida strikes a heavy blow to his self-image when she designates him not a knight but a page: "From this day on I appoint you as my page" (IX, 51). This epithet creates a bond between the child motif, which enters directly into the verbal exchange between Volodya and Zinaida, and the horseman-knight motif. It enters also into the plot and serves to generate another confrontation between father and son. Since Volodya has been designated page, Malevsky can urge him on to the garden rendezvous. Thus Volodya is put into the ludicrous position of holding the train of the princess as she goes to meet her lover. In the garden Volodya once again attempts to fantasize himself as an adult, this time as Othello. Upon seeing his father, just as when he first saw Zinaida, he drops his weapon: "Othello suddenly turned into a schoolboy" (IX, 61).

The father believes in the power of the dominant will. This will puts him in control of every situation and enables him to tame the wildest of horses—and Zinaida as well. It is the strength of will which Volodya would like to develop but is powerless to do so. The rivalry between father and son is played out in terms of horsemanship. Volodya likes to ride with his father but is only rarely permitted to do so. (Compare the infrequent and encouraging conversations.) Horsemanship becomes identified with masculine successes, and Volodya is deliberately excluded by both Zinaida and Pyotr Vasilich. As

Volodya becomes more and more attached to Zinaida, in a way suggested by the captured-beetle image cited above, he ceases riding horseback ("I even stop walking around the environs and riding horseback"; IX, 35). Zinaida is thus an emasculating force. This impotence is further dramatized by the riding episode. Zinadia asks Belovzorov to procure a horse for her. Underestimating her riding ability, Belovzorov is afraid that the horse which he offers will be too spirited. But she is every bit as commanding as Pyotr Vasilich. The next day when Volodya sees Zinaida riding with his father, she is quite able to keep up with him, but Belovzorov and the other suitors, including Volodya, are left far behind.

A final incident summarizes this theme. It occurs after the family has returned to Moscow and Zinaida has supposedly been forgotten. Volodya is riding with his father and for the first part of the ride, with a considerable exertion on the part of his little horse, is able to pace the father's more powerful animal. However, after Volodya sees his father deliver the whiplash to Zinaida, he is no longer able to ride with him as an equal. On the return trip he is left behind, like Belovzorov earlier. The pattern of his personality as developed throughout the story is here reinforced. Volodya has learned that his father has continued a liaison which he has not even been able to begin. He will never be the equal of his father either in horsemanship or in overall capabilities. This is the last deadly blow to his maturation.

Although the plight of Volodya may be considered a secondary theme of "First Love," Turgenev, as we have seen, has thoroughly integrated it into a complex system of symbols and themes, and this structural unity gives "First Love" the harmony for which it is justly esteemed.

Notes

1. Richard Freeborn, *Turgenev: The Novelist's Novelist, a Study* (London: Oxford University Press, 1960), 133.

2. J. A. T. Lloyd, *Ivan Turgenev* (London: Robert Hale, 1942), 36.

3. David Magarshack, *Turgenev: A Life* (London: Faber & Faber, 1954), 30.

4. André Mazon, "L'Elaboration d'un roman de Turgenev: à la Veille, Premier amour, Fumée," *Revue des études slaves*, 5 (1925), 244–68.

5. D. N. Ovsyanniko-Kulikovsky, "Natury irratsionalnye: Zinaida," *Etyudy o tvorchestve I. S. Turgeneva* (SPb.: Orion, 1904), 131–45.

6. Nina Brodiansky, *SEER*, 32 (1953), 80.

7. Charles Morgan, "Turgenev's Treatment of a Love Story," *Essays by Diverse Hands: Transactions of the Royal Society of Literature of the United Kingdom*, 25 (London, 1950), 107.

8. Irving Howe, "The Politics of Hesitation," *Politics and the Novel* (New York: Horizon Press, 1957), 117.

9. I. S. Turgenev, *Polnoe sobranie sochinenii i pisem* (Moscow: AN SSSR, 1960–68); volume and page references in the text are to this edition.

Typical Images in the Later Tales of Turgenev
James B. Woodward[*]

Although the short story is clearly the genre that Turgenev most favored in the last fifteen years of his life, his attitude toward his short narrative works during this period was consistently and curiously ambivalent. In his correspondence he often appears to concur with the widely held contemporary view that they are marred by a certain triviality. Such at least is the impression conveyed by his reference to "Lieutenant Yergunov's Story" (1868) as "that whimsical tale,"[1] to "The Watch" (1875) as "a frivolous piece" (*P.*, IX, 217), and to "A Strange Story" (1870) as "a trifle" (*P.*, VIII, 171), a term he also applied to "The Dream" (1877) (*P.*, XII, 53). Contrasting, however, with these unsolicited derogatory remarks is the stubbornly defensive attitude he adopts whenever he is responding to the critical observations of others. "This poor wretch, whatever you might say, is not so bad," he wrote to Annenkov in November 1868 in reference to "Lieutenant Yergunov's Story" (*P.*, VII, 239), and in stronger terms we see him defending "Knock, Knock, Knock" (1871) in letters of 1874 and 1877 respectively to A. P. Filosofova and S. K. Bryulova (*P.*, X, 282; XII, 58), declaring it in the latter to be "one of the most serious works I have ever written."

These intriguing volte-faces doubtless admit more than one explanation. It is significant, however, that in expressing himself in this contradictory manner Turgenev was repeating a procedure he had already employed in referring to earlier works of the sixties ("Phantoms," 1863; "Enough," 1864; "The Dog," 1866), in which the role of the sociopolitical issues is also not immediately apparent.[2] Since the importance he attached to these works, particularly the first two, is beyond question,[3] it may plausibly be deduced from this consistency of practice that the ambivalence was by no means unintentional. He came to regard it as the most effective means of disarming a potentially hostile public. His irreconcilable judgments may reflect the predicament in which he repeatedly found himself after the publication of *Fathers and Sons* and the protracted controversy to which the novel gave rise, the predicament of a writer torn between natural inclination

[*] From *Slavic and East European Journal* 17, no. 1 (1973);18–32. Reproduced by permission of AATSEEL of the U.S., Inc.

and the pressure of critical and public demand. His natural inclination was to observe the principle he formulated simply and concisely in a letter of January 1882 to Zh. A. Polonskaya: "Write about what enters your soul and take no account in advance of public opinion" (*P.*, XIII, 180). There can be no doubt that by 1870 the emphasis placed by the more vocal sections of Russian critical opinion on the writer's obligation to develop the political and social self-awareness of Russia's citizenry had become distinctly irksome to him.[4] It is equally evident, however, that while determined to pursue an independent course, Turgenev was anxious that it not be purchased at the cost of alienating the public, which had come to expect from him significant responses to major developments in the evolution of Russian society. Therefore, his task was to satisfy this demand while devoting himself to the themes to which his creative faculty responded, to devise a means of masking the genuine implications of these themes with a veneer of overt social or topical relevance, just as he masked his true attitude to the works concerned with the kind of disparaging comments cited above.

The most convincing support for this interpretation of Turgenev's intentions is provided by an ambivalence or equivocation in his remarks on the purpose behind the composition of these works and by the difficulty encountered in matching stated purpose with actual achievement. The chief source of difficulty is generally the same throughout, namely, determining the precise meaning of "a type" and "the typical," terms which are frequently employed during this period by Turgenev, both in his general statements on art and in his references to individual works. Perhaps his best known pronouncement on this question is his June 1876 injunction to the writer and publicist V. L. Kign: "Through the play of accidents you must aspire to create types, and at the same time always remain faithful to the truth" (*P.*, XI, 280). Does he mean "universal types" whose social relevance is merely incidental, or "types" specifically related to sociopolitical conditions in nineteenth-century Russia? One would think that Kign almost certainly understood the latter, and criticism has generally taken the same view. The Soviet critic A. N. Dubovikov, for example, is in no doubt on this point; he writes: "In the short novels and tales of his last years, as in the works which precede them, Turgenev's attention is concentrated mainly on the creation of typical images produced by typical circumstances of Russian life."[5] The term typical image is clearly employed here to denote a fictional character designed to highlight or synthesize some particular aspect of Russian social life. Dubovikov's claim also implies that the types portrayed in the works of which he speaks are not without some relevance to the period in which they were created, even though Turgenev drew them from the past.

Criticism in the West has for the most part not questioned this interpretation. A recent study of Turgenev's novels contains the following observations on the shorter narratives of the period from 1867 to 1877: "Practically all of them were nostalgic, evoking experiences from his own past, or from earlier periods in the century, with a clarity and perception of detail that immediately related them to the present. It is in these years that past and present seem to fuse in Turgenev's work."[6] Support for this observation can easily be culled from the remarks of the author himself. Thus his description of "Knock, Knock, Knock" in the above-mentioned letter to Filosofova as "a study of *Russian suicide,* which rarely represents anything poetic or pathetic but on the contrary is almost always carried out as a result of conceit and narrow-mindedness, with an admixture of mysticism and fatalism" (*P.,* X, 282) suggests that it was not his intention to restrict the relevance of Second Lieutenant Teglev's story to the 1830's. Similarly, the central character of the later story "The Desperado" (1881), Misha Poltev, who was born in 1828, is described by Turgenev in his letter to Polonskaya of January 1882 as "a type whom I find significant in relation to certain contemporary phenomena" (*P.,* XIII, 180).[7] To all appearances, then, the creation of social types would appear to have been of paramount importance for Turgenev.

A feature of his later fiction that gives cause for thought, even if no effective counterargument can be based on it, is his almost complete avoidance of a device which had occasionally served him in the past (e.g., in "Andrey Kolosov," 1844; "Yakov Pasynkov," 1855; and *Rudin,* 1858) as a means of identifying his protagonists as social types: using their names as titles. Only two works, in fact, have proper names as titles, "Punin and Baburin" (1874) and "Klara Milich" (1882), and the latter received its title not from Turgenev, who had called it "After Death," but from its publisher Stasyulevich, the editor of *The Messenger of Europe.* Stasyulevich was soundly rebuked for his pains by Annenkov in a letter to Turgenev of December 1882: "I am annoyed with Stasyulevich for changing the title of your story 'Klara Milich.' He could have done nothing more stupid. It did not occur to him, the ass, that titles *containing names* express the author's intention of representing this or that *type,* and that the main point here is not a type, but a rare and remarkable psychic phenomenon" (*S.,* XIII, 578).[8] He might have added that it is represented not through the heroine but through the hero Aratov. If Annenkov's definition of the main point of "Klara Milich" is accepted (and few would disagree with it), the problem of reconciling it with Dubovikov's general statement immediately arises. Only two conclusions can logically be drawn: either "Klara Milich" must be regarded as an exceptional departure from the practice advocated by Turgenev in his letter to Kign, or its connection with the other short fiction of his last years is based on an understanding of the term type that differs radically from the social interpretation that Dubovikov places upon it.

First of all, in order to decide whether "Klara Milich" is in fact an exceptional work, we must examine the extent to which the term social type adequately describes the protagonists of the other stories written during the fifteen-year period in question, above all the stories which on Turgenev's own testimony were specifically devoted to the creation of types. Of particular interest in this connection is "The Desperado," the second and last of a projected cycle of works entitled "Excerpts from Memoirs—My Own and Others."[9] It has been observed that in his letter to Polonskaya Turgenev was intent on stressing the connection between his hero and "certain contemporary phenomena" (by which he apparently meant the young radicals of the seventies), and his statement implies that he attached considerable importance to this connection. Elsewhere, however, he expressed himself rather differently on this subject: "I am attributed with the hostile intention of belittling the young protesters of today by connecting them genetically with my 'Desperado.' I simply depicted a type from the past which I recalled. Am I to blame that the genetic connection is self-evident, and that my 'Desperado' and those of today are two related types merely living in different social conditions— the same recklessness, the same restlessness, weakness of will, and vague desires?"[10] Here again Turgenev defines Misha as a type and indicates the particular aspects of his character which relate him to the younger generation of the present, but now he conveys the impression that the connection is to be regarded as little more than incidental. His primary purpose, he states, was simply to depict "a type from the past," and he refers to his cousin Mikhail Alexeevich Turgenev as the model on whom he based his hero.[11]

It might be thought that this apparently inconsistent attitude toward the work was prompted by the sharp criticism it had incurred.[12] But this would not explain the presence of similar equivocation in the work itself, in the opening and closing paragraphs. The brief introduction to the story takes the form of a discussion on young people of the day, in the course of which one of the speakers notes their alarming susceptibility to despair and claims that it is an unprecedented phenomenon in Russian social life. His remark is swiftly countered, however, by an elderly member of the group who states, "There have been despairing people in the past as well, though they were unlike those of today" (S., XIII, 30). In order to illustrate his point he relates the story of his nephew Misha, which he eventually concludes with the works: "He was unlike the despairing people of today, though it may be assumed that some philosopher would find related features between them. In both cases there is a craving for self-destruction, anguish, dissatisfaction. . . . But I leave it to the philosopher to judge the cause of it all" (*S.*, XIII, 52). Again the question of the relationship is enigmatically blurred. Misha simultaneously merits comparison with and is distinguished from the young Populists of the seventies.

If we pursue the enquiry and examine the intervening narrative in the light of the author's claim that he created a type, albeit "a type from the past," the enigma, far from being resolved, is rendered doubly perplexing. The portrait that emerges, in fact, is no less devoid of socially typical features than that of Aratov, and one wonders whether Turgenev was himself alluding to this fact when he expressed the fear, in a letter to Annenkov in November 1881, that the work was "too much a *study*" (*P.*, XIII/1, 152; Turgenev's italics). In any event, eighteen years later the story was used as a case study by an eminent psychiatrist,[13] just as the story of Aratov was used in the Soviet period.[14] The reasons are not difficult to perceive, for the emphasis throughout is on manifestations of behavioral abnormality which are completely devoid of social motivation. As in "Klara Milich,"[15] "Phantoms," and "Faust" (1856),[16] the motivation provided by Turgenev for the curious behavior of the protagonist is primarily genetic: Misha is the offspring of an epileptic father and a "very nervous and sickly" mother (*S.*, XIII, 31). The first eighteen years of his life, that is, while his parents are still alive, offer no hint of the transformation to come, though a note of warning is perhaps sounded by the discordant element in his physical portrait to which the poet Polonsky apparently took exception:[17] the large, sharp, "bestial" teeth that contrast with his otherwise effeminate appearance. With the removal of parental control, however, he immediately sells the family estate far below its value and embarks on a round of debauchery which leaves him penniless and an unrepentant alcoholic.

The subsequent episodes from Misha's life recounted by his uncle combine to portray a unique individual whose abnormality is indisputably psychic. Numerous critics, it is true, have sought to explain his condition by reference to social discontent, presumably basing their judgment on Misha's invariable reply to his uncle's questions about the reasons for his metamorphosis: "You come to and recover your senses, and you begin to think about the poverty, the injustice, Russia. And that does it! The anguish is so great that you feel like blowing your brains out, and involuntarily you take to drink" (*S.*, XIII, 37). But this expression of concern for social evil is so patently inconsistent with his customary attitudes that it can only be regarded as an empty pretext. Not for nothing does the narrator refer on two occasions to his stilted style and way with words; the reviewer of the story for *The Voice*, mystified by this inconsistency, was understandably prompted to ask whether Misha's words had been inserted merely to enhance the interest of the story (S., XIII, 559). The most conclusive confirmation of the shallowness of Misha's principles is provided by his confrontation with the new owner of his estate, who has merely to offer him a bottle in order to drive these noble sentiments from his head and lips. Misha's life is entirely dependent on alcohol, for which he is prepared to sacrifice almost everything. Marriage alone induces him to abstain, and his death quickly follows.

"The Desperado" therefore raises the same problems as "Klara Milich." It portrays a character who is defined by his creator as a "significant type" but whose bizarre conduct can only be ascribed to psychic abnormality. One can only register astonishment at the response to Misha of Annenkov, who referred to him in a letter of November 1881 as "a universal nephew" who "will receive a rapturous welcome from all our uncles in Russia" (S., XIII, 555). In reality the reader is again faced with the problem of reconciling the rare or abnormal with the typical, and once more a question mark is raised against the customary interpretation of Turgenev's statement to Kign.

No such problem, however, appears to be presented by a story written ten years earlier, "Knock, Knock, Knock." Here at last is a work that would seem to support Dubovikov's judgment, and it is in the spirit of this judgment that it has generally been interpreted. Perhaps the most detailed analysis belongs to the Soviet critic S. E. Shatalov. After a persuasive defense of the proposition that Turgenev was guilty of "deviating from the logic of his own work" when, as we have seen, he described the story as "a study of Russian suicide," Shatalov claims that it reveals "the intimate psychological depths of the well-known type of fatalist who grew up and developed under the influence of the romatic images of Marlinsky."[18] The claim would seem to offer little cause for dispute. Teglev's story is preceded by the narrator's general observations on the social type to which Shatalov refers, the romantic poseur of the thirties popularized by Marlinsky, the devotee of Byron and Napoleon, liberally endowed with faith in his destiny and willpower; and in chapter 2 he duly introduces Teglev as a representative of this type. Noteworthy, however, is the immediate addition of the proviso, seemingly unimportant, that in appearance he differed from the type quite markedly. Only later do we realize that this initial proviso, like the discordant element inserted into the physical portrait of Misha, prepares the way for a whole succession of more significant distinctions between the hero and the type to which he allegedly belongs. Teglev, we are told, believes in presentiments, predictions and signs, lucky and unlucky days, and in an alternately benign and malevolent fate. The narrator comments: "True men of destiny should not display such beliefs; they should inspire them in others" (S., X, 271). Significantly, however, the narrator's conception of the protagonist is totally unaffected by this thought. In fact, Teglev's unusual superstitiousness is most important among those aspects of his character which continually deceive the narrator. Not only does it ultimately, in combination with a guilty conscience, impel the lieutenant to commit suicide, but it is invariably the source of the chilling seriousness that underlies those aspects of his behavior which the narrator can only regard as marks of the poseur, that is, of the social type.

Teglev's account of the event which produced the crisis of conscience elicits the following remark from the narrator: "The very sound of his voice, his glances, the movements he made with his fingers and hands—in a word everything about him seemed unnatural, unnecessary, false." It is true that the narrator has become somewhat less impulsive in his judgments in the time since these events, and he is careful to add at this point: "At that time I was still young and inexperienced, and I was unaware that the habit of expressing oneself in rhetorical fashion with false intonations and mannerism can eat into a man to such an extent that he is no longer capable of shaking them off: they are a kind of curse" (S., X, 280). Although the lesson has been imperfectly digested, experience has since taught him that form can be deceptive. Consequently, this brief digression is tantamount to an admission that in the case of Teglev the form characteristic of the type conceals an individual of a quite distinctive cast. But it requires the tragedy of Teglev's suicide, for which the narrator's playful knocking on the wall during the ill-fated night in the barn is largely responsible, to make him fully aware of this fact. For Teglev the knocking is a call from the dead, a summons from the girl whom he had abandoned and, he mistakenly believes, driven to her death. His decision to answer the call with his own death is characteristically ascribed by the narrator to the pose from which he is still unable to disassociate his mysterious acquaintance. As before, however, the melodramatic form of Teglev's announced intention veils his complete sincerity, and the threat is duly carried out.

This brief synopsis is sufficient to invalidate Shatalov's interpretation of the story and to highlight the pervasive tension between the central character's true image and the image superimposed on him by the myopic narrator, whose role is by no means confined to merely offsetting the hero, as critics have suggested.[19] Showing negligible regard for Turgenev's habitual delight in frustrating expectations based on conventional experience, Shatalov assumes (47) that the superior education of the narrator, Ridel, invests his judgments with an unchallengeable authority. He ignores the possible significance of the fact that Ridel is from German stock. The story was written at the time of the Franco-Prussia War, and the anti-German sentiments that Turgenev conceived during this period are clearly reflected in "Spring Freshets," which was completed in the same year (1871).[20] Essentially, Ridel's story records the tragedy of an abnormally superstitious individual, and the title duly underlines the episode which causes his abnormality to overwhelm him. Ridel's attempt to relate him to a social type with which he displays certain superficial affinities is continually, though obliquely, exposed as misguided. In consequence, the individual and the type are once more clearly distinguished. It has been noted that, like "The Desperado," the work was termed by the author "a study," and it reveals a similar progressive dissociation of the protagonist from the type with which he is initially associated. For final confirmation that social concerns were far from Turgenev's mind when he wrote the story, we might turn to his reference to it in the context of an indictment of contemporary criticism in his letter to Filosofova of 18 August 1874: "I wished merely to direct your attention to the right and appropriateness of treating purely psychic (not political and not social) problems" (P., X, 282). With equal justification, as we have observed, he could later have employed "The Desperado" to demonstrate this point, not to mention "The Song of Triumphant Love" (1881) and "Klara Milich," in which his undeviating concern with purely psychic problems requires no substantiation.

The two later stories of Turgenev in which the presence of specifically social types is perhaps least open to dispute are "Punin and Baburin" and "The Watch," the action of which is set respectively in the forties and in 1801. Both works are usually regarded as "laboratory exercises" preceding the creation of Virgin Soil.[21] Both present portraits of strong personalities who have emerged from the lower strata of society, types reflecting "the increasing importance of the new type of raznochinets who was to be typified by Turgenev in the figure of Solomin."[22] Baburin and Davyd are both men of action and inflexible will, free from the guilt-ridden complexes of the gentry, mindful of their duty to their fellow men, and eminently successful (after initial problems in the case of Baburin) in the test of love to which, like their predecessors in Turgenev's fiction, they are duly subjected. Even so, aspects of at least the latter of these seemingly uncomplicated stories cause one to wonder whether the reincarnation of the virtues of Don Quixote was in fact Turgenev's sole objective.

Once again the title is worthy of note. It is undeniable that the function of the watch in the story is primarily compositional. This innocuous birthday present received by the narrator links together the diverse episodes and characters of the work. It is also used astutely as a basis for characterization. However, in the relatively few other instances that Turgenev elevated phenomena in his stories to the status of titles, in no case did he limit their function to serving composition alone. The dream in "The Dream" and the song in "The Song of Triumphant Love," not to mention other examples from the period which concerns us, lie at the very center of the dramatic action and provide the main motivation for events. And when in "The Watch" the narrator, looking back on the events of his story and, in particular, on the role of the watch, remarks: "The thought involuntarily enters one's head that it contained some mysterious power" (S., XI, 255), he merely confirms the reader's growing suspicion that perhaps this tenuous strand linking the various elements of the fiction was not selected without some ulterior motive. One is repeatedly struck by the extent to which actions and attitudes of the characters appear to be determined by the existence of this mundane but ubiquitous object. Like time itself, it is omnipresent, constantly erupting into their thoughts and indirectly even shaping their lives.

This point by no means exhausts, of course, the significant content of "The Watch." It is stressed merely to indicate that even here, in one of the two shorter narratives from Turgenev's later period which appear to conform most closely to Dubovikov's interpretation of Turgenev's general purpose, one can detect an element totally unrelated to the creation of social types; the title itself would seem to allude to it, so that some critics have gone so far as to pronounce it "symbolistic."[23] In other stories of the seventies such conflicting elements are far more obtrusive. In "Father Alexey's Story" (1877), for example, we encounter another instance of the basic pattern identified in "The Desperado" and "Knock, Knock, Knock." The first few paragraphs of the work induce the reader to believe that the protagonist Yakov, son of the unfortunate priest named in the title, will be portrayed as the type of *raznochinets* who emerged from the ranks of the rural clergy with considerable social impact in the fifties and sixties (most notably in the persons of Chernyshevsky and Dobrolyubov) and whose materialistic approach to the problems of life and society evolved from study of the natural sciences. In accordance with family tradition Yakov obediently commences his education in a seminary, but after a period of academic success he suddenly confronts his father with a confession of incipient religious doubt and a request to embark on a secular education. "I feel a strong inclination towards science," he remarks (*S.*, XI, 294).

The association thus far sustained between Yakov and the *raznochintsy* of the fifties is abruptly terminated with the cessation of his initial successes at the university. His education is left incomplete, like that of Misha in "The Desperado" and Aratov. So sharp in fact is the deviation at this point from the anticipated scheme of development that the rest of the tale provides more than adequate justification for the contemporary V. F. Chizh calling it "the story of a sickness."[24]

It records the progressive disintegration of Yakov's mind, culminating in his death under the influence of increasingly obsessive hallucinations of the devil. The motivation for the transition is supplied by two passing references in the foregoing part of the text: to the brief episode involving the "old green hunchback," who has been interpreted as an objectivization of the unvanquished ancient paganism with which Yakov's family for generations has been in conflict;[25] and to Yakov's weak health and to the death of six of Father Alexey's eight children, bearing witness to Turgenev's resumed interest in problems of heredity. Regarded in toto, therefore, the story displays the sequence observed in other works of the period: association with a clearly defined social type and dissociation from the type. It offers further evidence of Turgenev's overriding concern at this time with abnormal forms of experience.

Turgenev's distinctive treatment of love as a paralyzing and destructive obsession is well-known, and the theme receives further development in two stories from the fifteen-year period in question, "The Brigadier" (1868) and "Spring Freshets." However, the motif of hallucinations and visions is introduced into the love theme in two instances ("The Song of Triumphant Love" and "Klara Milich"), and it represents an element in his art which, though anticipated in "Faust" and "Phantoms," acquires prominence only in this period. In each case, as in "Father Alexey's Story," the effect of the motif is either to reduce or to eliminate any recognizable social implications in the characters and situations depicted. In "A Misfortunate Girl" (1869) and "A King Lear of the Steppe" (1870) the role of the motif is admittedly limited, though it is significantly inserted in both works at crucial junctures in the course of events; in the former it performs the same function it does in "Faust" (S., X, 141) by presaging the imminent death of the heroine Susanna. It also provides the sole motivation in the latter for Kharlov's fatal decision to divide the ownership of this property between his formidable daughters.[26] In "A Misfortunate Girl" the theme of heredity again plays a notable part (the legacy of misfortune bequeated by the heroine's Jewish mother, which prompts the parallel with Sir Walter Scott's Rebecca), perhaps explaining Turgenev's comment that the work contained "too much pathology" (P., VIII, 63). The epilogue's introduction of the theme of the power of love to conquer death clearly points the way to "Klara Milich."[27]

In "A Strange Story," the title of which discloses the "abnormality" of its content, the function of hallucinations and visions is somewhat more complex and certainly more important. Briefly summarized, the story is divided into two main sections, the first of which centers on the narrator's hallucination, during a visit to a provincial village, which is induced by the hypnotic stare of a local celebrity named Vasya. In the second section the author's attention turns to the fate of Sofi, the daughter of a local landowner and friend of the narrator, whose conviction that the sole purpose of life is self-renunciation impels her to accompany Vasya and minister to his needs when he assumes the chains and self-inflicted sufferings of a holy fool. Sharing the hardships of his vagrant life, she voluntarily condemns herself to premature aging and death.

Although the action of the work is set in the midfifties, the story of Sofi has been interpreted by critics (e.g., Shatalov, 46) as a reflection of Turgenev's interest during the sixties and seventies in Russian religious sects (as in "The Dog" and "Father Alexey's Story"), or more pertinently, as a response to the appearance of a new, fanatically inclined type of young Russian woman in the social conditions of the postemancipation period. The most cogent support for the latter interpretation is provided by a statement in the narrator's postscript: "I did not understand Sofi's action, but I did not condemn her, just as subsequently I did not condemn other girls who likewise sacrificed themselves for what they considered to be the truth and what they saw their calling in" (S., X, 185). The defect of this interpretation, however, is that it fails utterly to account for the events in the first section of the story. In addition, Turgenev himself disclaimed the presence of any ulterior motives in the work (P., VII, 285); it was precisely this story which prompted his well-known plea of January 1870 to M. V. Avdeev for the right of artists to create "noncontemporary types" (P., VIII, 171). It is plain that Sofi's story cannot be considered in isolation; the evidence of the fiction itself, despite the inadequate development of the "psychological motifs" which Turgenev acknowledged (P., XVIII, 240) and Annensky later found so disturbing,[28] indicates that the division of the story was dictated by the author's desire to juxtapose two contrasting illustrations of the conquest of the individual will: the subjugation of the narrator's will by Vasya's hypnotic eyes and Sofi's self-conquest, which similarly involves Vasya. The enigmatic Vasya is the connecting link between the two seemingly unrelated episodes.[29]

A careful reading of this work suggests, therefore, that even here the relevance of the issues raised and characters portrayed to any specifically Russian problem is merely incidental. The author's primary concern is again with experiences of a totally exceptional nature. And this is more clearly the case in two other shorter narratives from the period, to which only passing reference has been made thus far: "the "fantastic tale"[30] "A Dream" and "Lieutenant Yergunov's Story." In the former even the location of the action is no longer recognizably Russian, and the theme of heredity is again combined with that of visions and dreams;[31] "Lieutenant Yergunov's Story," which Shatalov and I. Vinogradov have pronounced devoid of "important problems" and a "central, generalizing idea,"[32] was described by the author himself as an attempt "to represent the imperceptibility of the transition from reality to dream" (*P.*, VIII, 172), a process in which hypnotism again plays a notable part.

Thus the main conclusion to be drawn from this brief survey of almost all Turgenev's shorter narratives of the period 1868–82[33] is that with the exception of "Punin and Baburin" and to a more limited extent "The Watch," they all hinge in varying degrees on experiences and states of mind in which a distinctly pathological element can often be detected and to which the epithet typical, at least in the sense of socially typical, is singularly inapplicable. It must be assumed that herein lies at least one reason for the almost complete absence of titles consisting of proper names. In almost every case the titles indicate the state of mind or condition of the central character ("The Desperado," "A Misfortunate Girl"), the stimulus that induces the state of mind concerned ("Knock, Knock, Knock," "A Dream," "The Song of Triumphant Love," and, in part, "The Watch"),[34] or the entire sequence of events which records the given state of mind, its background, and consequences ("Lieutenant Yergunov's Story," "A Strange Story," "Father Alexey's Story"). Moreover, although these various states of mind and psychic experiences are in most cases projected against a Russian backdrop, it has been observed that their connection with specifically Russian settings is invariably tenuous or incidental.

Are we then to conclude that Turgenev, with his seemingly ineradicable sensitivity to the demands of criticism, was intent on deceiving his contemporaries when he pledged himself to the creation of types and either indicated explicitly or alluded indirectly to the social implications or peculiarly Russian character of the problems raised in some of his works? The works themselves and the occasional inconsistencies in his comments on them suggest there may indeed be some grounds for regarding such indications and allusions, at least in part, as concessions to public demand. At the same time a possibility exists that there is in fact no contradiction between Turgenev's advocacy of the creation of types in his letter to Kign and his practice in the stories surveyed for the simple reason that, contrary to Dubovikov's contention and the impression conveyed by some of the author's other remarks, the term in that context is totally devoid of social implications. In order to test the vailidity of this suggestion, we must consider the precise nature of the recurrent abnormal or socially untypical elements in these stories to discover, if possible, affinities in them that cast light on an underlying nonsocial concept of the typical. Looking back over our survey, the sole common factor that merits serious attention is the characters' varying degrees of dependence on forces over which they have no conscious or rational control. The presence of this interest in individual works of Turgenev's last years has been recognized, but its pervasiveness and the variety of forms it assumes have yet to be appreciated. Had Turgenev conceived such characters as Misha, Yakov, and Aratov in the forties and fifties, he most likely would have added them to his gallery of "superfluous men," but by the late sixties he was concerned with a radically different dilemma.

"Only now did I realize that ever since morning I had been guided by unknown forces," remarks the narrator in "A Dream" (*S.*, XI, 285), and in a sense these words define the predicament of all the characters whose stories have been considered. Heredity, entrancing music, fateful combinations of circumstances, hypnotism, extreme superstitiousness, and narcotics—such are the forces to which Turgenev subjects his heroes and heroines, and in each case the dikes of self-control or rationality are fatally breached. Herein lies the vital connection between such apparently dissimilar works as "Lieutenant Yergunov's Story" and "The Desperado," "A Dream" and "A Strange Story," "Knock, Knock, Knock" and "Father Alexey's Story." Each individual story adds a new chapter to Turgenev's exposé of the limited powers of human reason, and it is their expression of this essentially universal theme which renders typical the elements we have examined in these works. They reflect and dramatize in a manner wholly consistent with Turgenev's characteristic objectivity an aspect of human existence which is independent of prevailing sociopolitical circumstances. Both the repeated projection of events into the past and the occasional parallels between past and present are surely related, in the final reckoning, to the universal character of this theme. "A Dream" and "The Song of Triumphant Love," in which the Russian setting is entirely abandoned, represent the logical conclusion of this process, and the theme is completely universalized. Here the insignificance of the time and place is unmistakably apparent; nineteenth-century Russia is replaced by sixteenth-century Ferrara.[35] Thus, Nina Brodiansky has appropriately remarked that "Turgenev, to all appearances the most time-bound, the most 'Victorian' of the Russian classics, is least of all concerned, in his psychological stories, with the conditions and values of his time."[36]

It is Turgenev's intention in this group of works to present, not a gallery of social types in the conventional, restricted sense, but illustrations of a particular aspect of the human "type." These illustrations in most cases lack the pervasive social implications of his novels and the majority of his early stories; they are unrelieved by any semblance of religious faith, unblemished by facile philosophical palliatives,[37] and characterized by a concluding interogative note which is a mark of his intellectual integrity. Only in this sense can these shorter narratives be reconciled with his statement to Kign. At no point, however, was Turgenev disposed to make an unequivocal statement to this effect or to abandon his position of defensive ambivalence. Both within the fiction and in his references to it he endeavored to cloud the issue in the hope that the more demanding sections of his socially conscious public might at least be placated, if not convinced.

Notes

1. I. S. Turgenev, *Pisma* (M.-L.: AN SSSR, 1961–68) VI, 144. References to Turgenev's works will be to I. S. Turgenev, *Sochineniya* (M.- L.: AN SSSR, 1960–68). References in the text preceded by *S.* or *P.* are to this edition (*Polnoe sobranie sochinenii i pisem v 28-i tomakh*). Dates of letters are Old Style.

2. Cf. his references to "Phantoms" as "rubbish" in letters of January 1857 to M. N. Longinov and Annenkov (P., III, 71 and 73) and again of September 1863 to Annenkov (P., V, 157), as well as his remark to Annenkov in a letter of May 1864: "According to all the news 'Phantoms' has suffered a general fiasco. Yet it seems to me that the deceased was not a bad fellow" (P., V, 258). For a discussion of these statements, see A. Andreeva, " 'Prizraki' kak ispoved Iv. S. Turgeneva," *Vestnik Yevropy*, LXIV, 9 (1904), 6.

3. See my "Turgenev's 'Phantoms': A Reassessment," *Slavonic and East European Review*, LX (1972), 53–54.

4. See his letters of 13 January 1870 to M. V. Avdeev (P., VIII, 171) and 18 August 1874 to Filosofova (P., X, 282).

5. A. N. Dubovikov, "Vstupitelnaya statya k kommentariyam," in *S.*, XI, 451. My italics.

6. Richard Freeborn, *Turgenev: The Novelist's Novelist* (London: Oxford Univ. Press, 1960), 162–63.

7. Cf. his remarks in a letter to Polonsky written four days later (P., XIII, 184).

8. It may be objected that Turgenev's generally limited use of names in the titles of his works invalidates this point, but it is difficult to believe that Annenkov, his closest confidant, would have expressed himself so forcefully on the matter had he not known that the author recognized the convention.

9. See Turgenev's letter to Annenkov of 22 November 1880 (P., XIII, 15).

10. N. M. "Cherty iz parizhskoy zhizni I. S. Turgeneva," *Russkaya mysl*, IV, 11 (1883), 319. Quoted in *S.*, XIII, 557.

11. Letter to Annenkov of 1 December 1881 (P., XIII, 154). He refers to Mikhail as his nephew; in fact, Mikhail was his paternal uncle's son, i.e., his first cousin.

12. "The story of Bazarov has been repeated on a small scale," Turgenev wrote to Annenkov in February 1882 (P., XIII, 201).

13. V. F. Chizh, "Turgenev, kak psikhopatolog," *Voprosy filosofii i psikhologii*, X, 4 (1899), 624–48.

14. V.I. Rudnev, "Turgenev i Chekhov v izobrazhenii gallyutsinatsii," *Klinichesky arkhiv genialnosti i odaryonnosti*, III, 3 (1927), 181–91.

15. See Rudnev, 182.

16. See N. Ammon, " 'Nevedomoe' u Turgeneva," *Zhurnal Ministerstva Narodnogo Prosveshcheniya*, CCCLII, 4 (1904), 274.

17. See Turgenev's letter to him of 28 January 1882 (P., XIII, 190).

18. S. E. Shatalov, " 'Tainstvennye' povesti I. S. Turgeneva," *Uch. zap. Arzamasskogo gos. ped. inst.*, V, 4 (1962), 47; hereafter cited in the text.

19. For example, M. A. Rybnikova, "Odin iz priemov kompozitsii u Turgeneva," in N. L. Brodsky, editor, *Tvorchesky put Turgeneva* (Petrograd: Seyatel, 1923), 122.

20. See N. A. Kuznetsova, " 'Veshnie vody' I. S. Turgeneva," *Uch. zap. MGU*, 127 (1948), 155–71.

21. Thus M. Turyan, " 'Punin i Baburin' v ryadu pozdnikh proizvedenii Turgeneva," *Russkaya literatura*, VIII, 4 (1965), 150.

22. Freeborn, 163.

23. For example, M. Gabel, " 'Pesn torzhestvuyushchey lyubvi' Turgeneva," in *Tvorchesky put Turgeneva*, 202.

24. V. Chizh, "Turgenev, kak psikhopatolog," *Voprosy filosofii i psikhologii*, X, 5 (1899), 738.

25. See V. M. Fisher, "Tainstvennoe u Turgeneva," in *Venok Turgenevu, 1818–1918* (Odessa: A. A. Ivasenko, 1919), 98.

26. *S.*, X, 203; see Ammon, 259.

27. See L. M. Polyak, "Istoriya povesti Turgeneva 'Klara Milich,' " in N. K. Piksanov, editor, *Tvorcheskayaistoriya: Issledovaniya po russkoy literature* (M.: Nikitinskie subbotniki, 1927), 240.

28. I. F. Annensky, *Vtoraya kniga otrazhenii* (SPb.: Br. Bashmakovy, 1909), 40–41.

29. The corollary of arguing the relevance of such events to social issues during the sixties and seventies is surely to confront oneself with the unenviable task of repeating the process when considering a figure so manifestly noncontemporary as Valeriya in Turgenev's "Italian pastiche" of 1881. See Turgenev's letter to Stasyulevich of 11 September 1881 (*P.*, XIII, 119).

30. See Turgenev's letter to P. V. Zhukovsky of 11 May 1876 (*P.*, XI, 261).

31. Turgenev wrote (in English) in reference to this work in a letter to William Ralston of 10 January 1877: "I have tried to solve a psychological riddle—which I know to a certain extent from my own experience" (*P.*, XII, 63). The suggestion is that his treatment of the mysterious relationship between a mother and her son was prompted in part by his own uneasy relationship with his mother in his youth.

32. Shatalov, 44, and I. Vinogradov, "Povesti i rasskazy Turgeneva shestidesyatykh godov," in I. S. Turgenev, *Sobranie sochinenii* (M.: GIKHL, 1962), VII, 252.

33. The only works in this category that have not been mentioned here are "Old Portraits" (1881), "The Quail," and the later additions to *Notes of a Hunter* "The End of Chertopkhanov" (1872), "Living Relics" (1874), and "There's a Knocking!" (1874).

34. This type of title in Turgenev's fiction can be traced back to "Faust," which though a proper name indicates the force from without which intrudes to destroy the heroine.

35. It might be noted, however, that even the choice of Ferrara as the setting in "The Song of Triumphant Love" has been construed by one ingenious Soviet critic in purely sociopolitical terms. M. Baysgolova, "K voprosu o realizme pozdnikh proizvedenii I. S. Turgeneva ('Pesn torzhestvuyushchey lyubvi')," *Trudy Tbilisskogo G. U.*, ser. filolog. naku, LXXXIII, 2 (1959), 3.

36. "Turgenev's Short Stories: A Revaluation," *Slavonic and East European Review*, XXXII (1953–54), 76.

37. See K. D. Balmont, "Mysli o tvorchestve: Turgenev," *Sovremennye zapiski*, XXII, 4 (1921), 289.

Turgenev, the Dramatist   Richard Freeborn°

Turgenev's career as a dramatist occupied a period of scarcely more than half a dozen years—approximately 1846–52—at an early stage in his development as a writer. Before this period he had written youthful verses, a number of long poems, the most famous of which is "Parasha," published 1843, and several critical articles.[1] Later, of course, he was to turn to prose fiction, especially the novel, for his major work. In consequence, it is not difficult to see that Turgenev's interest in the theater occurred at a transitional period in his development, when he was no longer the young man writing pleasant, though hardly very original, lyric poems, nor the author of such famous novels as *Rudin* and *Fathers and Children*. So it is hardly very surprising that his plays should be experimental. They may be considered experimental in two senses, as experiments, that is, in the art of writing for the theater and in the more important sense that they illustrate the way in which Turgenev was experimenting with his own talent, searching for a means of expression, exploring new forms. There is, for instance, a similar air of experiment about the form and content of the other major work upon which he was engaged at this time, his *Sketches from a Hunter's Album (Zapiski okhotnika)*.[2] When one contemplates Turgenev's career as a whole one sees that Turgenev's experiments in the theater and those in the sphere of the *Sketches* were complementary; they were to blend after a further half-dozen years into that balanced, finely wrought harmony of theatrical form and realistic manner, of truth and poetry, which were to be such important properties in his novels as works of art.

    Turgenev was never a "dramatic" dramatist. He referred to his plays as no more than "Scenes and Comedies," and it is under this title that they are still known. His diffidence about his plays shows itself in the Preface that he wrote to the collection of his *Scenes and Comedies* published in 1869: "I consider it my duty to explain my motives to my readers. Realizing that I have no dramatic talent, I would not have acceded to the request of my publishers who wished to print the fullest possible edition of my works had I not thought that my plays, although unsatisfactory as pieces for the stage, could be of a certain interest as pieces designed for reading."[3] He was reinforced in this view by the opinion of, among others, Prosper Mérimée. In 1866, Mérimée had impressed upon Turgenev that "drama" was the latter's main concern, but had added in qualification: "I am not speaking about drama for the stage or drama which might

° From *Transactions of the Association of Russian-American Scholars in the U.S.A* 16 (1985):57–74. Reprinted by permission of the author and the Association of Russian-American Scholars in the U.S.

be presented on a stage, but drama for intelligent people, the happy few, armchair reading. . . ."[4] Turgenev acquiesced in this opinion about his plays to the end of his life and, despite evidence to the contrary, this view was the prevalent view among his friends and critics both during his lifetime and for many years after his death. His plays were generally considered "unstageable." They were "actors' pieces," suitable for the repertoire of domestic theaters or for actors' "benefits," but they were not regarded as pieces suited to have a place in the permanent repertoires of the major Russian theaters.

There was some truth in this view. Turgenev's is an intimate theater; it demands the subtlety and imagination of a Stanislavsky for it to be fully appreciated, and it was only when Stanislavsky directed and played a major role in *A Month in the Country* in 1909 that this, Turgenev's finest play, was recognized for what it was, a brilliant piece of intimate psychological theater. When, in the 1840s, Turgenev began his career as a dramatist, the Russian theater was, like other forms of literature, subject to government censorship. It was also dominated by the actors themselves, whose choice of play depended upon the effectiveness of a play's main role. The parts played by a director, producer, or scenic designer in the staging of a play were either non-existent or negligible. Similarly, the dramatist himself was regarded as little more than the man who provided a plot and dialogue which could be manipulated by the actors to suit their needs. The main attraction was the leading actor or actress. An actor or actress of talent could do much, of course, to raise theatrical standards. The most famous actor of the period, Shchepkin, succeeded in creating a brilliant constellation of actors at the Maly Theater. He staged Gogol's plays and he was also to make a great success of Turgenev's three-act play *The Bachelor*. But this state of affairs, though it helped Turgenev's lighter pieces, was to prove a serious hindrance to his more important work. Government censorship was to prevent the production of *A Month in the Country* for many years and even when it was eventually admitted to the theatrical repertoires, after the abolition of the monopoly of Imperial Theaters in the 1880s, the dominant position enjoyed by actors in the Russian theater had caused the art of acting to stagnate until, in Nemirovich-Danchenko's graphic description, "it had become as immovable as a battleship encrusted with barnacles after standing too long at anchor."[5] Consequently, the view that Turgenev's plays were "unstageable" was in part due to the conditions prevailing in the Russian theater during the second half of the last century, but it was also due to an absurdly widespread critical misunderstanding of the nature of Turgenev's work for the theater—a misunderstanding which Turgenev himself did little to dispel.

His first play, *A Lack of Care (Neostorozhnost,* 1843), is a curiosity. It precedes the bulk of his plays and it appears on the face of it to have little connection with them. It tells how Doña Dolores, the young wife of an elderly husband, Don Baltasar, feeling bored with her life, is momentarily tempted by the attentions of a young dandy, Don Rafael. This momentary "lack of care" is noticed by a maidservant, who informs Don Baltasar. The latter consults his trusted friend, Don Pablo. Steps are taken to ensure that Don Rafael does not leave the grounds of Don Baltasar's house. In a situation of this kind, when it might be expected that the rendez-vous between the young wife and the amorous dandy would produce a romantic de-nouement, Turgenev intentionally, it seems, introduces an element of parody which is to lead to an ironically tragic conclusion. Doña Dolores and Don Rafael do not confess their love for each other. They are so uncaring in their feeling for each other that their rendez-vous is quickly discovered by Don Pablo and the young Don Rafael is dispatched from the house. The original assignation becomes instead an occasion for Don Pablo to confess his long-concealed passion for the beautiful Doña Dolores. The ironic outcome is that Don Pablo murders Doña Dolores at the moment that Don Baltasar succeeds in breaking down the door to her apartment.

The melodramatic ending tends to conceal the fact that this short play contains several points of interest. For example, it can arguably be said to parody the Romantic concept of drama, which is one reason, no doubt, why it was commended by Belinsky. More signif-icantly, it also broaches themes, such as two men attracted by the same woman, of unreciprocated passion or passion long concealed, which Turgenev is to use later, more subtly and to greater effect, in his plays and his novels. Despite these pointers to the future, the play is basically derivative. A year previously in 1842, a second edition of Mérimée's *Théâtre de Clara Gasul; comédienne espagnole* had appeared in Paris. Turgenev admitted that the appearance of this work "gave me the idea of writing a little piece of the same kind."[6] He even took the names of his characters from Mérimées work, though, as he admitted in another connection, a Spaniard to whom he once read his play remarked that his "dramatis personae" bore as much resemblance to Spaniards as they did to Chinamen. The derivative features and the fact that it differs so obviously from what he was to write subsequently have tended to confuse critical opinion. They play was either ignored or condemned as imitative or dismissed as the unsuccessful work of Turgenev during his supposed Romantic phase at the beginning of his career. Perhaps a more sophisticated reading would stress the arresting mixture of tragic and comic dis-cernible in the play. Turgenev may have derived his ideas from Mérimée, but he appears to have brought to it his own awareness of the tragi-comic uses of irony. Belinsky attempted to express a definition of such comedy when reviewing Russian literature for 1843:

> Comedy, humor and irony are not accessible to everyone, and what arouses laughter is generally considered by most people to be of less importance than whatever arouses lofty passion. Everyone finds it much easier to understand an idea expressed in a direct and positive fashion, rather than an idea which contains a meaning opposed to the sense of the words used to express it. Comedy is the flower of civilization, the fruit of a society that has grown to maturity. In order to understand comedy, one must have attained a high level of culture. Aristophanes was the last great poet of ancient Greece. The crowd can only understand what is externally comic; it does not understand that there are points where the comic fuses with the tragic, giving rise to a laughter that is not easy and joyous, but sick and bitter.[7]

These remarks refer to Gogol and occur in a passage towards the end of a review in which Belinsky is speaking of the need for the writer to choose his subjects from reality. Turgenev's first work for the theater clearly bore no relationship to reality in the sense that Belinsky intended. It was, as Belinsky himself described it, "a dramatic essay, remarkable as a masterly sketch, but no more."[8] There is no doubt, though, that the example of Gogol's satirical comedies and the influence of Belinsky's teaching on the importance of literature as a mirror of society were bound to have their effect on Turgenev. If his first play seems a curiosity, it is because it contains so little hint of that satirical social comment which is to be so marked in the majority of his works for the theater.

Bearing this in mind, his first real contribution to the contemporary Russian theater is no doubt his short one-act play A *Lack of Money (Bezdenezhye,* written 1845, published in *Otechestvennye zapiski* in 1846). It is also a derivative work, in the sense that it is constructed on the lines of the vaudevilles so popular at the time and in its social comment it follows, roughly speaking, the pattern already established by Gogol. It depicts a morning in the life of a young St. Petersburg nobleman, Timofey Petrovich Zhazhikov, who is beset by money problems. His faithful servant, the serf Matvey, urges him to abandon his penniless existence in the capital and return to his home in the country. Zhazhikov wavers and finally, under the influence of a country neighbor visitng St. Petersburg for the first time, decides to stay where he is. It seems that he prefers to live a feckless and precarious day-to-day existence in the big city rather than return to the humdrum, though more useful, life of a landowner. Matvey's bitter comment on his master's conduct reveals the moral of the play: "Long gone are the good old times! You exist no more, you once noble tribe!"

The social comment in this short piece is not acid, but it is pointed enough. The censor, for instance, took exception to Matvey's remark and it was omitted from the version of the play published in 1846. When it was first staged in 1852 the censor played havoc with it. All references to Zhazhikov's status as a member of the Russian nobility or Matvey's as a serf were excised. The result was, one critic observed, "an extraordinarily weak thing" redeemed by some well-observed characterization and some instances of artistry.[9] It was taken off after its second performance. The same fate befell Turgenev's third play when it was produced in 1852. These failures were to be the main reason for Turgenev's decision to give up writing for the theater.

Neither of his first two plays provides much evidence of the way in which his talent was later to develop. Both works are immature and unoriginal; both betray a certain skill in characterization, theatrical craftsmanship and felicity of dialogue; they have a period charm lightened by intelligent irony and an artist's eye. On the debit side, neither has depth, subtlety, or atmosphere. These characteristics, which lend such grace to Turgenev's art, become discernible for the first time in his work for the theater only in his third play, *One May Spin A Thread Too Finely (Gde tonko, tam i rvyotsya,[10] 1848)*. Like his greatest play, *A Month in the Country*, for which it is in many respects a trial sketch, this third play is not "Gogolian" in its subject-matter or in its treatment. It is the first "Turgenevan" play and an example of intimate theater in the sense that no Gogol play is "intimate."

The play is witty, ironical and sophisticated in the French manner. The influence of de Musset's "theatrical proverbs" may perhaps account for the this, since Turgenev wrote the play in Paris in July, 1848, at a time when de Musset's work was arousing almost as much interest as the revolutionary events of that year. It has a favorite Turgenevan setting, that of a country house, and its theme is also a familiar one, in that a girl of nineteen, Vera Nikolaevna Libanova, has to choose whether she will marry Gorsky, a witty, well-educated, sophisticated young man, or her staid neighbor, Stanitsyn. Gorsky is amused by his rival's devoted and scarcely articulate attachment to Vera and decides to play upon the girl's emotions. Despite his professed coldness, he is not entirely impervious to her charms, and Vera herself is not unaffected by his attentions. Gorsky is the one spinning a fine thread. Though simply wanting to make things difficult for his rival, he is not for his part contemplating love and marriage. When put to the test by Vera, he backs down in favor of Stanitsyn, and he does so perhaps with considerably more regret than he had earlier supposed. The story is less important than the manner of its telling, but as a study of the emotional relationship between two intelligent people it is neat, engaging and plausible, never at any point tending to mawkishness or sentimentality. The fascination of this short work lies chiefly in the way Turgenev has embroidered it with passages of ironic, evocative dialogue which convey with characteristic deftness both the atmosphere of the country house, its leisurely pursuit of culture and pleasure, and the growing intimacy between Vera and Gorsky. This growth of intimacy is accompanied by the realization on Vera's part that, despite his elegance and his wit, Gorsky is not likely to be a suitable husband for her. There is no hint here of the crudeness which is only too clearly apparent in the form and manner of Turgenev's first two plays. His contemporaries recognized this at once. Nekrasov, for example, had favorable, even flattering, comments to pass on the play: "I will tell you," he wrote to Turgenev, "without exaggeration that it would be hard to find a more graceful and artistic piece in present-day Russian literature."[11] Ogaryov referred to the "percipience, talent and grace" in the play and prophesied that Turgenev would "do something *important* for Russia."[12] The critical reception that the play received in the press when it was first staged was favorable, but it was withdrawn after its second performance in December 1851 in St. Petersburg. There appears to have been a general agreement that it was more suitable for reading than acting.

Turgenev's next three plays—*A Poor Gentleman (Nakhlebnik,* 1848), *The Bachelor (Kholostyak,* 1849) and *Breakfast at the Marshal of Nobility's (Zavtrak u predvoditelya,* 1849)—are all comedies in a less sophisticated, more Gogolian, vein. They all touch on social matters and they contain also an element of the grotesque reminiscent of Gogol's humor. *A Poor Gentleman* is a two-act play in which Turgenev depicts the dilemma of an elderly hanger-on in a country household. Kuzovkin, the old man in question, is obliged to drink too much, baited and eventually crowned with a dunce's cap by the party of country squires who have gathered to welcome the return of the mistress of the house, Olga Yeletskaya, newly married to a St. Petersburg official. Driven to an extremity of humiliation by the taunts and horseplay of the guests, Kuzovkin finally blurts out that Olga is really his daughter, to everyone's astonishment and disbelief. In the second act it transpires that this is the truth. Kuzovkin confesses the details of his affair with Olga's mother twenty or so years earlier and thus explains why he has been for so long an impoverished hanger-on in her family's house. The new husband decides that Kuzovkin must be paid off, for his presence in the household would be too blatant a reminder of Olga's illegitimate birth.

Although the most striking feature of the play is the portrait of the elderly Kuzovkin, it contains many features which link it to the critical manner of Turgenev's portraits of the provincial nobility in his *Sketches.* The critical picture of the nobility naturally offended the censorship, causing it to be banned throughout the reign of Nicholas I. Turgenev had written the play specifically for the actor Shchepkin and was deeply angered by the ban imposed on it. Even later, after its publication in 1857 and its first staging in 1861, there was a tendency to regard it as an "actor's piece," which meant that only its first act was produced. In such an emasculated form it, of course, lost much of its critical point.

Angered by the censorship's treatment of the play, Turgenev wrote a second work for the actor, Shchepkin, and took care on this occasion to be more cautious in his handling of the social problems. This play, *The Bachelor,* was Turgenev's first critical success. It contains one major role designed for Shchepkin, that of an elderly St. Petersburg official, Moshkin, who has generously become a foster-father to two young people: Vilitsky, a weak, indecisive, ambitious young man and a young girl, Masha, whom Moshkin hopes that Vilitsky will marry. Moshkin's hopes prove fruitless. Vilitsky has fallen under the influence of a certain von Fonk, a pompous bureaucrat of German extraction, who suggests to Vilitsky that he would be lowering himself socially if he were to marry Masha. Vilitsky follows this advice, and Masha, in the end, accepts a proposal of marriage from none other than Moshkin himself, the "bachelor" of the play's title. It is a contrived and artless work with several amusing scenes, some pointed caricatures of officialdom and a light-hearted skit on the hardly very exacting criteria for literary success in St. Petersburg. Dostoevsky found it "disgracefully bad. . . . It has no originality: it's an old, well-worn path. It's all been said before and better than he's said it."[13] The condemnation clearly reflects the rivalry between the two writers and it is for that reason too harsh, but the comment on the play's lack of originality is justifiable. It was probably this lack of originality that accounted for its success. When Turgenev saw the play for the first time in December 1850, he wrote of the experience to Pauline Viardot:

> The public gave it a warm reception; the third act in particular had a remarkably good success. I confess that this was pleasant. Shchepkin was magnificent, full of truth, inspiration, and sensibility; he was given an ovation after the first act, twice in the course of the third and twice after it. But how instructive it is for an author to be present at the performance of his own play! Whatever one may say about it, one becomes a member of the public, and every suggestion of longwindedness, every false effect strikes one at once, like a stroke of lightning. The second act was undoubtedly a failure, and I found that the public was being too kind to me. Nevertheless, I am in general very satisfied. This experience has shown me that I have a

vocation for the theater and that in time I will be able to write good things.[14]

Had it not been for the censorship, this prophecy might well have come true. In his plays Turgenev was unable to assume that pose of detached, objective portraiture which gave so many of his *Sketches* such an innocent or unassuming appearance. In the theater he had to rely on burlesque to sugar the pill of social indictment. *The Bachelor* skirts the deeper implications of its subject, particularly the question of Masha's social inferiority, by couching it in purely humorous, even caricature, terms. It is probable that by concentating on the burlesque manner Turgenev hoped to evade the censorship in the case of his short one-act play *Breakfast at the Marshal of Nobility's*. Like *A Poor Gentleman* it is set in the milieu of the provincial nobility and depicts the superficially quite innocent quarrel of two landowners, a brother and sister, over the division of some inherited property. The Marshal of Nobility attempts to arbitrate between them, but the sister indulges in such tantrums that no one can persuade her to come to terms. The humorless censorship found that the play presented the nobility in an unfavorable light and, like *A Poor Gentleman,* it was banned until after the death of Nicholas I. Of all Turgenev's comedies it is the one most obviously written for laughs. Although the critical implications are discernible, they obtrude very little into what is scarcely more than a burlesque entertainment.

Whatever critical claims can be made for these early plays, they have to be regarded as minor and experimental. Turgenev's only major work for the theater was *A Month in the Country (Mesyats v derevne,* 1848–50). This five-act comedy is the only play by Turgenev to have achieved an international reputation and to have become an acknowledged classic of the Russian theater.[15] Yet it is also a derivative work and can be seen to be experimental in two main senses: first, in the sense that it blends the social element of his "Gogolian" plays with the delicate, psychological manner of his *One May Spin a Thread Too Finely,* and second, in the sense that it paves the way for the theatrical form of the novels.

What are the likely derivative features? The most obvious, and the one most often quoted in the critical literature about the play, is the possible debt that Turgenev owed to Balzac's *La Marâtre*.[16] Turgenev was in Paris in April 1848 when Balzac's play had its premiere. Both plays can be shown to have an approximately similar plot. A young woman finds that her adopted daughter is a rival to her in her love for a young man. The young woman decides to marry her adopted daughter off to an obviously unsuitable older man with the help of the local doctor. The plays further resemble each other in being a new kind of intimate theater. At this point, though, the resemblance largely ceases. Whether or not Turgenev was directly influenced by Balzac's play cannot be ascertained on the available evidence. What can be said in demonstration of the lack of influence is that the title which Turgenev first gave to the play in draft form was *The Student*. This suggests that from the start Turgenev was more concerned to emphasize the importance of the young student in the play, Belyaev (the first name Turgenev used was apparently Andrey Kolosov, after the title of his first published short story of 1844), than the figure of Natalya Petrovna, the *marâtre* or stepmother in his comedy. The social element, the realistic social reference of the play, seems then to have assumed as much importance for Turgenev as the element of the "amorous duel," the link between them being the young student, Belyaev. Through him Turgenev has brought to his comedy a representative of what Isaiah Berlin has called "that classless dissident intelligentsia with which Turgenev was in sympathy all his life."[17]

A Month in the Country describes how Natalya Petrovna Islayeva, loved and admired by her husband and her friend of long standing, Rakitin, falls in love with Belyaev, who has been engaged to teach her son, Kolya. Belyaev meanwhile is attracted to the orphan girl Verochka, Natalya Petrovna's adopted daughter. Unaware perhaps of the true nature of her intentions, Natalya Petrovna resolves to marry Verochka to an elderly neighboring landowner, Bolshintsov, and uses as a go-between in this matter the local doctor, Shpigelsky. In consequence a number of misunderstandings arise. Natalya Petrovna does not know that Verochka is in love with Belyaev; Belyaev does not know that Natalya Petrovna is in love with him; Islayev, the husband, does not suspect that Rakitin is really in love with his wife. When the truth about these emotional relationships becomes known, Rakitin and Belyaev are both obliged to leave. The outcome of this "month in the country" is that Natalya Petrovna loses both her admiring, patient lover of four years' standing and that vision of a younger and perhaps rejuvenating love which she feels Belyaev may be able to offer her.

Although it deals with amorous relationships, the play broaches no important moral issues. It sets out to explore and illumine, in the subtlest and least didactic of ways, the absurdity of human passion. In doing this, it touches upon social differences which are a clue to the play's deeper meaning. The catalyst is the young Belyaev. Like the later Bazarov, for whom he is clearly a trial sketch, Belyaev is not only a *raznochinets,* classless, dissident, whose status in social terms is dependent upon his intelligence and education, he is also—to judge from what he says in the play—scornful of poetry and evidently biased towards science.[18] Like Bazarov, he has a common touch, it seems, which gives him an inherent social mobility, so that he can move with equal ease among children, servants and the landowning gentry. To him is contrasted the figure of the "superfluous man" Rakitin. Natalya Petrovna recognizes this contrast at once. In her eyes Rakitin is unduly "sensitive," but it is a sensitivity, like Rudin's, which lacks the spontaneous, untutored perception so necessary for a proper understanding of the ways of the heart. When Rakitin, in Act II, speaks eloquently of the beauty of the dark green oak, Natalya Petrovna reproves him by saying:

> Do you know what, Rakitin? I've noticed this long ago. You have a very sensitive feeling for the so-called beauties of nature, and you talk about them very eloquently, very intelligently, so eloquently and intelligently that I imagine nature must be unspeakably grateful to you for your exquisitely felicitous expressions of admiration; you chase after her like a perfumed marquis in dainty red shoes chasing after a good-looking peasant girl. The only pity of it is that it seems to me nature can't understand or appreciate your sensitive comments, just as the peasant girl wouldn't be able to understand the courtly blandishments of a marquis; nature is much simpler, even coarser, than you imagine, because it is, after all, healthy."[19]

This contrast between nature's healthiness and Rakitin's sensitivity emphasizes the difference between the healthy youthfulness of Belyaev and the middle-aged, introspective character of the "superfluous man." As in so many works by Turgenev, the heroine is given the role of evaluating the relative social merits of the hero to whom she is juxtaposed, and here there can be no doubt about Natalya Petrovna's preference for the young Belyaev. It is a preference due as much to the fact that Belyaev represents for her a kind of social release from the stifling, hot-house atmosphere of the Islayev household as to the fact of his youthfulness. Both are equally unobtainable for her, of course. Equally she is unable to perceive the further contrast between Rakitin and her husband. Turgenev took pains in many of his works about the provincial nobility to indicate the difference between the man who was "superfluous" and the man who was practical—in *Rudin,* for example, a contrast posed in the clearest terms between her hero and Lezhnyov. Here the contrast between Rakitin and Islayev is less clearly drawn, but it is one that nevertheless points up the superfluity of the one and the practicality of the other within the limited ambience of Natalya Petrovna's experience.

Other social disparities must explain other features of behavior in the Islayev household. The social disparity existing between Natalya Petrovna and her adopted daughter Verochka must partly explain her readiness to contemplate such an unequal match as the one between Verochka and Bolshintsov. Similarly, there is the socially dependent position of the go-between, Dr. Shpigelsky. Shpigelsky has a role approximately similar to a Gogolian matchmaker and chorus. He is a peripheral figure whose comments, when they are not directly related to the question of the match and often seem in that connection more burlesque than serious, contain beneath their laconic exterior a deliberate censure of the upper-class milieu in which he is obliged to pass his time. His remarks to Lizaveta Bogdanovna in Act IV endow his role with a degree of forceful asperity that makes him the most serious critic of the mores of the serf-owning nobility in the play.

The social contrasts are there to be discerned and Soviet criticism has not failed to point them out, but they are for the most part implied rather than overt. They acquire importance only when they are related to the intimate psychological contrasts which form the weave of the play. At the center of them is Natalya Petrovna. Her love for Belyaev, Rakitin's love for her, her jealous feeling towards Verochka, her husband's devotion to her—these are the emotional axes about which the principal relationships revolve. It is here that the element of amorous duel, which Turgenev had first exploited in *One May Spin a Thread Too Finely,* becomes so conspicuous. The relationship between Natalya Petrovna and Rakitin is an amorous duel, conducted in Act I against the background of the card game and in later acts to the accompaniment of Natalya Petrovna's increasing love for Belyaev, of Belyaev's love for Verochka, of Natalya Petrovna's growing jealousy and Rakitin's growing despair. As in all amorous duels, the participants are not evenly matched. Natalya Petrovna has all the advantages at the beginning, as it were, and loses them in the end. Rakitin starts with the disadvantage of being her devoted admirer, the friend enslaved to her affections, and ends by witnessing her defeat—a defeat which ironically frees him from a self-imposed four years' enslavement. There is a similar amorous conflict between Natalya Petrovna, Belyaev and Verochka, in which Natalya Petrovna ostensibly starts with all the advantages, but overreaches herself and ends by destroying the likely happiness of all three participants. Yet even though she must be regarded as the prime cause of the unhappy denouements in the play, hers is by no means an unpleasant or evil nature. Although her desire for love is not exactly innocent, she is innocent of real malice in her attempt to gain it. She repents quickly of her plan to match Verochka with Bolshintsov. Her complex motives, like her complex nature, are the result of an unhappy childhood, as she explains to Belyaev in Act I. Dominated by an overbearing father who eventually went blind, she became fearful of him and the embarrassment and shyness deriving from this fear have remained with her into adulthood. Her love for Belyaev springs from a sense of loss. It is a craving for affection, self-indulgent, pitiable and hurtful, giving pain as much to herself as to Belyaev, Rakitin, and Verochka. It is also a genuine and sincere love which is fruitless because Belyaev cannot be expected to respond to it. The incongruity of Natalya Petrovna's love for Belyaev is paralleled by a similar incongruity in her relations with Rakitin. She cannot respond to his love in the same way that Belyaev cannot respond to hers. The emotional needs of all the play's chief characters remain unfulfilled. In ths respect, as a study in human incompatibility, *A Month in the Country* anticipates Chekhovian comedy much more obviously than it reflects the comedy of Gogol.

But, in contrast to Chekhov's work, Turgenev's play illustrates a definable attitude to such a human dilemma. Love, nature and freedom are the ingredients. As Stanislavsky pointed out in discussing the play, Natalya Petrovna is drawn to Belyaev and, for that matter, to Verochka, because their love is

> natural, naive, simple and, as it were, field-fresh. In seeing these lovers and admiring the simplicity of their relations, Natalya Petrovna is involuntarily drawn to such simple and natural feelings and thus towards nature itself. The hot-house rose sought to become a field flower, started to dream of meadow and woodland; she fell in love with the student Belyaev. From this there came the general catastrophe: Natalya Petrovna frightened away the simple and natural love of poor Verochka, dismayed the young student, but did not go after him, was deprived of her faithful admirer Rakitin, remained forever with a husband whom she could respect but could not love, and retreated once more into her hot-house.[20]

Indeed, *A Month in the Country* is a study, as it were, of love in two climates: the climate of the stuffy, restricted, hot-house world in which Natalya Petrovna lives and the field-fresh, "natural" climate to which Belyaev and Verochka belong. Natalya Petrovna wanted to free herself from the hot-house world, but found she could not survive in the astringent, purer air of the fields. Rakitin, on the other hand, had no desire to leave the hot-house, but was eventually forced to leave if after the failure of Natalya Petrovna's attempt. Both find themselves denied what they most want; both are involved in a choice between love and freedom; both are obliged in the end to opt for a lesser rather than a greater happiness. And what, after all, is love? Rakitin passes the typically Turgenevan verdict on this absurd human emotion which has been the cause of such happiness and such misery during the course of the comedy. In Act V, instead of praising love as earth's greatest blessing, Rakitin instructs Belyaev in its pitfalls and dangers:

> In my opinion, any love, whether it be happy or unhappy, is a real calamity if you give yourself up to it utterly. You will learn perhaps how those soft fingers can torture, with what gentle considerateness they can tear your heart to shreds. You'll learn what burning hatred

is hidden in the most passionate love! You'll remember me when, like a sick man thirsting for health, you'll thirst for peace of mind, when you'll envy any other man his unconcernedness and freedom. You'll learn what it means to belong to a woman's skirt, to be enslaved, infected—and how shameful and wearisome such slavery is! You'll learn finally what worthless joys are bought for such a high price.[21]

The moral of these words, for all their whiff of sour grapes, is that lack of freedom is too high a price to pay. Rakitin bows gracefully out of his relationship with Natalya Petrovna and gains what one assumes is an unwanted and rather profitless freedom, but it is at least better than enslavement. These are the contrasts, then, from which the comedy is made: the contrast of youth and age, of one social status with another, of the hot-house climate and the climate of the fields, of the artificial and the natural, of love and freedom. Out of these contrasts Turgenev "wove a fine lace," as Natalya Petrovna described it. In the weave of the play itself one can easily discern the experimental blending of the element of Gogolian social satire from such earlier plays as *The Poor Gentleman* and *The Bachelor* with the delicate psychological manner of *One May Spin a Thread Too Finely*. It is also not difficult to see that *A Month in the Country* is a turning point. The social element, though important for an understanding of the play, is clearly secondary to the study of emotional relationships. The laconic, oblique, subtly emotive dialogue, the peaceful country-house setting, the summer atmosphere, the intrusion into this world of a disruptive influence from outside, the resultant emotional conflict which is, on the face of it, no more than "the flaring up and dying away" of a spark, as Belyaev calls it, and beneath these superficially slight occurrences the tragic comedy of human incompatibility, inadequacy, and heartbreak—these are to be, along with the theatrical form, the ingredients of Turgenev's later novels, added to which is that dimension of social-political biography, the chronicle element, which his work for the theater always lacked. The subsequent history of *A Month in the Country* must largely account for Turgenev's decision to abandon the theater. Originally entitled, *Two Women*, it was banned by the censorship when it was first submitted in November 1850. Despite this, it enjoyed considerable success in St. Petersburg salons during the autumn of that year. However, it was not published until 1855, in *Sovremennik [The Contemporary]*, when it was prefaced with the following words by Turgenev:

This comedy was written four years ago and was never intended for the stage. It is not really a comedy, but a short story in dramatic

form. It is clearly not suitable for the stage; the well-disposed reader
must decide whether it is worth printing.[22]

These words tended to mislead both critics and readers. They also
concealed the fact that Turgenev had been obliged by the censor to
cut out the figure of Islayev and to make Natalya Petrovna into a
widow. The curious moral scruples which must have guided the censor
in demanding such changes can only be guessed at. It was not until
almost twenty years after it was written that the play was published
in an "authorized" version, in the collection of *Scenes and Comedies*
which Turgenev published in 1869. By this time he had already made
his reputation as a novelist and few people remembered that he had
been a dramatist. His insistence, moreover, that he had no dramatic
talent and that his plays were to be read rather than acted did not
help. But during the 1870s these injunctions were overlooked. The
play was given a public performance for the first time in January
1872. Real success first came in 1879, when it was produced at the
Alexandrinsky Theater in St. Petersburg by the young actress Savina.
She took the part of Verochka. Turgenev was delighted by her
performance and fell in love with her. "Did I write the part of
Verochka?" he exclaimed. "I didn't even pay any attention to her
while I was writing. Everything centered on Natalya Petrovna."[23]
Reactions to the play were mixed, but audiences on the whole seem
to have applauded the merits of this half-forgotten and long unrecognized comedy.

It was not until many years after Turgenev's death that his comedy
was to be recognized as a major theatrical work. The association of
the work with Chekhovian comedy has become a commonplace of
criticism,[24] though it is very likely that in terms of theatrical history
Turgenev's work should be regarded paradoxically as owing more to
Chekhov's influence than exerting any prior influence of its own. The
success of Chekhov's plays in the first years of this century was to
provide the kind of theatrical atmosphere in which an intimate,
psychological comedy like *A Month in the Country* could be properly
appreciated. Stanislavsky recognized this. He was particularly sensitive
to the extremely delicate skeins of amorous experience which form
the weave of Turgenev's comedy. He felt that his own acting method
could be applied successfully to the creation of the role of Rakitin
(the part which he played in the famous 1909 production of the
Moscow Art Theater) and to the other roles. For, as he described it,
a particular kind of acting was required "which would allow the
theater-goer to appreciate the delicate psychological patterns made
by the loving, suffering, envying hearts" of the play's characters.
"Let the actors sit motionless and feel and talk and infect thus the
thousand-fold audience with their experiences. Let there be no more

than a garden bench or a divan on the stage, on which all the characters sit, so that everyone can see the unfolding of the inner essence of their souls and Turgenev's complex picture of psychological interrelationships.''[25] In this way the inner picture of *A Month in the Country* would be revealed and the actor's concern would be to reveal the spiritual activity defined by the psychological picture of his role. Only a generation of actors nurtured in the tradition of Chekhov and the Moscow Art Theater would be suitably equipped for such a task.

Turgenev wrote three other works for the theater after *A Month in the Country,* the most important of which is *The Provincial Lady (Provintsialka,* 1850). It is a short one-act play which describes how the wife of a provincial official exercises her charms upon an elderly roué, Count Lyubin, to obtain a position for her husband in St. Petersburg. By the end it seems that she has succeeded. A delightful, neatly observed piece, it was written originally for a "benefit" performance by the actress Samoylova and, though atrociously acted at its first performance in 1851, was greeted with rapturous applause. Sterner critics, such as Druzhinin and Apollon Grigoriev, were less favorably disposed to it. Absence of serious content in the work dismayed them; it was ephemeral and compared badly with the prose work, particularly the *Sketches,* which Turgenev was publishing at the time in *Sovremennik.* The other two works for the theater are *Conversation on the High Road (Razgovor na bolshoy doroge,* 1851), written for the actor Sadovsky, in which Turgenev made use of various dialect words from the Oryol region, and *An Evening in Sorrento (Vecher v Sorrente,* written 1852). It was never published during Turgenev's lifetime. Shortly before his death he apparently gave it to the actress Savina, who presented it for the first time in 1885. It is quite the slightest of Turgenev's dramatic works, relating quite simply the brief amorous encounters and the eventual pairing off of four Russian tourists on their last evening in Sorrento.

With the exception of *A Month in the Country* all Turgenev's plays are minor pieces. Though this play stands apart as the one important work for the theater by which Turgenev is still remembered, it lacks the stature and majesty as a work of art which may legitimately be claimed for his work as a writer, especially as a novelist. It is a work which, no matter how brilliant the production, inevitably betrays its immaturity, its experimental blending of disparate elements, when it is staged. It can never fully satisfy in the way one feels a Turgenevan work should satisfy because it lacks two characteristics which contribute so greatly to Turgenev's appeal as a novelist. First, from the technical point of view it cannot have the pervasive descriptive atmosphere, so enriching, prolific, and infectious, which supplies the emotional frame to his months in the country when they become novels. Second, it lacks the philosophical purposefulness, that special view of man's condition and destiny, which expresses itself through the fictional lives of Rudin, Lavretsky, Elena and Bazarov and suggests not only the ephemeral character of human happiness, even perhaps its impossibility, but also the ultimate dignity of all human endeavor when confronted by an indifferent nature and a desolating eternity. For these reasons alone, not to mention the greater maturity of craftsmanship and characterization, the greater range of social and political commitment in his novels, Turgenev's work for the theater must seem merely part of his apprenticeship for future greatness, at its worst no more than very gifted improvisations on the lines of the vaudevilles so popular during the 1840s, at its best, in *A Month in the Country,* adding a dimension of rare and forceful psychological insight, reinforced by a sharp edge of social criticism, to a form of intimate stage comedy that had its origins in the Parisian theater of the time.

Notes

1. This is not to deny claims by many critics and commentators about the significance of Turgenev's early work, which frequently rises above "juvenilia" in its range and accomplishment. As a recent study of the subject has claimed, "the total number of Turgenev's early works is comparable in volume to the complete literary heritage of Gogol or Lermontov." Walter Smyrniw, *Turgenev's Early Works: From Character Sketches to a Novel* (Oakville, Ont.: Mosaic Press, 1980), p. 11.

2. The title is taken from my own translation of a selection of the *Sketches* for Penguin Classics.

3. Quoted from I. S. Turgenev, *Polnoe sobranie sochinenii i pisem,* 28 vols. (M.-L., 1960–68), *Sochineniya,* II, 551. References to this edition are hereafter cited as *Soch.* or *Pis'ma.* All translations are my own.

4. *Ibid.*

5. V. I. Nemirovich-Danchenko, *Iz proshlogo* (M.: Gosizdat, 1938), p. 29; quoted from *Turgenev i teatr,* edited by G. P. Berdnikov (M.: Iskusstvo, 1953), p. 82.

6. *Soch.,* II, 558.

7. V. G. Belinsky, *Polnoe sobranie sochineniy,* 13 vols. (M.: Akademia nauk, 1953–59), VIII, 90.

8. *Ibid.,* 96.

9. For this and other reactions, see *Soch.,* II, 563–64.

10. The translated title is taken from a version by M. Gough of 1909.

11. *Soch.,* II, 570.

12. *Ibid.,* 569.

13. *Ibid.,* 611–12.

14. *Pis'ma,* I, 420–21.

15. The production at the National Theatre in London in February 1981 with Francesca Annis as Natalya Petrovna and Michael Gough as Shpigelsky proved to be extremely successful. The new translation by Sir Isaiah Berlin undoubtedly contributed to the success. I have chosen to make my own translations of the Turgenev text for

this paper, based on *Soch.*, III, though I have used Isaiah Berlin's transliteration of the names.

16. For a full discussion of this, see L. P. Grossman, *Teatr Turgeneva* (Petrograd: Brokgauz-Efron, 1924), 67–83.

17. *A Month in the Country: A Comedy in Five Acts* by Ivan Turgenev, translated and introduced by Isaiah Berlin (London: Hogarth Press, 1981), 13.

18. In his first draft of the play Turgenev described him as belonging to the "department of political studies" of Moscow University. These references to what might seem to be Belyaev's radical sympathies were deleted from the first publication of the comedy, although it appears likely that Turgenev originally conceived the character as a politically conscious member of the younger generation. See *Soch.*, III, 412–13.

19. *Soch.*, III, 75–76.

20. K. S. Stanislavsky, *Moya zhinz' v iskusstve*, 3rd ed. (L.-M.: Academia, 1931), 562–63.

21. *Soch.*, III, 145–46.

22. *Sovremennik*, 1 (1855), 29.

23. *Soch..*, III, 422.

24. See, for example, Marc Slonim, *Russian Theater: From the Empire to the Soviets* (London: Methuen, 1963), 68.

25. Stanislavsky, *op. cit.*, 563–64. A little known but interesting discussion of Turgenev's work as a dramatist may be found in O. Adamovich and G. Uvarova, "Turgenev-dramaturg," in *I. S. Turgenev: K pyatidesyatiletiyu so dnya smerti, 1883–1933, Sbornik statey* (Leningrad: Gosizdat, 1934), 272–328.

Foreword to the Novels   Ivan Turgenev[*]

Having decided to publish all the novels I have written (*Rudin, A Nest of Gentlefolk, On the Eve, Fathers and Sons, Smoke,* and *Virgin Soil*) in sequential order in a forthcoming edition, I consider it relevant to explain, in a few words, why I have done this. I wanted to give those of my readers who take upon themselves the labor of reading these six novels in a row the opportunity to satisfy themselves clearly about just how fair those critics are who have reproached me for a change in the orientation I once adopted, for apostasy, and so on. I think that on the contrary, I could be reproached more accurately for excessive constancy and a sort of straightforwardness of orientation. The author of *Rudin,* written in 1855, and the author of *Virgin Soil,* written in 1876, are one and the same person. Over the course of this whole time I have striven, insofar as strength and skill have sufficed, conscientiously and dispassionately to depict and embody in appropriate types both what Shakespeare calls "the body and pressure

[*] From *Polnoe sobranie sochinenii i pisem,* vol. 12 (Moscow-Leningrad: AN SSSR, 1960–68), 303–10. Translated from the Russian for this volume by the editor.

of time" and that rapidly changing physiognomy of the Russian people of the cultured stratum that has primarily served as the subject of my observations. How successful I have been is not for me to judge; but I venture to think that readers will not now doubt the sincerity and uniformity of my aspirations.

I will allow myself to add a few short remarks about each of the six novels—remarks perhaps not devoid of a certain interest.

Rudin, which I wrote in the country, at the very height of the Crimean War, had a purely literary success not so much in the editorial office of *The Contemporary,* where it was published, as outside it. I recall that the late Nekrasov,[1] after hearing my reading, said to me: "You have conceived something new; but just between us, as secret, your *Rudin* is boring." True, a few weeks afterwards the same Nekrasov, talking to me about the narrative poem *Sasha* he had just written, remarked, "You'll see, in it I imitate your *Rudin* to a certain extent—but really, you won't get angry." I also remember that I was very surprised by a letter from Senkovsky (Baron Brambeus),[2] whom I shunned, as did the whole young school then, and who regarded *Rudin* with great sympathy.

A Nest of Gentlefolk had the greatest success that has ever fallen to my share. Beginning with the time of that novel's appearance I began to be considered among the writers deserving the public's attention.

On the Eve had a much lesser success, although no other of my novels produced as many articles in journals. (The most outstanding, of course, was Dobrolyubov's article.)[3] The late N. F. Pavlov criticized me strongly, and another critic, also deceased now, a certain Daragan, was even given a dinner by subscription in gratitude for a quite stern article about *On the Eve,* in which he especially insisted on the main characters' immorality. Several epigrams appeared; one witticism was repeated particularly often: my work was entitled *On the Eve,* it was said, because it came out on the eve of a good novel.

I ask the readers' permission to tell—specifically apropos of this *On the Eve*—about a small episode from my literary life.

I spent almost all of 1855 (just like the preceding three years) without leaving my village in the Mtsensk District of Oryol Province. Of my neighbors the person closest to me was one Vasily Karateev, a young landowner of twenty-five. Karateev was a romantic, an enthusiast, a great lover of literature and music, endowed, moreover, with an original sense of humor, quick to fall in love, impressionable, and direct. He had been educated at Moscow University and lived in the country with his father, who was overcome every three years by a fit of spleen resembling insanity. Karateev had a sister, a very remarkable creature, who also ended in insanity. All of these people are long since dead; that is why I am speaking of them so freely.

Karateev forced himself to look after the estate, a business in which he understood absolutely nothing, and he especially loved reading and conversations with people he liked. Few such people turned up. The neighbors did not like him due to his freethinking and his mocking tongue; moreover, they were afraid to introduce him to their daughters and wives, since he had acquired a reputation—in essence not at all deserved—a reputation as a dangerous ladies' man. He came to see me often—and his visits gave me almost the only entertainment and pleasure at that not very happy time for me.

When the Crimean War came and there occurred a recruitment for a gentry levy, called the home guard, the gentry of our district, who did not like Karateev, agreed, as they say, to give him his marching orders—and elected him an officer of that very home guard. After learning of his appointment, Karateev came to see me. I was immediately struck by his distraught and alarmed appearance. His first words were "I won't come back from there; I won't survive this; I'll die there." He could not boast of good health; his chest ached continually, and he was of a weak constitution. Although I feared for him myself because of the difficulties of the campaign, I tried to dispel his gloomy premonitions and began assuring him that not even so much as a year would pass before we would again meet in our backwater, would again be seeing each other, talking and arguing as before. But he stubbornly stood his ground—and after a rather long walk in my garden he suddenly addressed the following words to me: "I have a request to make of you. You know that I spent several years in Moscow, but you don't know that I was involved in a story there that aroused in me the desire to tell about it—both to myself and to others. I tried to do that, but I was forced to conclude that I have no literary talent, and the whole business concluded with my writing this notebook, which I am placing in your hands." After saying that, he took from his pocket a small notebook about fifteen pages long. "Since I'm certain," he continued, "in spite of your friendly consolation, that I won't come back from the Crimea, please be so good as to take these sketches and make something of them that would not vanish without trace, as I shall!" I was going to refuse, but seeing that my refusal grieved him, I gave him my word to carry out his wish, and that very evening, after Karateev's departure, I glanced through the notebook he had left. In it, in cursory strokes, was outlined what later made up the contents of *On the Eve*. The story, however, had not been brought to an end, and broke off abruptly. During his stay in Moscow, Karateev had fallen in love with a girl who reciprocated his feelings; but after becoming acquainted with the Bulgarian Katranov (a person, as I subsequently learned, once quite well known and not yet forgotten in his homeland), she fell in love with him and left with him for Bulgaria, when he soon died. The story of that love was conveyed sincerely, though unskill-fully. Karateev really had not been born a writer. Just one scene, namely, a trip to Tsaritsyno, was sketched rather vividly—and I retained its main features in my novel. True, at that time there were other images turning around in my head: I was preparing to write *Rudin;* but the task that I later tried to carry out in *On the Eve* occasionally arose before me. The figure of the main heroine, Yelena, then as yet a new type in Russian life, took rather clear shape in my imagination; but a hero was lacking, the sort of person to whom Yelena, with her as yet vague but strong yearning for freedom, could give herself. After reading Karateev's notebook, I involuntarily ex-claimed: "There's the hero I've been looking for!" There was not yet that sort of person among the Russians of that time. When I saw Karateev the next day, I not only confirmed to him my decision to fulfill his request, but also thanked him for leading me out of difficulty and shedding a ray of light on my at that time still vague plans and imaginings. Karateev was happy about that, and after repeating once more, "Don't let this all die," he left to serve in the Crimea, from where, to my regret, he did not return. His premonitions came true. He died of typhus while stationed near the Gniloe Sea,[4] where our Oryol home guard, which did not see a single enemy during the entire war and which nonetheless lost about half of its people from various diseases, was quartered—in dugouts. I postponed the keeping of my promise, however; I had begun another work; after finishing *Rudin,* I undertook *A Nest of Gentlefolk;* and not until the winter of 1858–59, once again finding myself in the same village and in the same circumstance as during my acquaintance with Karateev, did I sense that the dormant impressions had begun to stir; I found his notebook and reread it; the images that had retreated to the back-ground again came to the foreground—and I right away took pen in hand: a few of my acquaintances became aware at that time of everything I have just told about; but I consider it my duty now, in connection with the definitive edition of my novels, to share this with the public as well, and in so doing to pay at least a belated tribute to the memory of my poor friend.

And that is how a Bulgarian became the hero of my novel. But the critics reproached me concertedly for the artificiality and life-lessness of that character, were surprised at my strange idea of choosing specifically a Bulgarian, and asked, "Why? What's the point? What's the sense?" A tempest in a teapot began brewing, but at that time I did not consider it necessary to enter into further explanations.

I think there is no need to speak of *Fathers and Sons* in detail: an entire chapter of my *Memoirs of Literature and Life* is devoted to that novel. I will remark on just one thing: seventeen years have now passed since the time of the appearance of *Fathers and Sons,* and, as far as can be judged, the critical view of the work has still not been settled—and as recently as last year, apropos of Bazarov, I was able to read in a certain journal that I was nothing but a "bandit who finished off people wounded by someone else." True, that was said by Mr. Antonovich,[5] who, soon after the appearance of *Fathers and Sons,* asserted that Mr. Askochensky[6] anticipated the contents of my novel.

Smoke, though it had a rather significant success, aroused great indignation against me. Especially strong were reproaches for a lack of patriotism, for insulting my native land, and so on. Again epigrams appeared. F. I. Tyutchev himself, whose friendship I had always been proud of and which I continue to be proud of to this day, considered it necessary to write a poem in which he deplored the false road chosen by me. It turned out that although from different points of view, I had equally offended both the left and right parties of the reading public. I began to doubt myself somewhat and fell silent for a time.

As for *Virgin Soil,* I imagine that there is no reason to belabor the concerted condemnation that greeted this last work of mine— one that cost me such effort. With the exception of two or three opinions—written, not published—I have not heard anything but abuse from anyone. First people averred that I had made it all up; that because I lived abroad almost continually, I had lost all comprehension of Russian life and of Russians; that only petty vanity and an inclination to chasing after popularity had guided my pen; one journalist hastened to declare that any decent person ought definitely to spit on my book and trample it under foot.[7] And then, after a certain trial which justified the greater part of what had been called my fabrications,[8] my judges began arguing something else: they alleged that I myself had nearly participated in those disloyal designs and, of course, knew of them, since otherwise how could I have foreseen and foretold it ahead of time, and so on and so forth. This all gradually came into balance; and during my last stay in Russia I was able to satisfy myself that without retreating from certain indubitably fair accusations based mainly on my remove from my native country, the majority of my compatriots do not consider my last novel entirely useless or harmful or worthy of nothing but contempt.

And so the deceased Belinsky's words, which he often loved repeating, came true: "Every person sooner or later winds up in his berth."

"Was ist der langen Rede kurzer Sinn?" "What is the point of this speech?" one reader or another may ask. First, the defense of that intention that was expressed by me in the first lines of the present foreword; second, the following conclusion instilled in me by the experience of many years:

Our criticism, especially recently, cannot lay any claims to infallibility—and the writer who listens *to it alone* runs the risk of ruining his talent. Its main sin consists of the fact that it is not free. I cannot pass up the opportunity to express my opinion about "unconscious and conscious art," "preconceived ideas and tendencies," "the utility of objectivity, directness, and naiveté," and about all those "pathetic" words that no matter from whose authoritative lips they issue always seemed commonplaces to me, rhetorical common coin that fails to be taken as a counterfeit only because too many people take it for the real thing. Any writer *who is not devoid of talent* (that is the first condition, of course), any writer, I say, tries first of all to reproduce accurately and vividly impressions gained from his own and others' lives; any reader has the right to judge how well he has succeeded at that and where he has made mistakes; but who has the right to instruct him as to precisely which impressions are appropriate for literature and which ones are not? If he is veracious, he is right; and if he has no talent, no "objectivity" will help him. We have now produced writers who consider themselves "unconscious creators" and chose only plots "from life," but meanwhile are permeated through and through with precisely that ill-starred "tendency." Everyone knows the saying "*a poet thinks in images*"; that saying is quite indisputable and true; but on what basis do you, his critic and judge, allow him to depict graphically a picture of nature, or let us say, the life of the people, an integrated character (There is another *pathetic* word!), but if he touches on anything vague, psychologically complex, even pathological—especially if it is not a particular fact, but extracted from its very depths by that very same life of the people, the life of the society, you yell, "Stop! That won't do. That's morbid self-analysis, a preconceived idea, that's politics! Non-fiction!" You assert that the non-fiction writer and the poet have different tasks. No! They can be identical for both; it is just that the non-fiction writer views them with the eyes of a non-fiction writer, and a poet, with the eyes of a poet. In the matter of art the question of how is more important than the question of what. If everything that you reject lodges in a writer's soul as an *image*—note: as an *image*, then why should you suspect his intentions, why do you expel him from the temple where the priests of "unconscious" art sit on splendidly decorated altars—altars before which incense burns, often lighted by the hands of those very priests? Believe me: true talent never serves extraneous goals, and finds its satisfaction in itself; the life surrounding it gives it content—it is its *concentrated reflection,* but a true talent is just as little capable of writing a panegyric as a lampoon. In the final analysis, that is beneath it. Only those who do not know how to do anything else or anything better can submit to an assigned topic or carry out a program.

Paris, August 1879

Notes

[1. The poet and publisher Nikolay Nekrasov (1821–78).]

[2. O. I. Senkovsky (1800–58), writer, journalist, publisher.]

[3. For information about Dobrolyubov, see the introduction to this volume.]

[4. Part of the Sea of Aral.]

[5. M. A. Antonovich (1835–1918), radical critic whose bilious review of *Fathers and Sons* perhaps represents the nadir of Russian literary criticism in the nineteenth century. See following note.]

[6. V. Askochensky (1813–79), whose antinihilist novel *Asmodey nashego vremeni* (An Asmodeus of Our Time) provided the title for Antonovich's review of *Fathers and Sons*.]

7. One reviewer went even further. Apropos of certain articles about translations of *Virgin Soil* that had appeared abroad, he made the following pronouncement: "Let foreigners write articles about him; we refuse even to spit on him." Such stinginess, just imagine!

[8. Turgenev is referring to the trial of fifty young revolutionaries in 1877.]

Turgenev's Novels and the Novel
On the Eve   Lev Pumpyansky*

The novel *On the Eve*, like all of Turgenev's novels, belongs to a special variety of that genre which it would be most accurate to call the "heroic novel."

In a heroic novel the continuous trial of a person goes on—not of actions, but of a person—so that actions have only a symptomatic meaning. The question concerns the hero's general social quality, not the quality of individual acts.

That the word "heroic" in our usage needs to be understood in a formal, terminological sense (cf. the literary history term "heroic epic"), rather than as praise ("a heroic act," "heroic struggle"), perhaps does not even have to be stipulated, so obvious is this. After all, a hero in the adulatory sense of the word is one who emerges victorious from life's trial of a person; a hero in the technical sense of the word is one who in general submits himself to the uncertainty of that trial. The variety of the European novel, a very great rep-

* From I. S. Turgenev, *Sochineniya*, vol. 6 (Moscow-Leningrad: Gosizdat, 1930), 9–26. Translated from the Russian for this volume by the editor.

resentative of which is Turgenev, concerns itself only with that latter sort of hero.

The heroic novel has received such enormous development in Russian literature, has come to occupy such an exclusive place in it (in comparison to Western literatures, the place is disproportionately large), that the Russian reader is inclined, first, to assume without saying so that any novel is more or less a heroic novel, and second, to see in a novel of the Turgenev type a typically Russian novel, one not characteristic of Western literature. Both views are mistakes, but quite natural ones. The second mistake is in particular understandable because, really, in no other literature is there such a relative number of novels whose theme is the trial of a person's social significance. We will say a few words later on about the reasons for this peculiarity of Russian literature; right now it is necessary to have a clear awareness of the signs of a heroic .novel, since all of Turgenev's work as a novelist is linked to them.

A trial is inseparable from literature if for no other reason than that any verbal statement is a judgment; a judgment about a fact of life is accompanied inevitably by an evaluation (very often wordless and assumed). Simple human speech is already a continuous trial; literature, which represents in general a qualified condition of human speech, is therefore inseparable from a trial (also qualified and complicated). The failure to understand the whole seriousness of this fact constitutes, by the way, the fundamental methodological defect in so-called formalism. The more so as the functions and signs of a trial are characteristic of a novel, which is constructed entirely on the plane of the socially appropriate and the socially significant, and differs from any other sort of simple narrative precisely in that the social aspect in it prevails over the narrative itself.

But it is precisely here that a bifurcation arises in the dependence both on the character and on the subject of this trial. Without going into a detailed analysis of this complex question of literary theory, we will cite a simple example that will demonstrate the whole distinctive quality of the Turgenev novel. In Dostoevsky's *Crime and Punishment* a trial also takes place. But of what? Of an act (and of the theory that caused the act), but of a person only in accordance with the preliminary evaluation of his act. In the novel it is not Raskolnikov on trial, but primarily the spilling of blood (and the Napoleon theory linked to it). Raskolnikov figures in that trial only as the anomaly of his inner development that led him to the act. The predominance of the act over the person is so obvious that the whole novel bears the name of an act rather than of a person (or an equivalent name from the category of personal names). But the inclination toward a "qualified" act, which is so typical for all of Dostoevsky, is in particular characteristic of the "novel of action." By qualified act we mean, for instance, its approaching what becomes a crime in the judicial sense of the word as well. The enormous role of murder, state trial, and state punishment (none of this plays any role at all in Turgenev) in Dostoevsky is striking, and the inclination of the novel to those sorts of plots is also directly proportional to their approaching the pole of the "novel of action." In Turgenev's novel, however, the hero's action in and of itself is never related to the category of qualified ones, but, on the other hand, reveals some qualified state of the personality (for instance, most often, a general bankruptcy in life). Such is the principal watershed between the novel of action and the novel of personality—although, of course, one needs to bear in mind the extreme simplication introduced by us into the question; in fact there are also such important varieties of the first class as the novel of event, or of the second class, as the novel of society (for instance, the satirical lampoon), and many others.

Furthermore, the novel of personality is not yet a Turgenevan novel in the specific meaning of that word. After all, the whole uniqueness of a Turgenev novel consists of the fact that it is not so much a novel about a hero as a novel about whether the hero really is a hero. If it turns out, as is most often the case in Turgenev, that he is not, then it is as if the whole novel disclaims itself at the end, admits the negativity of the result achieved by him and abandons its hero "in an evil moment for him . . . for a long time, forever." Before us is not a novel of the trial of a hero as a finished personality that has taken up a definite though perhaps incorrect position in life, but, rather, the search for a hero, in each individual instance, each individual episode in the history of the search. We call only that kind of novel heroic, because only in it does the question of the hero overwhelm everything else and turn all the secondary characters, the whole cultural, historical and psychological material, even all the events, into the literary background.

And so, the heroic novel in the narrow sense of the word is a novel of the hero being sought. The method is the construction of a field of life's action, scenes of life on which forces are tested, sides collide, a calculated social trial is carried out, accompanied by the author's constant commentary. At the outcome of the field passed through there is worked out, through the realization of all of its elements, a precise conviction about the question of the hero's social value and of the type of human represented by him; that conviction (identical, in the ideal case, for the author, for the hero, for his milieu, and for the reader) in the heroic novel is in fact a verdict, but again a verdict not on an action (as with Dostoevsky, and, by the way, in *Anna Karenina*, which also represents an extreme instance of a novel that judges not a person, but an act by that person), not on an act or a step, but on a person, or more precisely, as we shall see, on a qualified person.

That qualification (elevation) of an act, which constitutes, as we said, the main trait of Dostoevsky's poetry, is lacking in Turgenev the novelist. But on the other hand one may speak positively about the absolutely special, qualified character of his heroes. A qualified person is an *active figure* in the life of educated society. Absolutely all Turgenev's novels (with the addition of those of his stories that are obviously related to the novels, like "A Hamlet of the Shchigrov District," "The Diary of a Superfluous Man," in part "Spring Freshets," and others) are novels of social action, of course in the broadest sense of that concept, understanding by it a person's *social productivity.* That is why instead of the traditional poles of good and evil, virtuous and depraved, positive and negative, in Turgenev's novels (and in general in the pure heroic novel) the polarity is different: productive and nonproductive ("superfluous" in imprecise conversational language). Hence it is plain that the heroic novel (that is, in line with what has been stated above, a novel about whether the hero is a real hero) may be called with the same right a novel of social productivity.

From the above it is clear what an enormous absolutely special, social significance such a novel has. It is not simply needed by society, as is any other serious literary genre, but represents the realization of one of the most important social functions. It is truly the most social form of literature, because through it is carried out a trial of society's self-recognition; through it a society begins to understand what forces, what sorts of people, what types and categories of activists it has at its disposal, in other words, it becomes aware of the human material of its movers, activists and leaders. That sort of novel is received therefore with a special keenness, is immediately surrounded (as was always the case with Turgenev's novels) with especially passionate arguments, because society feels with a social instinct that the matter concerns a most important question for it on whose elucidation the accuracy of its knowledge of itself depends. It is noteworthy that neither a single novel by Dostoevsky nor a single work by Tolstoy became a social event immediately, at the moment of publication. Such very great works as *Crime and Punishment, War and Peace, Anna Karenina,* and *The Brothers Karamazov* were understood and even received with a significant time lag, very slowly; even the very fact of the significance of those works was not immediately grasped by society. Meanwhile, Turgenev's literary fate is remarkable precisely for the fact that the significance, need for, and interest of each of his novels was clear to one and all, friends and enemies, literally from the very first days of the novel's publication in a journal.

People argued in essence around the novel, but everyone agreed on the need to argue; no one argued about the need to argue.

This peculiarity of Turgenev's literary biography is not connected to the peculiarities of his talent (not a single of Turgenev's stories at the moment of publication produced anything even vaguely reminiscent of the clamor, arguments, and keen social interest that surrounded his first five novels), but rather to the peculiarities of the social genre par excellence to which those novels belong. They would have lost half their value and social significance if they had not immediately produced critical articles (we mean specifically social, not aesthetic criticism; Russian criticism was in fact purely social during those great decades) and the "oral literature" accompanying them and parallel to them: arguments, conversations, "twaddle" (Pushkin), and enthusiastic approval. Never was the social role of literature laid bare with such obviousness as in the history of Turgenev's novels. One can say positively that over the course of twenty years (approximately 1855–75) Turgenev fulfilled one of the most important functions in the development of educated Russian society, the function of social self-awareness, and he raised the "technique" of this function to an unprecedented height.

Thanks to Turgenev, the heroic novel seems to us to be a typically Russian literary genre. At first glance that seems to be indisputable, especially if one takes into consideration the fact that this genre includes *Eugene Onegin* (in particular chapter 8), *A Hero of Our Time*, Herzen's *Who Is to Blame?*, both of Goncharov's long novels (after all, it was apropos Oblomov that Dobrolyubov raised the question of Pechorin and Rudin, and Raysky's closeness to Turgenev's heroes is so great that the embittered, morbid accusations of plagiarism which Goncharov raised against Turgenev nonetheless had sense to them, if not foundation, i.e., they were groundless but not absurd), several pages by Pisemsky, Leskov, Boborykin, and in the opposite literary camp, Chernyshevsky's *What Is to Be Done?* and almost all the revolutionary novels of the 1860s and 1870s. All of this makes up a significant part of all of Russian literature, while it is impossible to name a single other nineteenth-century European literature in which the heroic novel occupied a similar place. And nonetheless it was not born in Russia!

Leaving quite aside the question of the origin in European literature of both the theme of social productivity and the heroic novel itself, we will remind the reader of a superb novel by Benjamin Constant, *Adolphe* (1816), which was so liked by Pushkin, Prince Vyazemsky, and all the elect minds of the 1820s. It has now been established beyond any doubt that it is precisely *Adolphe* that Pushkin has Tanya read in Onegin's study (chapter 6, 22) and that the characterization of a "contemporary person" "with his embittered intellect / Seething in empty action" refers to *Adolphe,* and that through *Adolphe* Tanya deciphers Onegin, in whom she suddenly sees a parody of Adolphe. Unfortunately, the enormous significance of the French book not only for Tanya, but for Pushkin himself as well, has not at all been elucidated: the whole eighth chapter of *Eugene Onegin* is written by Pushkin in the spirit of the new genre a model of which Benjamin Constant demonstrated. We will note that only of chapter 8 of *Eugene Onegin* may one say that it is close to Turgenev's novels (and really, it is very close to them), which absolutely cannot be said of the name day party, the dream, or the duel. Meanwhile, a number of passages in the eighth chapter represent a semi-translation from *Adolphe* (and part of Eugene's letters is a verbatim translation) and what is most important of all, Pushkin understood the novelty of the position of a trial of an individual's nonproductivity taken by Constant, and he transferred it in its entirety to the concluding chapter of his own novel.

Adolphe does not understand Ellenore's love. After possessing her, he very soon begins to find this integral, intelligent, profound creature's love burdensome. He does not understand that the judgment of life itself on him has been made at that moment, that it is not he who has rejected Ellenore, but life that has rejected him. Adolphe does not realize the seriousness of both this meeting and this moment in his life. After Ellenore's death he immediately realizes that he has left the choice of a path in life behind. All that he can do is carry on with the remaining segment of his physical life, which has been determined by preceding circumstances and is no longer needed by anyone, until he reaches death's door. The entire seriousness of the unrepeatable meeting that has not been played out in his favor suddenly becomes clear to him. He also comes to understand his true name; he is a barren egoist who has closed off within himself a life that normally would be spent productively.

The impression made by this short novel was enormous. As regards Russian literature, no matter how little the question has been researched, one thing may be said with certainty: *Adolphe* determined in any case the end of *Eugene Onegin* (chapter 8) and a number of passages in "Onegin's Journey," for instance, the well-known lines:

> Why, like an assessor from Tula,
> Do I not lie paralyzed?
> Why do I not feel in my shoulder
> Rheumatism at least. . . ?

Later the whole formulation of the question of Pechorin in Lermontov's novel, along with the very type of literary trial of a contemporary hero, of "a hero of our time," arose under the direct influence of Constant's novel. There are other Western European works of literature, as well, that testify to the fact that the malady of social nonproductivity was common to the cultural minority of the entire European ruling class, not just of the Russian gentry. The social death of the European aristocracy was sensed by its elect cultural representatives long ahead of time and moreover, at the time when the victory of European feudal reaction over Napoleon, the Restoration in France, and the Holy Alliance in all of Europe seemed to be able to guarantee the aristocracy many more decades of rule. It is all the more interesting that precisely at that time (*Adolphe,* 1816; the first chapter of *Eugene Onegin,* 1823) there arise the first works by the aristocracy's most intelligent and observant novelists expressing social doubt about itself.

The novel of social nonproductivity arose as a result of the blow that the French Revolution and the Napoleonic Wars delivered to the centuries-old rule and cultural influence of the cosmopolitan European aristocracy, the eastern wing of which, the Russian gentry (we mean its culturally progressive part), as a consequence of the peculiarity of local historical conditions, was shaken especially profoundly by the revolutionary era.

And so, the question of the nonproductive social individual (of the "superfluous man"), which it is customary for us to consider a local Russian social and literary question, needs to be raised in a general European context. D. Ryazanov was absolutely correct in noting that we will not move ahead in studying the Decembrists until we see in that remarkable gentry movement the Russian branch of an enormous general European phenomenon (the other branches were German, Italian, and in particular Spanish and others). Until the historians of the Decembrists go over to the methods of comparativism (as it is now customary to call the comparative study of historical phenomena), we will inevitably have a one-sided and distorted picture of the whole movement. This remark by D. Ryazanov may also be applied to a whole series of other Russian cultural phenomena; thus, for instance, it is methodologically incorrect to study the history of Russian philosophical thought of the 1830s and 1840s separately from the general movement of European philosophy; the whole history of Belinsky's rupture with Hegelianism (to take a well-known example) is crudely distorted and loses its whole enormous historical meaning if separated from the general European history of the crisis of Hegelianism in the 1840s (therefore, by the way, Belinsky's intellectual development remained incomprehensible until the appearance of Marxist historians; they alone—not to mention the superiority of their method—possessed the necessary pan-European perspective). We imagine that even such a seemingly purely local phenomenon as Slavophilism will turn out upon close study also to be a Russian branch of a general European phenomenon. The number of these examples could be increased. But of course we do not deny in the least that on Russian soil many of these phenomena acquired an absolutely special development, an unparalleled force and importance. This relates precisely to that phenomenon of social nonproductivity that occupies us just now. Why? Why did the "superfluous man," the hero of several novels of Western literature of the first half of the century, become practically the main hero of all of Russian literature during the period of its highest development and originality?

We have spoken about social self-awareness, about the heroic novel as an important instrument of self-awareness of society in its available progressive forces; but in a class society social self-awareness is *class self-awareness,* and moreover, in both senses of the word, in the subjective (class as the grammatical subject) and in the objective (class as a complement), that is, self-awareness of class (in the given case, of the gentry intelligentsia) in its social forces, but also the judgment of another class (in the given case, the *raznochintsy*[1]) on the gentry heroes. The Russian gentry began losing the ground under its feet almost immediately after the Napoleonic Wars; properly speaking, its serious role was ended together with the creation of the normal state territory, that is, already by the end of the 18th century. In accordance with the general law of the formation of ideologies, the question of self, social self-analysis, the social doubt about oneself lying at the basis of any class self-awareness, usually accompanies the process of a class outliving its own historical role. This enormous process has not yet been sufficiently studied; its economic aspect is best known; but the profoundly interesting facts of its political, philosophical, and literary history have not yet been reduced to a system. The question is complicated, in addition, by the contrary process of the growth of the *raznochintsy* and of their ideology, and beginning with the 1840s, and in particular in the 1850s and 1860s, both processes, that is, the fall of the gentry and the cultural growth of the *ranzochintsy,* take place simultaneously. In short, we do not yet have a general history of the ideology of the Russian gentry during the period of its historical fall, that is, for the approximately 100 years from the end of the Napoleonic Wars to the death of Lev Tolstoy. Meanwhile, only that sort of general history would explain for us the phenomenon we are interested in right now—the special development on Russian soil of the question of "superfluous people," and besides, the very social make-up of these people is unclear outside the general history of their class. By the way, only such a history would explain the mysterious flowering of Russian gentry literature precisely in those decades when the economic and social decline of the class was obvious and it was dealt such a blow as the abolition of serfdom. Someone as early as Solovyov-Andreevich recalled Hegel's words in this regard: Minerva's owl only flies out at night. That is in general a correct application of Hegel's profound idea, but precisely *in general,* since the *real* history of this paradoxical chronological coincidence of the decline of a class with the unprecedented flowering of its literature has not yet been studied. In general, the history of individual classes (in a certain period) is now waiting to be taken up by Marxist historiography.

In 1852 and the following years, while living in the country, Turgenev worked a great deal on the creation of the type of novel he needed. It is noteworthy that in his work he did not proceed from the then-reigning "Gogolian" school in its various branches and not at all from the state of Russian literature as it then existed. None of the tendencies and genres then reigning corresponded to that European genre, saturated with culture and themes of culture, that Turgenev desired. That year, one significant for his literary biography, even his own early works (i.e., peasant stories and anecdotal stories), had receded into the past. There already existed a rather substantial peasant and village literature; there was "physiological" literature; there was, finally, the democratic Gogolian grotesque school, to which the young Dostoevsky belonged. But for Turgenev all of these were genres that were precisely too democratic and too close to home, too Russian; Gogol was perceived in those years as the creator of a national Russian epic. The *raznochintsy* writers and journalists, for whom the Russian literature close to them, their own, began with Gogol's Petersburg stories, rather than with Pushkin, were drawn in particular to Gogol. That link between Gogol and his school and the groups of *raznochintsy* intelligentsia was clearly recognized by contemporaries, who sensed no less clearly that the process of the democratization of literature that led to the brilliant victory of the *raznochintsy* at the end of the 1850s had begun precisely with Gogol. A very interesting passage in Herzen comes right out and unites Gogol, Chernyshevsky, and Belinsky into a single social group: "The son of a minor bureaucrat, who did not wish to go into government service, like Belinsky; a priest's son, like Chernyshevsky; lastly, a petty provincial nobleman of modest means, a proletarian from the nobility, like Gogol—that was the stratum, the new people who were soon to play a great role."[2]

In a purely literary regard, the whole Gogolian era is characterized by the absence of an interest in the theme of the hero and the related theme of the trial of the hero who is being sought. Reading *Dead Souls,* one can sometimes imagine that it arose before *Eugene Onegin* or *A Hero of Our Time,* to such an extent is one struck by the complete absence of the hero problem (in the above-mentioned sense of the word).[3] Really, the first consequence of the Gogolian democratization of literature was the collapse of the Onegin and Pechorin question. Gogol transferred the interest of literature to collective units—estates, groups, professions, the people. The cultural saturation that characterized pre-Gogolian classicism and that turned Pushkin's poetry into a literary encyclopedia of his era also dropped away. In the second generation of the "Gogol" era, with writers appearing at the same time as Grigorovich and Dostoevsky, there set in an absolute oblivion about the riches of Pushkinian culture. But what in particular was subjected to oblivion in the atmosphere of Gogol's democratic literary culture was Pushkin's main theme, the theme of the trial of the social quality of a progressive figure, the great theme of Onegin. Turgenev had to restore a lost tradition over the head of literature of the 1840s. He constructed a novel that was in no way linked to the contemporary literature of the Gogolian school and that resumed the literary line where Lermontov had broken it off. Turgenev restored the chain of gentry literature that Gogol had torn asunder.

That Turgenev's novels directly continue the Pushkin school of the novel (and are in no way related to the Gogolian school of group poetry) was recognized very clearly by contemporaries but expressed, of course, not in the language of literary history but of criticism. "The Onegins and Pechorins were replaced by Rudins and Beltovs," says Yury Nikolaev (a now-forgotten journalist and critic of the 1870s), omitting, consequently, the Gogol era. In general, a listing of this type became a cliché in nineteenth-century criticism; moreover, two parts were always distinguished: "Onegin-Pechorin" and "Beltov-Rudin-Lavretsky," that is, a "Pushkin" half and a "Turgenev" half; moreover, it was impossible to name a single name from the material of the Gogolian school (except, as we have said, Tentetnikov and later, but in a somewhat different way, the elder Verkhovensky). Thus, the first task for the future investigator into the origins of the Turgenev novel is to elucidate the dimensions and character of the Pushkin legacy in it, and then the nature of and reasons for Turgenev's departures from the Pushkin norm. These are special questions. Nonetheless we will allow ourself to point out, with regard to the second question, the enormous role (noted by contemporaries) that George Sand's novel played in the formation of the Turgenev novel.[4] But the novels of George Sand, that is, those of them relevant for our question, belong to the literary progeny of *Adolphe* and represent the development and broadening of the methods of Constant's *roman d'analyse*. With regard to the first question, about the nature of the Onegin legacy in Turgenev's novels, we will point out such an important sign, common both to *Eugene Onegin* and, for instance, *Rudin,* as the identical role of intellectual culture. We mean, of course, the elementary aspect of this matter as well (the role of books, reading; book titles; arguments on philosophical and literary topics; and so on), but in particular that decisive trait thanks to which both novels may be called *culturally* heroic. We have in mind the hero's plot actions being conditioned upon the type of culture to which he belongs. So, for instance, the central plot action of *Eugene Onegin*— Onegin's rejection of Tanya's love—is profoundly linked to the dandy and skeptical intellectual culture acquired by Onegin, according to Pushkin's conception, in Saint Petersburg in the years of the highest flowering of Saint Petersburg dandyism (1817–20). That is why the precise elucidation of the level and type of the hero's culture (which purpose is served by the lists of books, the hero's opinion on various questions) plays such a role in *Eugene Onegin*. But the plot actions of Turgenev's heroes are no less profoundly rooted in culture; the cultural identification of Rudin (metaphysical idealism and German romantic poetry), Bazarov (so-called physiological materialism and the revolutionary orientation of *The Contemporary*), Bersenev (the idealistic understanding of history and Granovsky's optimism) and others are inseparable from their actions and, moreover, from such central actions (in the plot of the novel) as, for instance, the rupture with Natalya, love for Odintsova. Hence the role of such indicators of cultural typology as books, opinions, arguments, is no less than in *Onegin.*

Before us is the strict form of the gentry culturally heroic novel.

Turgenev's first two novels, *Rudin* and *A Nest of Gentlefolk,* constitute a special group that is closest to *Adolphe* and the Pushkin school. But as early as in *A Nest of Gentlefolk* Dobrolyubov's penetrating gaze saw a partial transition to the second group (which comprises *On the Eve* and *Fathers and Sons;* but Dobrolyubov did not live to see *Fathers and Sons;* he died a few months before its publication, but he predicted with striking distinctness the main features of the novel). Dobrolyubov subtly notes that Lavretsky is no longer a propagandist, in which way "he seems to betray one of the family traits of his type" (in particular Rudin and the hero of Nekrasov's *Sasha,* and from the point of view of propaganda content— philosophical idealism and the themes of German romantic poetry: "Rudin was entirely immersed in German poetry, in the German romantic and philosophical world, and carried it along behind him to those treasured lands" [chapter 6]); he also notes that, "beginning with his first meeting with Liza, he bows humbly throughout the whole novel before the firmness of her notions" (while in the typical culturally heroic novel the girl's meeting the hero usually brought with it the disaster of her former culture). But Lavretsky's main distinction lies in the fact that "in him there is something legitimately tragic, not spectral."[5] The latter remark by Dobrolyubov is important in the highest degree because it was precisely the hero's "spectral quality" that was exposed by the heroic novel from *Adolphe* to *Rudin;* if, however, the novel lingered with respect before Lavretsky's life fate, then, consequently, before us is the sign of some sort of beginning transformation of the whole genre. But, of course, only a sign, because on the whole Lavretsky belongs to the history of gentry culture, from which Dobrolyubov and Chernyshevsky in those years no longer expected anything, because they considered that all its themes (Slavophilism, liberal Westernizing, cultural Europeanism) had already been exhausted, and that everything of social need that there had been in these themes had already managed to become the property of everyone. "It is clear that in that sort of situation," says Dobrolyubov,[6] "the former sowers of good, people of Rudin's make-up, lose a significant share of their former credit."

But, of course, it still remains unexplained *how* the transition from the gentry hero to the *raznochinets* hero was accomplished in Turgenev's works. Meanwhile that is precisely the main scholarly task in a study of the novel *On the Eve:* after all, it is the *first* in the series of novels about the *raznochinets* hero, that is, properly speaking, about a revolutionary hero. In order to elucidate how the move from a "socially nonproductive" hero to a "revolutionary" hero began to take shape in Turgenev's work, a major research project, which has not yet been done at all, is needed. Dobrolyubov was quite correct in noting the fact of the change ("In Mr. Turgenev's new story we encounter situations and characters different from those to which we became accustomed in the works of his early period"), correctly understood that the matter concerned not an accidental departure for the norm, but a new *period* that Turgenev's art was entering, that in general, beginning with the novel *On the Eve,* a new period was beginning in all of Russian literature, with a different class definition of the hero. But to the question of the reasons for the shift from a nobleman to a *raznochinets* Dobrolyubov replies with a reference to some sort of class transformation of educated Russian society: "Recently [meaning the years 1857–60] in our society there have been revealed demands quite different from those that produced Rudin and all his fraternity. . . . New people have grown up. . . . Where 12,000 copies of Belinsky are bought up in several months, there is simply nothing for a Rudin to do. . . . Something different is needed, one has to go farther. . . ." This is all quite true, but it is precisely this link that Dobrolyubov notes between the selection of a new hero (Insarov) and the appearance of a new hero in the life of educated society itself that needs scholarly study. Dobrolyubov's explanation, rather journalistic, leaves untouched the question that is most important of all in a scholarly regard: the history of the *realization* of that link. That sort of link, as between a new social formation (the more so—the new man) and a corresponding transformation of a large old literary genre (the new hero) belongs to the category of complex links, with many intervening links, that is, to the category of procedural links. That process in fact should explain the history of literature, the more so, as in the given case, we repeat, the matter concerns the birth of the revolutionary heroic Russian novel, that is, a question of extreme importance.

Right away there are a number of points here that are as yet dark. We are still powerless to answer in a precise way the question that has always occupied readers of the novel and continues to occupy them to this day: why is Insarov a Bulgarian? "What does a Bulgarian mean here? Why not a Russian? Can it really be that among Russians there are no such personalities? Are Russians really incapable of loving passionately and decisively?" Dobrolyubov has already asked. His own reply is interesting in the extreme: a progressive Russian figure *"refuses to see a mutual guarantee in everything* going on before his eyes, and imagines that any evil he notices is no more than the abuse of an excellent law. . . . In view of such concepts Russian heroes can only limit themselves, of course, to *miserable little details* without thinking about *the whole,* while Insarov, on the contrary, always subordinates the particular to the general. . . ." That whole remarkable tirade obviously has a revolutionary meaning (we have underlined the most unambiguous passages), but nonetheless Dobrolyubov's idea is not clear: after all, he has explained the switch from a Rudin to an Insarov as *the appearance* of a new hero in the very life of educated Russian society; here it turns out, however, that this hero has *not* yet appeared, although there is a presentiment of him. All of this is unclear. Dobrolyubov is apparently hinting at some sort of circumstances known to the progressive intelligentsia of his day, quite possibly the very same circumstances that produced Turgenev's rejection of a Russian hero.

But Dobrolyubov leaves the second, positive half of the question absolutely unanswered: why precisely a Bulgarian? On this point we need a detailed study not of the whole political, but of the whole socioideological aspect of the history of the Balkan question in the mid-nineteenth century in Russia; we need a history of the views that both the Slavophiles and the liberal Westernizing part of the gentry intelligentsia had on both the Eastern question and the Balkan nationalities; a history of Russo-Bulgarian cultural relations, and so on. In questions of the chronological, topographical, and political circumstances of the action in his novels, Turgenev did not write a single line without a conscious and precise design. Insarov's nationality (as well as the chronology of the novel: 1853–54) was chosen by him, probably, in a quite calculated way, perhaps as the result of a profound knowledge of the peculiarities of the cultural history of the gentry during the years of the Crimean War.

A great novelty was the introduction of a *raznochinets* into the novel as the main hero. The fact of Insarov's being a *raznochinets* was more important than the question of his nationality. Obviously it was more important for Yelena's parents too:

> "Married! to that ragamuffin, that Montenegrin! The daughter of Nikolay Stakhov of the ancient nobility married a tramp, a *raznochinets!*" (chapter 30)

> "Have you heard? My daughter, because of her great learning, married a student." (end of chapter 31)

For the development of the Russian novel there is no doubt that the class question linked to the new hero was much more important than the accidental one of nationality. When at the end of his article Dobrolyubov spoke of a Russian Insarov, a hero close to the future, the most needed person then in Russia ("he is essential for us, without him our whole life somehow counts for nothing, each day means nothing in and of itself, but serves only as the eve of the following day"), he proved by that how profoundly he had understood Turgenev's novel. The point was the first appearance in the Russian novel of a *politician* hero, a person of political culture instead of gentry heroes, people of literary or philosophical culture. The gentry intelligentsia was a class group incapable of creating its own political activity; meanwhile the condition of the country was already such by the 1830s that formation of a progressive political party was essential. Jacobins were needed, but the gentry intelligentsia did not know how to produce them. The *raznochintsy* were beginning to realize more and more clearly that they were called upon to be Russian Jacobins; they felt within themselves a direct calling to large-scale Jacobin politics, and really, their superiority to the gentry in political talent was enormous. Dobrolyubov and Chernyshevsky were born politicians, with a clear understanding of the structure of society, of its needs, of the needs of the coming day. Meanwhile, one may doubt the political gifts even of Herzen (he was a brilliant political writer, but that is quite another matter).[7] The political nonproductivity of the progressive gentry was striking. Actually, that is what is meant when "superfluous people" are spoken of; people are speaking of a culturally influential, highly knowledgeable and talented social group *without its own politics;* meanwhile, this political aspect of the reproach, the only serious one, is obscured by the unfortunate appellation "superfluous." The matter concerns a group that turned out to be superfluous in the *political* selection of groups left to live without a political function, but the name is also appropriate for people who remained superfluous, for instance, in the sexual selection or in the selection of happy, successful people. In his well-known story (1850) Turgenev used it precisely in that last sense: Chulkaturin is a failure of sexual selection, defeated in the battle for biological happiness. But biological failure is not a class or group trait; in the ferocious battle for love, the biological person, not the class one, conquers and suffers defeat. Of course, very often (almost always in Turgenev) the political biography is linked to the biological (Rudin, for instance, is a failure both of political culture aod of sexual selection), but the *term* ought to be precise and ought not combine such different things. The word "superfluous," which corresponds precisely to Chulkaturin's biographical fate (we know how bitterly happy he is after thinking it up: the entry of March 23), gives birth to a number of misunderstandings when applied to heroes whose cultural and political biography (rather than the biological) is most important of all. Herzen seems more than anyone else to have facilitated the general dissemination of the word in this new, non-Turgenevan meaning (at any rate Herzen uses it any time that the subject concerns criticism of the gentry intelligentsia).[8] As a consequence the most important (the only historically important) circumstance has been obscured: the group of the progressive gentry intelligentsia, after breaking with serf politics and liberal-bourgeois politics, did not develop its own politics and was left without any political function in an enormous country, on the eve of the decisive years of its history. The center of the question is in this, while the word "superfluous" is infinitely broader and, most importantly, melds the *historical* fate of groups with the *personal* fate ("happiness") of individual people. Moreover, it is inaccurate: there are no "superfluous" groups; there are only groups with abnormalities of development, with atrophied functions. "The people of the 1840s" were just such an abnormal group.[9] It is curious to note that when, already in the twentieth century, the progressive bourgeois intelligentsia forced its own system of culture, symbolism (in many regards so close to the gentry culture of the 1840s), a similar story occurred: on the eve of even more decisive years, a large and culturally influential group revealed its total inability to orient itself actively in political activity and lived either entirely outside politics or—for all practical purposes—on the plane of the politics of capitalism.

And so, the appearance of the *raznochinets* in the Russian novel is the appearance of a political figure, instead of the earlier figure who because of intellectual interests common to a small group of people had not yet found a way out into the arena of real action. And since the Russians of the 1840s were the heirs of the philosophical and poetic culture developed in the milieu of European and in particular German romanticism, it can be said that with Turgenev's *A Nest of Gentlefolk* an entire era of European cultural development ends, an era characterized by the predominant desire to "explain" the world (*Natürphilosophie,* philosophical poetry, the great systems of classical idealism). "Philosophers have explained the world enough;

the time has come to transform it" is what the founders of Marxism said, but the Russian *raznochintsy* thought exactly the same way.

And so, the main theme of the novel *On the Eve* is the appearance of a political activist in Russian life; it is accompanied by a historico-literary theme (in general, all great, bellwether works are not only literary but historico-literary monuments as well): the transformation of the Russian socio-heroic novel from a novel about a hero sought and rejected (formal heroism) into a novel about a hero found and real (positive heroism), which created the basis for the Russian revolutionary novel, a process occurring on the basis of the enormous growth of the role of the *raznochintsy,* who were already taking upon themselves in part the function of Jacobinism. Dobrolyubov's article at the very end hints quite transparently at what the *raznochintsy* think the "real day" will be. The title of the novel, which Turgenev selected very cleverly, seizes precisely what is most characteristic in the political condition of the *raznochintsy* of that time: they lived on the passionate presentiment and expectation of their "real day" that would be coming soon, of their great historical role (they already recognized their power perfectly well). Dobrolyubov's article (which immediately became inseparable from the novel) was a purely revolutionary article, striking in its boldness and the clear formulation of the question.

The usual heroine of Turgenev's novels also underwent a change, a transformation, corresponding to that of the hero's social personality. But the question is not as simple as it seems: it is linked to George Sand's enormous but as yet little-studied role in Russia. Perhaps in no other country did the great Frenchwoman's novels have such a significance as in Russia, and one may say, in the history of Russia, because there is no doubt that they played a strong part in the formation of the type of woman that produced the unforgettable phalanx of women revolutionaries of the 1860s and 1870s. In truth, Sandism was also "the eve" of those unforgettable years in the history of Russian womanhood. That Yelena herself, a George Sand woman, and that the novel, at least in the parts relating to Yelena, was written by Turgenev in George Sand's manner, these things, as we have seen, were noted already by contemporaries: they remembered her novels well. Posterity ceased to notice the link, because it ceased to read George Sand. One of the most important sources of the formation of the "Turgenev maiden" has disappeared from our literary perspective. On this point a major project is needed hy researchers in order to restore the actual historical picture. Unfortunately, that special question exceeds the bounds of our short popular article. We will remark nonetheless that the George Sand woman has been combined by Turgenev with Pushkin's Tanya, the protoheroine of the Russian novel. The Pushkinian provenance of Yelena's portrait, characterization, and the history of her upbringing (in chapter 6) is striking; the very digression for such a detailed account of the heroine reveals the Pushkin school;[10] other traits have an Onegin ring, such as alms for beggars ("when I would help the poor," in Tanya's letter) or Yelena's usual pose at the window ("she began gazing through the open window into the night," at the end of chapter 6)—the classic and constant pose of Tatyana-Svetlana. Apparently a profound study of Pushkin also explains the introduction into the novel of Zoya (Olga).

The introduction of caricature traits into Bersenev's characterization and actions is very interesting. In accordance with the growth of the new *raznochinets* hero, the "rank" of the gentry hero, the cultural propagandist, is degraded. Rudin had been in constant touch with the sources of Germanic culture; he had lived at its centers; his knowledge of it was not second-hand; he has an indisputably philosophical cast of mind; he knows the main philosophical and poetic systems, so to speak, from inside, through living intellectual experience. Before us is an animated activist of philosophical culture, one of those people through whom the dissemination of any new type of thought is accomplished. Bersenev leads off the brilliant series of caricatures aimed at the epigones of gentry idealism and the culture of the 1840s in general that later led to the creation of the immortal caricature of the elder Verkhovensky (by the way, like Bersenev, he is also an epigone of the Granovsky school).[11] The fossilization of the metaphysical idealism of the 1840s had already led Granovsky, and all the more so his disciples, including Bersenev, to a profoundly antidialectical optimism in the understanding of history, more accurately, even to a dogmatic "faith" in the greatness of history, which represents a revelation, but of what, remained unclear, but all the more solemnly was service to the science of history carried out. The falsity of that position was revealed, by the way, in the fact that Granovsky's tendency contributed almost nothing to the development of the then-serious science of history (Ranke in the West, S. Solovyov and others in Russia). The oratorical style and the cultivation of artistic historical prose were a bad symptom. Before us is the fossilization of once living and influential systems of thought. Here too Dobrolyubov hit the bull's-eye brilliantly when he singled out Bersenev's conversation with Insarov in chapter 11: "In one passage in the novel mention is made of his discussing Feuerbach: it would be interesting to listen to what he says about Feuerbach!" That really would be interesting! But Turgenev apparently wanted to mark the absence of any philosophical commitment in Bersenev, his indifferently eclectic, slack attitude toward various systems.

Thus, in the novel the rising curve of the *raznochinets* line intersects the falling curve of the gentry hero, which in the person of Bersenev breaks off abruptly, away from Rudin toward Stepan Trofimovich.

Turgenev's construction of novels and the methods of his narrative art are still quite unresearched (although there are already many accurate individual observations).[12] Therefore (and also in view of the character and size of this article) we will limit ourselves to the most important remarks. As a novelist, Turgenev's basic method apparently is the melding of several types of novels. The culturally heroic novel (as we called it above) is melded first of all with the love novel (for the most part, with the woman's novel). That method had already been indicated by Pushkin and, following him, Lermontov. The love novel is treated *not* as a psychological one, but, rather, as a lyrical one. That remarkable peculiarity belongs to Pushkin too, and with him, perhaps, is linked to the verse language of *Eugene Onegin* (Tanya's love is narrated as though in a series of individual "poems," for instance, "Tatyana, dear Tatyana. . .," and in any case, in the style of lyrical love poetry developed by the great French love poets, for instance, "you drink the magical poison of desires" and others). Turgenev's most powerful love pages are either passionate erotic tirades or elegies. Later, this already composite novel melds with the novel of manners, or, at least with separate elements of the novel of manners, and usually the majority of secondary characters belong only to that novel of manners. That is also Pushkin's method, but Turgenev gave it unprecedented development: compare, for instance, the scarcely marked out theme of the parents in Pushkin (the Larins), with its broad development, sometimes even with an epic coloration, in Turgenev (Natalya's, Yelena's, Liza's parents, Tanya's aunt in *Smoke,* and so on). Herein lies one of the vital distinctions of the Turgenev novel within the general school of the Pushkin novel. With Pushkin the novel of manners already introduced satirical elements, sometimes extremely sharp ones (Zaretsky); Turgenev broadened that aspect greatly in his novels; he has hardly a novel without some repulsive or coarsely caricatured individual (Pandalevsky, Kukshina, Lupoyarov in chapter 24 of *On the Eve* and many others, not to mention *Smoke,* in which the satirical complication turns into a real political lampoon). Thus, Turgenev's novel represents, in the main, a three-tiered structure—the culturally heroic novel, the lyrico-love novel, and the satirical novel of manners—developed on the basis of Pushkin's "free" novel. That sort of combination of different genres is apparently characteristic of the "novel of culture." Let us note in addition that in Turgenev the manners "tier" is saturated with such a quantity of historical observations that his novels are a truly encyclopedic history of Russian manners; out of the thousands of examples we will mention, let us say, the remark about the Saint Petersburg type of house in Moscow, at the beginning of chapter 7 of *On the Eve*.[13] There is no chapter without several observations of that sort.

An important distinction between the Turgenev novel and *Eugene Onegin* is the powerful landscape orchestration of the whole action (in *Eugene Onegin* the landscape was *only* calendric). It has been noted, for instance, that in *A Nest of Gentlefolk* the atmosphere of a summer night dominates, and in *Fathers and Sons,* that of a hot, unbearably white, dry summer day. All of this is very true but needs detailed study. Especially unclear is the provenance of Turgenev's landscape. Landscapes of phenomena of nature also have an enormous orchestrating significance in Turgenev; such in our novel, for instance, is the thunderstorm introduced by the hand of a master into chapter 18, before the decisive meeting between Yelena and Insarov. That is the highest degree of the narrative art. But the role of the landscape is especially bared in Turgenev's stories (the whirlwind in front of Gemma's window in "Spring Freshets"; the thundery summer night in "First Love"); therefore it is more appropriate to lay aside analysis of the question.

The stories are also a more appropriate basis for analyzing the role of the "philosophical," pessimistic orchestration of all of Turgenev's works, which gives them the irresistibly beautiful character of tragically courageous hopelessness (the introduction to "Spring Freshets"). The question is complicated, but its resolution is important for understanding all of Russian gentry poetry after Pushkin (in whose *Eugene Onegin* a tragic orchestration is entirely lacking).

In conclusion—a few words about the possible significance of Dobrolyubov's article for our Soviet criticism.

"Placing as the main task of literary criticism the elucidation of those phenomena of reality that have called forth a certain artistic work"—that is what Dobrolyubov says; in another passage in the article he tries "to justify his device—to discuss the phenomena of life itself on the basis of a literary work." We consider it useful to recall these remarkable, clear words, because right now among us views on the purpose of literary criticism are very confused. Formalism is highly guilty in this matter because of the fact that it (not to mention the general doubtfulness of its methods) turned criticism into the historico-literary or linguistic or theoretical analysis of current literature. That is a major and socially harmful error. The analysis of contemporary literature in and of itself is quite legitimate (and in view of the current general intrerest in literary criticism, inevitable); the point is that what is required is the recognition that it is not criticism, has nothing at all to do with criticism: the contemporaneousness of the material does not make an analysis criticism. Criticism is the public's reaction to a contemporary work, "a correction on contemporaneousness," as one investigator of the question calls it, and strange to say, we do not now have such criticism. Chernsyhevsky saw in Gogol a realist; that is absolutely incorrect in a historico-literary sense, but *as a critic,* Chernyshevsky was absolutely correct, because the society that he represented, and in particular the *raznochintsy* party, strove for "natural" literature and found social satire in Gogol's grotesque. Of course, it is better not to make historico-literary errors than to make them; but the business of criticism does not lie at all in these dimensions. It is the voice of society's claims against a work: its only serious interest is the life of the community; therefore the transformation of literature into a means of cognition of the life of the community is the only possible path for it.

We possess a more precise instrument for that than Dobrolyubov and Chernyshevsky did: Marxism. But the *passionate commitment* of such criticism needs to be learned from its great classic representatives, the *raznochintsy* of the 1850s and 1860s. They are our ancestors in a number of regards. It is from them our young proletarian criticism must learn the extremely difficult business of "discussing the phenomena of life itself on the basis of a literary work."

Notes

[1. The *raznochintsy* were those members of the nineteenth-century Russian intelligentsia whose social roots lay elsewhere than in the gentry. The best-known *raznochintsy* were political radicals who hoped and sometimes worked for the destruction of the czarist regime.]

2. *La Cloche,* 1864, in *Polnoe sobranie sochineniy i pisem,* vol. 17, ed. M. K. Lemke (Petrograd, 1915–25), 214.

3. Nonetheless one should bear in mind that "rudiment" of it that turns up in Gogol's character Tentetnikov; he is of particular interest as a consequence of the (approximate) contemporaneousness with Herzen's novel. The frequent parallels between Tentetnikov and Beltov are striking.

4. "In George Sand's novels, which were read so zealously by Russians too, a similar type [Yelena] had long since been depicted, and perhaps, it was not without George Sand's influence that this female type was formed in Russian life too" (Yury Nikolaev). Here are additional comments by a (rank and file) literary critic of Turgenev's time: "Turgenev borrowed the basic material for composing the character Yelena to a significant extent from literary sources, perhaps most of all from George Sand's novels."

5. From the well-known article "When Will the Real Day Come?," *The Contemporary* no. 3 (1860).

6. Ibid.

7. As for Turgenev himself, that great chronicler of Russia's political history did not do anything in concrete politics but make a mass of mistakes. "Turgenev," said Herzen, "is not at all a political person; he has proven that just as brilliantly as everything else that he has tried to prove" (*The Bell,* 1863, 167).

8. The history of the word ought to be researched in detail.

9. We will take advantage of the chance to remark that it has long since been time to go over to a class point of view in the study of the nineteenth-century Russian

novel in school. Turgenev's novels provide an enormous amount of material for understanding the various groups in the social life of the time. We need to move from the naive position of a school trial of the hero ("Was Rudin really an unnecessary person, or did he contribute his share of usefulness?" and so on), the legacy of the intelligentsia era of the history of Russian literature, and take the material of the novels not as a subject for confronting "accusations" with "apologies," but as *profoundly historical* material. We need to proceed from the main fact of all of Russian literature: the nobleman's battle with the *raznochinets,* and treat the works themselves not in a naive pedagogical spirit but in a historical and materialist one.

10. Pushkin, in his turn, learned the art of introducing the heroine from Richardson and the novelists of his school (Rousseau, Mme. de Staël).

11. There is much in common in the methods of caricature as well. Compare, for instance, the parodic titles of Bersenev's historical works ("About Certain Peculiarities of Ancient Germanic Law" and so on), in the novel's epilogue, and Stepan Trofimovich's.

12. For instance, in V. Fisher's interesting work in the miscellany *Turgenev's Creative Path* (Moscow, 1920). [The article is excerpted in this volume.]

13. Schools should learn to use the inexhaustible wealth of observations on manners andd history in Turgenev's novels and stories.

On the Composition of Turgenev's Novels

Vasily Gippius[*]

In undertaking the examination of Turgenev's novels from the point of view of composition, let us agree to distinguish *static* composition from *dynamic* composition.

The static composition consists of the construction of a scene (that is, the development of action in *space*), the filling of that scene with characters, and the positioning of the characters in a certain specific order (by the will of the author)—in certain specific relationships.

The dynamic composition sets in action the springs necessary for motion, and the action of the novel begins to develop in *time:* what we call the novel's story and plot are properly spoken of here.

It goes without saying that although these two aspects can be distinguished by the clear critical eye, their following one another is not at all obligatory during the process of creation: an artist may first conceive the plot, then create the characters, and only then construct the scene—or he may do just the reverse. Thus, as far as can be judged, the point of origination in the creation of *On the Eve* was the story line (Karateev's manuscript about his fiancée's leaving with a Bulgarian), and in the creation of *Fathers and Sons,* the

[*] Excerpted from *Venok Turgenevu* (Odessa: Kn-vo A. A. Ivasenko, 1919), 25–55. Translated from the Russian for this volume by the editor.

personality of Bazarov, which reflected the personality of a "young provincial doctor." For the study of already given composition the difference in origin is not important. Although the term "dynamics," as far as we know, had not yet been used, one has to think that Turgenev had precisely dynamics in mind when he spoke of "the construction of novels," their "architectural aspect" (letter to Stechkina, 1878).

By singling out the main characters in Turgenev's six novels, observing the relationships that the author places them in, and comparing these relationships, we will see that all six novels have a noticeable and essential similarity.

At the center of action in each novel we see in sharp relief a single hero and a single heroine (with Tolstoy, as is well known, it is otherwise), and next to the hero three (it is that way everywhere almost without exception) characters set out in specific relationships to the hero. The hero himself is not just a psychological unit, but a sharply defined socioideological one as well. Of the characters standing next to him, one is a product of a lower social order, as though from a second, inferior socioideological plane, and at the same time, a rival in his relationship to the heroine (Volyntsev, Panshin, Kurnatovsky, Ratmirov, Kallomeytsev); the second either feels indifferently about him personally or is also in a relationship of rivalry, and in any case, for long or not for long, openly or secretly, is hostile to him and ideologically his antipode (Pigasov, Lemm, Shubin, Pavel Kirsanov, Potugin, Solomin); the third is his friend, a like-minded person as far as ideology or, at least, from the same ideological milieu (Lezhnyov, Mikhalevich, Bersenev, Arkady Kirsanov, Markelov). Just as the heroine stands between two characters of a different order, so the hero, in the majority of the novels, stands between two women who are also dissimilar. On a more remote plane are arranged the characters who can be called episodic: their disposition is also not accidental and is dependent upon the basic pattern.

Having agreed to designate the main hero as A, the heroine as B, the aspirants of the lower order as a1, the hero's ideological antipodes as a2, the like-minded friends as a3, and lastly, the second woman in the composition of the novel as b, let us examine each novel separately so as to become convinced that we have reached our conclusions about the unity of the pattern, the unity of their static composition, without stretching things—on the contrary, with all the necessary disclaimers.

In *Rudin*, the limited Volyntsev, an honest fellow and virtuous estate manager, who fears poetry and philosophy, doubtless belongs to the category of a1, that is, of those aspirants of a lower order with whom Turgenev's heroes are fated to struggle (usually not very hard). In spite of the fact that he plays practically no part in the novel's plot, I definitely assign Pigasov to the category of a2, moving him from the group of background episodic characters out into the forefront. Pigasov, a skeptic and a materialist, a nihilist in the bad sense of that term, definitely contrasts with—more than that—*is contrasted to* Rudin in purely compositional aspects. Over the whole course of the novel Rudin is as though a banknote of undetermined value, and Lezhnyov's story about Pokorsky's circle is important precisely because it discloses the background that assures Rudin's ideological worth and simultaneously establishes Pigasov's worthlessness. In other words, Rudin is attractive by virtue of his being remote from Pigasov. Rudin is not devalued if for no other reason than that Pigasov, his opponent, is completely devalued. In this common "fund"—in the milieu of the Romantic circles of the 1830s—are to be found Rudin and Lezhnyov's common roots. No matter how psychologically unlike Rudin Lezhnyov may seem, if we examine these two from the point of view of those socio-ideological bases as whose spokesman Rudin is presented, we will notice that the bases in them are the same—that is especially underscored in the epilogue. Let us note right away that Lezhnyov is a less complex but when it comes to life more stable personality than Rudin, assimilating romantic ideology in forms more muted and less contradicting life, mores, and "essence" (to use the terminology of the times). This epigone of romanticism is more characteristic for the historical moment than is its eloquent apologist who is at odds with everyday culture, his contemporaries, and himself. Let us note this trait in the like-minded characters—a3—they are typical, while the heroes represent an acute condition of the moment, untypical, like any acute condition, and a^3 represent remnants or exceptions that are either not at all typical or no longer typical.

The same ideological bases as in Rudin and Lezhnyov can be seen in Basistov, who is as though a second character of this compositional unit:[1] his idealistic naiveté complements what Lezhnyov lacks. Basistov is an addition to a3—similar additions will be encountered in other of Turgenev's constructions as well—but an addition only in regards to statics; in the dynamics of the novel Basistov's role, just like Pigasov's, is insignificant.

There is no "second woman"—b—in the structure of *Rudin;* there are only references to the heroines of Rudin's youthful romances—they are not given a role in the motion of the novel.

The composition of *A Nest of Gentlefolk,* which, unlike the others, has been well studied (Apollon Grigoriev touches on it in a remarkable article; chapters 7 and 8 of Ovsyaniko-Kulikovsky's *I. S. Turgenev* are devoted to it), becomes significantly clearer when compared to the composition of *Rudin.* Speaking for the time being only of one aspect of the structure—the grouping of characters—we will see how

indubitably similar the two novels are. There is no need to speak of
a1 and a3, so obvious is it that Volyntsev corresponds to Panshin and
Lezhnyov (together with Basistov) to Mikhalevich, who, by the way,
even fulfills the same auxiliary role of defining in words—even if
one-sidedly—the hero's character. Greater doubts may be raised by
the assertion that Lavretsky's ideological antipode—a2, who corresponds to Pigasov in *Rudin*—is Lemm. The doubts will be based,
however, on a misunderstanding, on a confusion of compositional
similarity and psychological similarity. There is no question that
Pigasov and Lemm are psychologically contrasted to each other, but
after all, Lavretsky does not correspond to Rudin psychologically
either; on the contrary, Apollon Grigoriev correctly notes traits of
Lezhnyov in Lavretsky and those of Rudin in Mikhalevich. The absolute magnitude of Pigasov and Lemm is different, but the former's
relation to Rudin is equal to that of the latter to Lavretsky. Lavretsky
is not Rudin, to whose romantic "fund" he is privy only through his
epigone Mikhalevich—rather remotely; his soul has been instilled
both with romanticism and with the salubrious poisons of "Russian
skepticism" (Prince Vladimir Odoevsky called the main hero of *Russian
Nights* "a Russian skeptic"), the latter historically infused in his
grandfather's Voltairism; and the reverse—this skepticism, by retaining all its salubrious and curative power, is significantly decontami-
nated by an admixture of late romanticism of the Slavophile variety,
and did not produce the deformed results of Pigasov's scepticism.
The offspring of a peasant (on his mother's side) and a Russian
nobleman—Russian even (and especially!) in his very imitativeness
and attraction to the West—Lavretsky unites in himself all that is
historically typical for a Russian: he is the *most Russian* of Turgenev's
heroes. Contrasting him to a stranger and specifically a German (when
Lavretsky's father was attracted to France, and later to England)
ought not therefore to be considered accidental. The "Russian skeptic" stands in contrast to the German romantic with the same acute
form of romanticism that leaves Rudin's romanticism far behind and
intertwines with sentimentalism. It is significant that he is a musician,
that his personality is defined precisely by music, that most revered
art in romantic mysticism, while Rudin's romanticism was defined
only obliquely by music (the arrival scene), and to a greater extent
by the "German poetry" in which he was "immersed," by "Goethe's
Faust, Hoffmann, Bettina's letters, Novalis" (chapter 6).

Lemm and Lavretsky's relationship represents a greater com-
plexity compared to that of Pigasov and Rudin; although we do
encounter here, as in all the relations of a1 to A, elements of hostile
repulsion, complicated even more by jealousy repressed and being
overcome,the mutual attraction of these two personalities is indub-

itable, which was not the case in Rudin (where there was not even any basis for that).

A new element in *A Nest of Gentlefolk* is b–Varvara Pavlova, a product of just as inferior an order in comparison with B–Liza as a1–Panshin, is a phenomenon of an inferior order in comparison to Lavretsky.

In *On the Eve* we will again fail to meet b, but otherwise we find the arrangement that is already familiar. Insarov's socioideological significance, consisting of his creative activeness, is complemented by the activeness of his friend Bersenev (a3), which is produced and directed in another way but is no less intense and is also creative. In his own way, a1–Kurnatovsky, is active, too, but he shows with the very quality of his activeness that it is activeness of a different, inferior sort compared to Insarov's heroic type (melodramatic type!— critics have corrected, but critics interested more in their own impressions than in Turgenev's goals, such as P. Basistov, the critic for *Notes of the Fatherland,* and V. Burenin, a later interpreter).

From the preceding two examples one can construct even a priori a2—the ideological antipode to Insarov, to his rectilinear, concentrated practicality. That will be an aesthete who is "broad" in the Russian sense: that is exactly what we see in Shubin, the first and only *young* antipode. But just as Basistov shared the role of a3 with Lezhnyov, so here the role of a2 is shared by Shubin and Uvar Ivanovich; the latter's epic maxims (which Nezelyonov risked taking seriously) in any case complement Shubin's opposition to the Bulgarian "hero" and simultaneously injects into a2's outward manner traits of worldly maturity familiar to us from other examples.

In *Fathers and Sons* the pattern outlined produces the fewest doubts, so obvious is it that for A–Bazarov, a3 is Arkady Kirsanov and a2 is Pavel Kirsanov; next to B–Odintsova, b is Fenichka; a1 here, unlike in the other novels, is missing, if one does not count the references to the deceased Odintsov.

In *Smoke* there is a different blank spot: in spite of the sharply defined a1–Ratmirov and a2–Potugin, there is absolutely no a3.

Litvinov is alone; he has no like-minded friend; one cannot consider, after all, that that role has been given to Bambaev! His significance is too paltry and there is too little like-mindedness to Litvinov in him; perhaps only one trait—the garrulous advertising of Litvinov ("Do you see this man? He is a stone! He is a rock! He is granite!") can be considered a caricature of Basistov's ecstatic exclamations, Bersenev's introductions, and Arkady Kirsanov's worship.

And so even here Turgenev has not entirely departed from the pattern adopted by him, but has merely reduced this componeme to a minimum and weakened it to the point of episodic quality. But if we ponder the bases of such a weakening, we will see that it is thoroughly consonant with our earlier observations. Componeme a^3 appears as an echo of the *socioideological basis* of the hero's psychic life—a muted echo, but one that often characterizes the era more than the hero himself does. Litvinov lacks such a companion precisely because he expresses no social idea—he is the least socially minded type of all the heroes of Turgenev's novels. All of concerned society, in its intensity, extreme this time, is moved back in *Smoke* into the depths, into the background—and against this vivid background the features of the bashful "practical Russian" who views with equal distaste the "right" and "left" phenomena of life (true, caricatured!) and who counters Potugin somewhat vaguely and flabbily, look pale. The central dynamics are transferred to the plane of personal psychology—that is why B and b (Irina and Tanya) are contrasted here with the same sharpness as in *A Nest of Gentlefolk;* but there the intimately psychological was harmonically merged with the socioideological, not mechanically blended, as here.

In that case—I will be asked—how can one explain a2–Potugin—in the novel? After all, that role is also conditioned by the socioideological mutual relations with the hero; once we have called that componeme an "ideological antipode," do we not have the right to ask what idea he is contrasted to? The answer will be—none, and that answer will disclose a serious artistic mistake of Turgenev's—an error in construction. Potugin is saturated with an ideological bent, saturated with a social concern that is sharp to the point of partisanship; he is perhaps the most *sectarian* of all the a2's known to us—the author has so *tuned* him (and conveyed that tuning to us) that we expect a complementary harmony without which this sounds dissonant. But Potugin's speeches are poured out into emptiness, and he is left in the old role of the ancient chorus or of the neoclassical authorial mouthpiece.

Virgin Soil produces first of all a question about the main hero. Turgenev himself called Solomin that (Letter to Polonsky), and Ovsyaniko-Kulikovsky (*Turgenev,* 99) did not consider it necessary to dwell on the question of the hero, considering Solomin's dominance "clear all by itself." Both Turgenev and his interpreter can hardly have in mind *compositional* dominance. From the point of view of authorial sympathies and his social goals one can, of course, single out Solomin in comparison to Nezhdanov, but even the author admits in that same letter to Polonsky that "Solomin—the main character—is hardly outlined," and it is not difficult to be persuaded by comparison that only Nezhdanov is *outlined* the way the *main heroes* of his other novels are; it is just that while drawing him Turgenev used the compositional devices that were systematically used while drawing the heroes, but he is allotted the greatest and central attention. Without going into detail, we will remind readers that Solomin does not appear until the sixteenth chapter, and up until his appearance we do not lose sight of Nezhdanov; let us remind readers, lastly, that the dynamics of the novels are created precisely by Nezhdanov. Solomin, however, in spite of all the author's sympathy, practically retreats into the background, and only authorial prompting and the readers' bias retain him even in the role that we recognize for him, the role of a2.

If one sees Nezhdanov's tragedy at the center of the dynamics of *Virgin Soil,* then the static correlations must be presented as applied to him: a1–Kallomeytsev, a2–Solomin, a3–Markelov, B–Marianna, b–Mashurina.

It must be noted that here, as earlier in *On the Eve,* the relationships of a1 and a3 seem to be confused, that is, a3 is also a competitor, one of the hero's rivals. The question arises of whether it is not arbitrary to designate precisely Kallomeytsev (like Kurnatovsky before) as a1, and to assign Markelov (and Bersenev) the role of a3. It is not arbitrariness, because by a1 we agreed to understand the rivals only of an *inferior* socio-ideological order as compared to the hero—such is Kallomeytsev. Markelov, however, is Nezhdanov's like-minded cohort, and our observation about this componeme's (a3) typicality for the era is most applicable to him: in memoirs and works devoted to "active populism" may be found parallels to Markelov.

Solomin is Nezhdanov's ideological antipode. Their like-mindedness, of course, is sham: the practical gradualist Solomin obviously is contrasted to Nezhdanov, a Hamlet who has thrown himself into the role of Don Quixote. True, we will not find any scenes in the novel where these two characters collide—nothing similar to the third chapter of *Rudin,* the sixth and tenth chapters of *Fathers and Sons,* or even scenes of a simple conversation, like Potugin's with Litvinov. But in the twentieth chapter (dinner at Golushkin's), when Solomin has pronounced himself a gradualist, and especially in the conversation with Marianna in the twenty-ninth chapter, Solomin definitely states his lack of sympathy for the politics of populist activeness, spurning it in favor of private beneficence and small deeds having nothing in common with populist ideology.

And so, we derive the following series (the ordering is chronological; missing characters are indicated by a line):

A (heroes): Rudin, Lavretsky, Insarov, Bazarov, Litvinov, Nezhdanov.

a1 (competitor of an inferior order): Volyntsev, Panshin, Kurnatovsky, ———, Ratmirov, Kallomeytsev.

a2 (ideological antipodes): Pigasov, Lemm, Shubin (Uvar Ivanovich), Pavel Kirsanov, Potugin, Solomin.

a3 (like-minded friends): Lezhnyov (Basistov), Mikhalevich, Bersenev, Arkady Kirsanov, ———, Markelov.

B (heroines): Natalya, Liza, Elena, Odintsova, Irina, Marianna

b (the second woman): ———, Varvara Petrovna, ———, Fenichka, Tanya, Mashurina.

The positioning of secondary characters does not seem to me accidental either. We can distinguish in them as well the three categories that were designated in our eyes with a1, a2, and a3—or, more accurately, six categories, since each includes both male and female characters. Designating the male *background* characters as c and the female ones as d, we will derive the outlined division:

> c1—*Pandalevsky, Gedeonovsky, N. A. Stakhov, Nikolay Kirsanov, the generals in* Smoke, Sipyagin.

Here we have grouped together those background characters who come closest to a1, that is, are types of a different—and inferior—social order from the hero, and therefore the hero's dynamic energy—correspondingly diminished, of course—is directed in the movement of the novel at them too; and the reverse—they contribute their are to the milieu's struggle with the hero, to opposing the hero. . . .

> c2—*(missing in* Rudin*), Anton, Uvar Ivanovich, the elder Bazarov (missing in* Smoke*), Paklin.* . . .
>
> c3—*Basistov (missing in* A Nest of Gentlefolk*), the Bulgarians, Sitnikov, Bambaev, Ostrodumov.* . . .
>
> d1—*Lasunskaya, Marya Dmitrievna, Anna Vasilievna, [Katya?], the ladies from Irina's circle, V. M. Sipyagina.* . . .
>
> d2—*Marya Timofeevna, Bazarov's mother, Kapitolina Markovna (in* Smoke*), and Tatyana (in* Virgin Soil*).* . . .
>
> d3 is defined by analogy with c3. They are *Lipina, Zoya, Kukshina, and Sukhanchikova.* There are no corresponding figures in *A Nest of Gentlefolk* and *Virgin Soil.* . . .

I have dwelled on such a detailed analysis of the arrangement of the componemes because putting them into order should help in the analysis of the dynamics of the novels, and the study of the dynamics will help most of all to bring us close to the author's goals. I do not know whether I need to explain that in observing the harmony and symmetry in the composition of Turgenev's six novels, I do not for a moment imagine that this symmetry was the result of a predetermined plan, that Turgenev mechanically arranged his characters, like chess pieces, on a board lined ahead of time. Of course not. Turgenev probably thought as little about being certain to give his hero and antipode and a like-minded comrade and about setting out the episodic characters in three series as Pushkin thought about having the fourth paeon predominate in his iambic lines. Creativity, in its very essence, is irrational, but even the irrational is subject to laws and accessible to study.

We will try to make a few observations about Turgenev's dynamics, and we will examine the remaining question—the construction of the scene—in connection with it.

Just as when looking at all six novels from a bird's eye view, so to speak, we found a general static pattern in the arrangement of the characters, so, examining them from the point of view of narrative movement, we will find in them that thing in common that we will agree to call the dynamic highway. That highway becomes clear in part from observing the positioning of characters: *the hero, arriving in a milieu that is new for him, struggles with it and, exerting a more or less noticeable influence on it, is himself influenced by it.* The motifs of victories and defeats fluctuate, and the conflict is resolved variously. It is necessary to note certain peculiarities in this connection: (1) the novel's temporal field of action is only a moment in the hero's life: we learn about his past from the author's story about him and only as much as is necessary for motivating the events in the "field of action." The same thing can be said of the hero's future in the novels in which the main action does not conclude with the death of the hero: like the past, it is portrayed in only the most essential features (*A Nest of Gentlefolk, Smoke*). (2) The confrontation with the milieu always coincides with another kind of confrontation— meeting the *heroine.* She stands out against this milieu (to one degree or another), being sort of a counter motion (head-on in the direction of the hero and the idea brought by him), and submitting (for long or not) to the influence of that idea. The movement of the novel consists in the struggle in store for each of the heroes with the opponents closest to them in term of composition: a1, a2, and a3; but A and B meeting is not the denouement, but the starting point of the plot, the center from which radiate the rays of further events leading away from this combination. In the denouement A and B are again (with a single exception) separated. . . .

Turgenev created a distinctive type of social novel the *statics* of which consist of a grouping of sociotypical componemes in relationships of ideological equality and inequality, conformity of ideas and divergence of them, and the *dynamics* of which consist of the relations of the hero to the milieu and his struggle with it. The more organically the psychological plot of the novel is linked to its socioideological goals, the more harmonious is its composition.

The dynamic highways of the novels are defined as follows:

Rudin: The hero, passing through a milieu that is obviously hostile or allegedly friendly, without managing to hold back the most reliable of his allies (B), continues his hopeless struggle with the environment in another plane, foreign with regard to the center of the novel. On the hero's side are B, c3, and d3; against him are a1, a2, a3 (temporarily), c1, d1. In the denouement A and a3—B + a1.

A Nest of Gentlefolk. The milieu is split into similar and alien character grouped around A and b as the centers. This split, having producing a tragic rupture between the heroine and the milieu, leaves the hero the passive participant in the newly defined ideological correlations:

$$A—B—a2—c2—d2—a3$$
$$b—a1\ c1\ d1.$$

On the Eve. The hero and heroine, isolated in their milieu, break the milieu's opposition in order to carry out another, "foreign" task. Here everyone—a1, a2, c1, d1, d3, and, in essence, a3—are against A and B. In the denouement—A + B, a1 + d3.

Fathers and Sons. Having cast himself off from the elements of his milieu, the obviously hostile ones as well as the allegedly friendly ones, the hero is left tragically alone. Here everyone is against A; the temporary allies are a3 and B. In the denouement—a3 + d1.

Smoke. The hero's hesitation between B and b, accompanied by the simultaneous rejection of the elements of the milieu close to a1 and opposite (c3—d3), has its outcome in the unions A + b, B + a1.

Virgin Soil. Having overcome the obstacles in one part of the milieu with the support of another, polar opposite part, the hero, without accomplishing further tasks in store for him, perishes.

Here only a1, c1, and d1 are obviously against the hero, but a new splitting off—B and a2—is outlined. In the denouement is complete isolation (and death).

The novels permit various groupings according on various bases. On the basis of historico-typical precision in drawing the milieu the first three novels differ from the last three, where the social relations are more sharply caught and their varieties are painted with greater diversity. In the words of one researcher (K. Istomin), here "the center of gravity is transferred from the heroes to the crowd, to the cultural reality which feeds and nourishes its heroes."[2] What Istomin considered a sign of the "Gogolian" streak in Turgenev's artistry (up to the 1850s) emerges with even greater clarity in the 1860s and 1870s. In other regards one may link *Rudin* and *Fathers and Sons*—in both novels the hero, after rejecting the hostile elements and being rejected by the friendly ones (Rudin by Natalya and Basistov; Bazarov by his parents), dies alone, retaining his ideological cast unaltered. *A Nest of Gentlefolk* and *On the Eve* share the figure of the uncompromising heroine; hence the irreparably tragic quality of both novels. *A Nest of Gentlefolk* and *Smoke* have in common the hero's attraction to patriarchal roots, which, however, are presented in a most profound and highly ideal expression in *A Nest of Gentlefolk* but in a flat and middling way in *Smoke.* Both novels are linked to *Virgin Soil* by the particular coherence of the group a1 c1 d1 (to which b belongs in the first novel), that is, by that banal milieu which in these three novels is painted with deliberate exaggeration, not at all as in *Fathers and Sons,* where the corresponding characters are presented in a significantly muted form, almost idealized, no matter how much Turgenev himself denied it. . . .

Notes

1. Let us agree to use the shortened form "componeme" in place of the awkward term "compositional unit."

2. K. Istomin, " 'Staraya manera' Turgeneva," *Izvestiya otdeliniya russkogo yazyka i slovesnosti Akad. nauk* 18, nos. 2, 3 (1913).

The Metaphysics of Liberation: Insarov as Tristan

Irene Masing-Delic°

I. S. Turgenev's third novel, *On the Eve* (*Nakanune,* 1860), set in 1853, is usually read as a novel dealing with contemporary political issues. In this interpretation, the freedom fighter Insarov appears as both a Bulgarian patriot who hopes to liberate his homeland from the Turkish yoke and also as a forerunner of future Russian liberators who would free their land from its inner Turks, the Czarist establishment. Elena, Insarov's faithful beloved, wife, and friend, then personifies young Russia, tired of superfluous men and searching for less cultured but more effectual suitors, men capable of bringing about real change.

There is much evidence to support the socio-political and prophetic reading of the novel initiated by N. A. Dobrolyubov's famous article "When Will the Real Day Come?" (1860).[1] The plot centers around Elena's search for a new type of man, one in whom thought and action are fused. She finds him in Insarov, for whom personal aspirations coincide with the interests of his nation. Insarov represents a new type of hero, modest and unassuming yet firm and unbending.

° Excerpted from "The Aesthetics of Liberation: Insarov as Tristan," *Die Welt der Slaven* 32, no. 1 (1987). Reprinted by permission of the author and Verlag Otto Sagner.

As such, he provides a dramatic contrast to the artist Shubin and the historian Bersenev, spiritual products of the aesthetic and idealistic 1830s and '40s, men who will not be the ones to free Russia from her inner Turks. That is a task for a Russian Insarov.

There is only one problem with this reading of the novel: the presentation of Insarov himself. This " 'iron man,' who does not know any discrepancy between word and deed, inclination and duty,"[2] has struck many critics as psychologically unconvincing. As early a critic as Dobrolyubov felt that Insarov remained alien to the reader: "even his love for Elena is not fully revealed to us" (123), Dobrolyubov regretfully noted. D. Pisarev, Dobrolyubov's contemporary, found Insarov entirely unconvincing. The critic was baffled by the purportedly heroic Insarov's constantly leaving all initiative to Elena, helplessly leaning on her while at the same time ready to sacrifice her "for the good of Bulgaria."[3] Insarov's death at the most interesting point of the novel, i.e., at the beginning of the struggle for Bulgaria's freedom, also provoked bewilderment. Contemporary critics in both Russia and the West have criticized Insarov's artificiality and his perplexing death. P. Brang sums up the general view when he points to a disharmony between the "fundamentally pessimistic mood" of the novel and its "heroic design."[4]

If Turgenev is to be spared the charge of faulty construction, one must view Insarov as a split hero: a positive patriot and a tragic hero. Critics often overlook the fact that Insarov becomes a different person after falling in love with Elena. A heroic figure only until he recognizes his love for her, he becomes a tragic and deathbound character after that event. Love marks a complete transformation of all values in his life. In undergoing a total metamorphosis through love, Insarov represents an archetypal Tristan figure, i.e., a hero who discovers that the heroic virtues of honor, duty, and valor possess but a secondary reality in comparison with that of love. Specifically, Insarov, a hero whose vision of the world is dramatically altered through love, shows a profound affinity to the hero of Wagner's opera *Tristan and Isolde*.

The striking parallels between Turgenev's Insarov and Wagner's Tristan begin with the pre-history of each hero. Tristan is pursued by death even before his own appearance in the world. His father dies before he is born, his mother as she gives birth to him. A constant awareness of death accompanies the sad man as a leitmotif wherever he goes. It is made audible in "the old earnest tune"[5] which he hears for the first time upon learning of his parents' death and which he hears again shortly before he dies himself. Insarov's childhood is also indelibly marked by the death of his parents: his mother had been abducted and killed by a Turkish aga, his father executed by the same man. These events leave him an orphan in an alien land, Russia, just as Tristan is an orphan in alien Cornwall.

Finding themselves in alien lands, both heroes devote themselves to deeds, rather than words; neither has time for conscious introspection. Both homeless heroes shun love, realizing on some subconscious level that it might confront them with dangerous insights. Tristan sets out to capture Isolde for King Marke, thus attempting to place her beyond reach. Insarov, as Pisarev noted with astonishment, literally runs away from Elena, planning to depart without paying her the obligatory farewell visit. Neither hero is quite ready to renounce his deeds of valor, those manly battles that scar the flesh but leave the spirit intact.[6] In *On the Eve* and *Tristan and Isolde,* man acquires true knowledge of death not in wars but in love.

Neither Tristan nor Insarov escapes his fate. The women they love are strong and determined not to let go of their chosen partners. Isolde forces Tristan to come to her cabin on the ship, and there she wrings a confession of love from him. Ostensibly it is the magic love potion she hands him that transforms him from an unblemished knight into a lover transgressing all conventions and boundaries, including the final demarcation, death. Most critics agree, however, that the love potion is but a catalyst that releases repressed emotions: believing that they are drinking a death potion, the lovers cast away inhibitions, certain they are about to die.

Elena is no less determined than Isolde to clarify relations with her fugitive lover. Although not a princess and lacking magic potions, Elena too pursues her hero, even defying a thunderstorm (just as Isolde does the sea), until chance (or Fate) brings the lovers together at a small chapel. There, by insisting on clarity, Elena also forces a confession of love from her reluctant lover. Magic plays a certain role in this realist novel also. Shortly before meeting Insarov, Elena speaks to an old beggar woman in the chapel; this woman calls herself a "sorceress" (*vorozheya*)[7] and promises to carry all of Elena's sorrows away in a handkerchief (which Elena has given her).[8] The magic here, as in the opera, serves to break down the fear of flouting convention, thus creating an unusual mood in which the impossible becomes possible.

In both declaration scenes, love, once admitted, wreaks a sudden and total (magic) change in the lovers. The man of principle, Insarov, suddenly behaves as if he, like Tristan, had swallowed a magic elixir, so instantaneous is his transformation (91): love "grinds his unbending soul to dust" (92). For the first time in his life, Insarov weeps. Ecstatic, he pronounces the name of his beloved. Similarly, Tristan exclaims "Isolde!" In both cases the exclamation seems to emphasize that a veil has been removed. Both heroes may at that moment retrieve some forgotten experience linked to maternal love; both perhaps approach the realm "out of which the mother once sent them" (55) and where she now dwells.

In these scenes both women point out to their heroes that brave as they are in battle, they are cowards in love. Isolde calls Tristan "bold and cowardly" (14). Elena justly states that she acted with "more courage" then did Insarov (91).

The most important parallel between the love scenes is the impact they have on the subsequent existential and ethical attitudes of the lovers, especially the men. For Tristan, love brings a total "revaluation of all values"; he now realizes that honor, convention, morality, and even life itself are but dreams, at least in comparison with the reality he has uncovered through love ("Was träumte mir/ von Tristans Ehre?" [27]). Insarov does not articulate his inner transformation, but all his subsequent behavior testifies to the fact that he too has discovered that life is a dream, and that even the noblest issues, such as the liberation of a nation, possess but a secondary degree of reality in comparison with the one he has found through love. As far as Insarov is concerned, the unity of thought and action, the harmony between the national and personal issues, has been disrupted forever: he no longer identifies his destiny with Bulgaria's. After his surrender to love, Insarov is no longer a positive hero fighting for Bulgaria's freedom. Instead, he becomes a tragic lover possessed by a longing for the realm of total freedom, where no limitations exist.

After assimilating a new system of values and confronting death for the first time (the death of the old self), Insarov and Tristan prove equally incapable of returning to their former activities. Tristan seeks and receives his never-healing wound; Insarov contracts his incurable malady, tuberculosis. Like Tristan, Insarov is predisposed to experience life as an illness, but the accurate diagnosis of these heroes' illnesses is not a fatal wound or tuberculosis, but yearning (*Sehnsucht*), a yearning so strong that it can be cured only by a liberation from all desire. In this liberation love plays a double role, as it temporarily cures searing desire through erotic fulfillment but also stirs ever more powerful longings that ultimately only death can still. Insarov's passion for Elena is intense, but he soon discovers that passion not only liberates but also "enslaves" (125). There is but one final cure for *Sehnsucht,* Insarov realizes, as does Tristan. Insarov's final insight comes to him in Venice, where he is cured of the sickness of life forever.

Venice is inextricably bound up with ships and the sea, as is *Tristan and Isolde.* In Venice, Insarov waits for his ship as impatiently as Tristan does in his forefathers' castle. Both tormented heroes yearn to make their final passage to the ultimate homeland, which Insarov still calls "Bulgaria," but which clearly lies beyond her borders. Neither ailing hero can quite make his journey "across the sea"

(Turgenev, 80, 147), however, since their female partners still tie them to the shore. Tristan cannot die as long as Isolde remains "in the realm of the sun" (61); Elena, "blossoming" in her love (146), dwells in sunlit lands and thus prevents Insarov from making his final journey.

In Venice Insarov and Elena go to the theater to see Verdi's *La Traviata*. The role of the tubercular heroine is played by a soprano whose performance is so moving that it helps Insarov make his passage from life to death, reconciling him with both. When the soprano "suddenly passes that borderline which cannot be defined, but beyond which beauty lives" (151), Insarov too makes this transition. The title of Turgenev's novel thus suggests many types of transitions and passages: that of a society assumed to be moving toward a dawn and that of an individual entering the realm of night; that of social change and political struggle; and that of a transition from all-round struggle to a realm of eternal peace, revealed on *this* side of existence in a vision of beauty. Insarov, like Tristan, goes to the "wondrous realm of night" across the bridge of aesthetic experience.

Although Wagner's *Tristan and Isolde* had its premiere in 1865, several years after the publication of *On the Eve*, Wagner's libretto was completed in 1857 and published two years later. In that same year, 1859, Turgenev began writing his novel. In December 1858 Franz Liszt invited Madame Viardot to Weimar. In view of Liszt's ardent support of Wagner, it seems probable that he and Viardot spoke of the composer of *Tristan and Isolde*. Moreover, they may even have talked about that particular opera, since Liszt had made a transcription of Isolde's "Liebestod" in 1858.[9] Although Turgenev and Viardot met less frequently in the years 1857–1860, he was at Courtavenel in July 1859. During the two weeks he spent there before going to Russia, where he would write *On the Eve*, the topic of Wagner is likely to have come up. Thus, it is not impossible that Wagner and his libretto, or at least the general plan of the opera, could have been on Turgenev's mind during his stay in Russia.

Ultimately, Wagner's influence on Turgenev's hero must remain a hypothesis, but even as such, the Insarov-Tristan parallel may be functionally useful. The prevailing view of Insarov as a Don Quixote type in Turgenev's gallery of archetypes leaves many aspects of his character unexplained. Insarov, for instance, is far more passionate, erotic, and "fatal" than Quixote. Brang notes Insarov's Byronic aspect (95), and indeed, the taciturn, mysterious, and uncompromising In-sarov is essentially a romantic hero, closer to Tristan than to Quixote. As such, he undergoes existential reversals, to which Quixote is immune. Unlike Quixote, for example, who takes his dreams to be reality, Insarov learns that dreams can be more real than life, witness his nightmare about the shabby lawyer whom he consults before marrying Elena. In his dream the vulgar lawyer personifies a trivial world of whose existence Insarov had been unaware and which he cannot accept. Dreams reveal the triviality of life to Insarov, but so does life itself. A few hours before he dies, he receives a visit from a certain Lupoyarov, a ludicrous hypocrite usually found in a state of verbose and tiresome enthusiasm for some new fashionable cause. This vulgar pseudo-liberal gives Insarov the last impetus to leave a world where everything can be trivialized and nothing remains sacred.

Insarov's ultimate choice is for metaphysical rather than physical reality, spiritual freedom rather than political rights. With her thirst for active good, does Elena arrive at the same conclusions as Insarov, thus proving to be a true Isolde to her Tristan? Such is indeed the case, as Elena unhesitatingly declares her readiness to go to "the end of the world" with Insarov (90), and as she ultimately also joins him in that realm which "embraces the whole world" (Wagner, 56). She sets out for that realm during her last vigil at Insarov's bedside, in the strange dream she has then.

Elena sees herself in a boat with many people whom she does not recognize. As the boat enters the open sea, a terrifying monster rises out of the depths, the monster of omnipotent death. At that moment Elena recognizes her father among her fellow passengers, the father she used to despise. The scene changes, and Elena finds herself in a sleigh, rushing through a desolate wintry landscape, a landscape of death. Next to her in the sleigh is the orphan Katya, a childhood friend raised by an abusive relative. Apparently Elena, herself a child then, had closely identified with Katya, feeling spiritually maltreated in her own home and regarding herself as an orphan too. Both little girls had dreamed of running away from home. The juxtaposition of Elena's father and little Katya points to a reappraisal of values stirring in Elena's consciousness; it indicates her growing awareness that moral indignation is a dubious sentiment, that good and evil are diffuse categories. Her dream makes her understand that her father perhaps spoke the truth when accusing her of theatrical philanthropy. Perhaps her own ostensible goodness toward Katya derived not only from noble impulse but also from egocentric self-dramatization.

Still in her dream, Elena suddenly realizes that her husband is locked in a cloister cell and that she must free him immediately from his imprisonment (156). But it is too late; his voice, mingled with Katya's laughter (perhaps the genuine child victim mocking a counterfeit one?), emerges "from the abyss" (159). Insarov is calling out at that moment that he is dying (159). Elena wakes up and sees his facial expression, one of "terror mingled with a searing tenderness"(159). He has made the terrifying but ultimately liberating passage.

Is the novel's final message, then, that political liberation and social reform are meaningless? that there must be no struggle, as all struggle inevitably involves causing some evil, without necessarily producing some lasting good? This of course is not the case, since for one thing, there are no messages in the novel; instead, there is a broad and multifaceted dramatization of the concept of liberation. Individuals, countries, classes are entitled to political and legal freedom, and all genuine efforts to secure those goods are clearly positive. These efforts should be accompanied by moral freedom, however, an ethical integrity which liberates one from righteousness and the desire to judge, and which comes with the knowledge that no one is free from guilt. There may be those who go beyond even this freedom, choosing ultimate liberation in metaphysical spheres which alone offer total liberation from egotism and guilt; this alternative is limited to those few who tolerate no compromise, however. Clearly, this is not and should not be a choice for all, but the Tristans and Isoldes are few and far between, and thus their example does not threaten mankind with extinction, while their insights remain valid without being translated into popular truths. To sum up, Turgenv's novel *On the Eve* celebrates social and political liberation but also broadens the often too narrowly defined concept of freedom.

Notes

1. N. Dobrolyubov, "Kogda zhe pridet nastoyashchii den'?" *Sobranie sochinenii v devyati tomakh* (Moscow-Leningrad: Gosizdat, 1963), VI, 96–140; hereafter cited in the text. Turgenev disapproved of Dobrolyubov's article because he felt that it attributed subversive political messages to his novel. He even broke off relations with the journal *The Contemporary* because it published Dobrolyubov's article. This article has retained its significance, however, particularly for Soviet criticism.

2. A. Batyuto, *Turgenev-romanist* (Leningrad: Nauka, 1972), 9.

3. D. Pisarev, "Zhenskie tipy v romanakh i povestyakh Pisemskogo, Turgeneva i Goncharova," *Sochineniia v chetyrekh tomakh* (Moscow: Gosizdat, 1955), 270.

4. P. Brang, *I. S. Turgenev. Sein Leben und sein Werk* (Wiesbaden: Harrassowitz, 1977), 98; hereafter cited in the text.

5. Richard Wagner, *Tristan und Isolde*, in *Gesammelte Schriften und Dichtungen* (Leipzig: E. W. Fritzsch, 1871), VII, 65; hereafter cited in the text.

6. Insarov has a scar (*rana*) on his neck from a wound received in his homeland. The scar saddens Elena. Sad Tristan is scarred by many wounds and ultimately receives one that cannot ever be healed. The tuberculosis from which Insarov dies invites interpretation as a kind of wound, too.

7. I. Turgenev, *Nakanune*, in *Sobranie sochinenii v dvenadtsati tomakh* (Moscow: Gosizdat, 1954), III, 89; hereafter cited in the text.

8. This incident has the flavor of a fairy tale. Elena is first tested, as it were, for moral worth. She passes the test by giving the beggar woman the only thing she carries, her elegant handkerchief, and is then rewarded by accidentally meeting the

man she previously could not find, the fugitive Insarov. As Soviet scholars have noted, *On the Eve* is rich in folklore.

9. S. Sitwell, *Liszt* (New York: Philosophical Library, 1967), 346.

[Comedy and Tragedy in *Fathers and Sons*]

David A. Lowe°

Sometime during the first months of 1862 the poet Afanasy Fet sent Turgenev his reactions to *Fathers and Sons*. Fet's letter has not survived, but we have Turgenev's reply, which reinforces the often expressed conviction that one need not necessarily give credence to what authors say about their own works. In his letter of 6 April 1862 Turgenev writes: "You also mention parallelism; but where is it, may I ask?"[1] Turgenev's protests notwithstanding, parallelism is one of the basic principles at work in shaping the novel. The other is contrast. No doubt there are few works in world literature that do not depend to some extent on parallels and contrasts to mold them and give them coherence. In *Fathers and Sons,* however, their significance is all-inclusive, extending to matters of composition, characterization, and thematics. In *Fathers and Sons,* a novel whose very title both links and contrasts the generations, form and content are one. An analysis of the novel's structure will demonstrate the validity of this assertion.

One might describe the novel's structure as determined by a sequence of trips. In such a scheme, Arkady and Bazarov are thus examined and illuminated in a variety of environments. At Marino Arkady is at home and Bazarov is the stranger. Both Arkady and Bazarov are thrown into an unfamiliar environment in town and at Nikolskoe. At Bazarov's parents' Arkady is the stranger (though in some ways he is less an outsider there than is Bazarov). Parallelism and contrast are immediately evident in such an analysis: Bazarov is the newcomer in one milieu, Arkady in another. Even within the series of trips, however, cycles can be established. Brazhe writes of two cycles of trip from Marino to Bazarov's home.[2] Such a calculation takes into account only Bazarov's point of view, however. It would be more accurate to identify three overall cycles. In the first, Arkady and Bazarov travel from Marino to town, then on to Nikolskoe and Bazarov's home, after which they go back through Nikolskoe to Marino. In the second, Arkady makes his way to Nikolskoe on his own. In a later and analogous development, Bazarov also arrives at

° Adapted from *Turgenev's "Fathers and Sons"* (Ann Arbor, Mich.: Ardis, 1983), 15–27. Reprinted by permission of Ardis Publishers.

Nikolskoe on his own. Finally, in the last cycle, Bazarov returns home alone, as does Arkady. The interesting structural note here is that Arkady's and Bazarov's travels consistently dovetail with each other, even when the two protagonists are not together. Implicit in this view of the novel's structure is one of the major themes: children cannot forever deny their parents' world, which, for better or worse, represents the mainstream of mankind. Children ultimately return home and, willingly or grudgingly, become reconciled to it. At that point, as Joel Blair notes, "the lives of the fathers become patterns for understanding the lives of the children."[3]

A second way of viewing the structure is as a series of confrontations. Such an interpretation is particularly widespread, since it provides abundant opportunities to discuss the ideological battles of the 1860s that form the socio-historical backdrop for the novel. Thus, the structure of *Fathers and Sons* may be mapped out as a series of ideological duels between Bazarov and Pavel, the ideological duels then capped by a real duel in which ideology and social values are as much at stake as personalities. Doubling the ideological battles is a series of erotic confrontations with Odintsova. All discussions of the structure of *Fathers and Sons* in terms of confrontations are ultimately spin-offs of Gippius's Formalist analysis of composition in Turgenev's novels.[4] For all its sophistication, however, Gippius's analysis is limited, because like most analyses of *Fathers and Sons,* it proceeds on the assumption that the novel is a tragedy and that Bazarov is the only significant protagonist therein. Such assumptions have led critics in the past to attempt to identify a single, all-embracing structural pattern in the novel, whether it be trips, confrontations, or love stories. But the supposition is flawed. *Fathers and Sons,* a novel whose structure is wholly dependent upon parallels and contrasts, is not a tragedy pure and simple—it exhibits traits of comedy as well. Furthermore, Bazarov, though he is the novel's most arresting figure, spends as much time in the wings as he does on stage.

The structure of *Fathers and Sons* is dualistic: it features two parallel but contrasting patterns. The first is that of tragedy, the second, that of comedy.[5] Since readers may find controversial the notion that *Fathers and Sons* is in any way comic, it makes sense to begin with this, the less obvious structural pattern in the novel. In using the word comedy, what is intended is not comedy in the popular sense (a funny play with a happy ending), but in the Aristotelian sense, specifically in its modern formulation by Northrop Frye. Frye uses comedy as a term denoting a literary mode, as he calls it, not a genre. Thus, as defined by Frye, the term is equally applicable to drama and narrative prose.

Basing his treatise on Aristotle's *Poetics,* Frye suggests that comedies deal with the integration of society. The standard comic formula involves a young couple—the technical hero and heroine, whose marriage is blocked by other members of the cast (society). In realistic fiction employing the comic mode, the hero and heroine tend to be dull but decent people, while the blocking characters are the truly interesting ones. The blocking characters are normally, but not necessarily, parental figures. They are consumed by a single passion (usually absurdly so), and they are in control of the society into which the hero and heroine seek entrance. The blocking characters are likely to be imposters, as Frye calls them, people who lack self-knowledge. At the conclusion of comedy the blocking characters are either incorporated into or expelled from the society, as a result of which the hero and heroine are free to wed. Thus, comedies often conclude with a wedding and births, and have a rural setting (an escape to a simpler, less corrupt society). At the conclusion of comedy the audience feels that justice has triumphed, that the people who should have been united are together, and that everyone will live happily ever after in a freer, more flexible society.[6] This is a somewhat primitive reduction of Frye's Aristotelian description of comedy, but it should be sufficient to demonstrate that the comic mode is at work in *Fathers and Sons*. However, Turgenev spins some fascinating variations around the timeworn comic pattern.

Arkady is the technical hero about whom the comedic plot revolves.[7] And true to comic type, Arkady is a rather bland but not unattractive personality. As in Roman comedy, we have not a single hero, but a pair of heroes. Instead of the typical pair of young heroes, however, Turgenev presents a father and son, both of whose marriages are blocked, as is a genuine reconciliation between the two of them. The blocking characters are Pavel and Bazarov, and consistent with the traditions of comedy, both of them are considerably more interesting than the technical heroes and heroines, and both of them are removed from the stage at the culmination of the comic plot line.

Bazarov's influence on Arkady forestalls an accommodation between him and his father, just as it temporarily blocks Arkady and Katya's marriage, largely because Bazarov's attitudes, which Arkady attempts in vain to adopt, prevent the latter from coming to terms with himself and his true nature. Bazarov's obstructing influence is apparent as early as the third chapter. Arkady, riding along in a carriage with his father, waxes lyrical, thus betraying his very unnihilistic enthusiasm for the beauties of nature. He abruptly breaks off in mid-sentence, discouraged by Bazarov's presence from being himself. As a result, the relations between father and son are strained. Bazarov is a blocker, and by the end of the novel there is no doubt that it is precisely Bazarov's sway over Arkady that temporarily thwarts mutual understanding between father and son. Furthermore, Arkady's distorted image of himself as a fire-breathing, militant disciple of

Bazarov's impedes his progress toward the realization that his love is not for Odintsova, as he imagines, but for her sister Katya. Katya in fact articulates what the reader has sensed all along: Arkady has been under Bazarov's thumb. "My sister was under his [Bazarov's influence then, just as you were" (364), Katya tells Arkady.

Arkady's transition from his false role as Bazarov's protégé to his true status as his father's son is signalled in his proposal to Katya: Arkady has recognized himself and has expressed his true feelings. It is appropriate that Arkady should proclaim his love for Katya in the shaded garden portico. Alexander Fischler has noted that the architecture of *Fathers and Sons* is linked to a garden motif, and that "the garden is a microcosm of nature, foreshortening its laws to uphold *what ought to be.*"[8] Bazarov's dramatic farewell and rejection of Arkady are really no more than a recognition that "what ought to be" has come to pass: he no longer has any influence over Arkady. Bazarov retires to his father's house, removing himself from the comic plot line and freeing Arkady to marry Katya and to be reconciled with his father.

Pavel is a blocking character with regard to Nikolay and Fenechka. His presumed hostility to the idea of their marriage has dissuaded Nikolay from regularizing his liaison with Fenechka. Note Nikolay's reaction when Pavel asks him to marry Fenechka: "But don't you know that it was only out of respect for you that I haven't fulfilled what you so rightly call my duty!" (362). So Pavel encourages Nikolay to marry Fenechka—an act that will assuage Nikolay's pangs of conscience and allow him to feel more at ease with his son.

Thus, at the culmination of the comic plot line the blocking characters have been expelled or have expelled themselves. Pavel prepares to spend the rest of his days in Europe, while Bazarov retires to his father's home. To complete the paradigm, the pairs who belonged together all along are at last united.

Some critics have noted the importance of couplings, uncouplings, and recouplings in the novel. Reeve writes: "Characters in pairs. . . relate to each other through a succession of still other people, each relationship forming a temporary triangle, each triangle imperfect. . . . The third person's action always in some way splits the original pair."[9] Or as Blair formulates it, "The principle of composition operating in the novel is the grouping and regrouping of characters; our understanding of the novel develops as we observe the initial groups of characters dissolve and perceive the formation of new pairs. Eventually, those characters who seemed most unalike are aligned; their similarities become more important than their differences" (556).

The general movement toward the final, inevitable pairings is the stuff of comedy. The double wedding noted in the epilogue underscores the emergence of a new, pragmatically freer society, a

salient feature of comedy. The crystallization of this less rigid society
is underlined by Pavel when he urges Nikolay to marry Fenechka:
"No, dear brother, enough of high-mindedness and thinking about
society: we're already old and peaceful people; it's time we put aside
empty pretense" (362). The new society, though not earthshakingly
different from the old, is a little less rigid, a little more spontaneous:
Nikolay, a member of the gentry, has become free to take Fenechka,
a peasant, as his lawfully wedded wife. In this respect Shklovsky
overstates the case in arguing that "what is new in Turgenev's novel
was that he understood the love story as the confrontation of the
new people with a world built on old principles."[10] It is really Nikolay
and Fenechka who confront old social values with new ones, Arkady
and Katya's thoroughly conventional marriage with their own socially
"progressive" one. Shklovsky's assessment nonetheless shows that he
perceives a comic base in the novel. Fischler, who emphasizes the
classical bases of *Fathers and Sons,* also sees comedy at work here.
He writes of the epilogue as "*prostodushnaya komediya,* 'artless
comedy'—life itself or a play in which the author's strings no longer
matter. In such comedy, the naive pursuit of happiness by the characters remaining on the stage blends with the timeless designs, overwhelming what momentarily stood out and was disturbing because
of its alien, fortuitous, or fateful appearance" (244).

What are the implications of the novel's comic structure? One,
obviously, is that the comic mode is extraordinarily hardy and adap-
tive. But more importantly, an analysis of *Fathers and Sons* as comedy
explains in formal terms why many critics read the novel as an
affirmation of life and nature. Strakhov, for instance, argues: "Although
Bazarov stands above everyone in the novel, life stands above him."[11]

But what kind of life stands above Bazarov? Some critics dismiss
the life led by Katya, Arkady, Nikolay, and Fenechka as banal,
mediocre, *poshly.*[12] Pisarev, for one, suggests: "The life of a limited
person always flows along more evenly and pleasantly than the life
of a genius or even of just an intelligent person."[13] A less petulant
interpretation results if one notes that the mediocrity represented by
the two couples is that of the middle way, the golden mean. Turgenev
himself spoke of Goethe's Faust as the defender of "the individual,
passionate, limited person" who still "has the right and the opportunity to be happy and not to ashamed of his happiness" (I, 235).
Vinogradov asserts:"The novel in essence is a battle of 'cerebral'
negative theories with the mighty power of love, with the inexpres-
sible beauty of nature, with all the intermix of human feelings which,
though 'old,' are alive and warm—a battle that ends with the triumph
of 'humanness,' 'nature,' beauty,'' over 'nihilism.' ''[14] The comic couples may be limited, but they are hardly vegetables, nor is their
existence gray. Arkady is a competent estate manager, and all the

Kirsanovs' lives, ordinary as they may be, are enriched by an instinctual and profound attraction to nature, art, and their fellow humans. They represent an ideal that Turgenev himself was unable to attain.

It is nonetheless beyond question that in most of his works Turgenev displays a contemptuous, despairing attitude toward bourgeois domesticity. It is also the case that Turgenev claimed to have taken a similar stance in *Fathers and Sons.* In a letter of 14 April 1862, to Sluchevsky, Turgenev responds to Sluchevsky's report on how Russian students in Heidelberg had read *Fathers and Sons.* The students' reactions are indicative, as is Turgenev's reply: "What was said about Arkady, about the rehabilitation of the fathers, etc., only shows—forgive me—that I haven't been understood. *My whole novel is directed against the gentry as a progressive class.* Examine Nikolay Petrovich, Pavel Petrovich, Arkady closely. Weakness, flabbiness, or limitedness" (4, 380). Later in the same letter Turgenev expresses bewilderment at the Heidelberg students' having found Arkady "a more successful type [than Bazarov]" (4, 380). Thus we have Turgenev's own testimony that he did not intend to portray Arkady or Nikolay in a flattering light. But authors' intentions are one thing (as is their hindsight), reader's perceptions quite another. As noted earlier, more than one critic has found a healthy, optimistic note in the depiction of Nikolay, Arkady, and their wives. In this connection Gippius, discussing groups of *poshly* characters in *Smoke* and *A Nest of Gentlefolk*, points out that these characters are "portrayed with exaggerated distortion, not at all as in *Fathers and Sons,* where the corresponding characters are presented in a significantly muted form, no matter how much Turgenev himself denied it" (54).

Arkady and Nikolay are not men of great stature, nor are they great thinkers, but Turgenev's having infused them with a love for Schubert, Pushkin, evening sunsets, their families, and their fellow humans makes it difficult to dismiss them and the life they lead. Turgenev portrays the Kirsanovs in a positive, if subdued light. In the novel's comic epilogue, where life and love are celebrated at Pavel's farewell dinner, Turgenev leads the audience to recognize that "this is how things ought to be."

Not all critics, of course, find positive notes in *Fathers and Sons.* Most would probably argue that the novel is a tragedy. Such a bromide of Turgenev criticism should surprise no one, but how and why *Fathers and Sons* is a tragedy—these are questions that remain largely unexplored. Once again Northrop Frye provides useful tools for exploration.[15]

The basic movement of tragedy, according to Frye, is toward the exclusion of a hero from a given society, with an emphasis on the hero's tragic isolation. Here Gippius's analysis of the structure of *Fathers and Sons* seems particularly apt. He describes the novel's "dynamic highway" in this way: "Having cast off the elements of his milieu, the obviously hostile ones as well as the pseudo-friendly ones, the hero remains tragically alone" (53).

According to Frye, the tragic hero must be of heroic proportions: "The tragic hero is very great as compared with us, but there is something else, something on the side of him opposite the audience, compared to which he is small."[16] Surely this is the case with Bazarov, whose greatness (implied, rather than shown) is, as Strakhov argues, less than the sum of life forces represented by the Kirsanovs and their spouses (207).

In addition, Frye conceives of the tragic hero as an impostor, someone who is deceived about himself. Significantly, Charles Bachman writes of "tragedy and self-deception" in *Fathers and Sons,* pointing out that "false self-images are crucial to the tragic view which the action of the novel seems to demand. . . ."[17] Most of the characters in the novel suffer from identity crises: this is true not just in the case of the strong characters, as Bachman suggests, but also in that of such a protagonist as Arkady. But Bazarov's self-deception is the most extreme and his journey toward self-discovery the most painful and tragic. He believes himself above the laws that govern human life; his fatal infection, leading him to summon Odintsova for a last meeting in which he confesses that he is not the "giant" he had imagined himself to be, demonstrates that finally he understands the extent of his self-delusion.

The movement toward tragedy is generally toward a revelation of natural law, "that which is and must be" (Frye, 207), so that the audience's reaction to the hero's fall is paradoxical: we feel a sense of rightness (the tragic hero represents an imbalance in nature and thus must fall) and horrible wrongness (how sad that this man must fall). Such indeed is our reaction to Bazarov's death. Poignant as it may be, we nevertheless perceive, as Richard Freeborn formulates it, that Bazarov is a "usurper of divine right whose arrogant self-will proclaims for itself a self-sufficiency in life which contravenes the limits of human experience and gives rise to a dilemma which is only to be resolved in death."[18]

Comedy and tragedy coexist in *Fathers and Sons.* It is of course the tragic side that impresses us most deeply. Such is human nature. Moreover, Turgenev takes pains to reinforce the novel's tragic overtones by placing the description of Bazarov's aged parents weeping inconsolably at their son's grave as the last element in the novel, the final chord of a tragic symphony, as it were. Yet the novel's last lines speak of "eternal reconciliation and life without end" (401). If these lines are read against the context of the interplay between the novel's tragic and comic structures, they may be seen to underscore the triumph of those life forces that find their apotheosis in comedy.

Perhaps the most balanced assessment, however, is that the novel's tragic side predominates without overwhelming. Significantly, critics who write of tragedy in *Fathers and Sons* often stop short of actually labelling the novel a tragedy, pure and simple. Helen Muchnic, for instance, calls the work "tragic in its implications, but not in its tone."[19] Such hesitation can be accounted for on the formal level by recognizing the coexistence of comic and tragic modes within the novel.[20]

Observing the relationship between the comic and the tragic in *Fathers and Sons* helps make understandable the initial and continuing controversy over the novel. In "Apropos of *Fathers and Sons*" Turgenev writes that he has an interesting collection of documents and letters from reader who accuse him of doing totally contradictory things in the work. By combining the comic and tragic modes he seem to stand behind two diametrically opposed views of life and one and the same time. If the novel's comic structure is taken out of context, one concludes that life is triumphant, rewarding, and meaningful. And in *Fathers and Sons* the portrait of the Kirsanovs, their babies, their joyous participation in the natural cycle, all lead the audience to infer that all's right with the world. If the novel's tragic side is taken out of context, however, one is led to the bleak view that life, ruled by fate and the irrational, is essentially meaningless: death is triumphant. Where does Turgenev stand? "Where is the truth, on which side?" one may ask, as does Arkady (324). "Where? I'll answer you like an echo: where?" (324). An analysis of the novel's dualistic structure shows that the truth is on both sides. Such a conclusion is supported by one of Turgenev's letters to Annenkov, in which he asserts: "I know that in nature and in life everything is reconciled one way or another. If life cannot do the reconciling, death will" (2, 144). Thus, Turgenev's own view is dualistic but not contradictory. This dualism lies at the heart of *Fathers and Sons,* a novel whose ambiguities have their roots, first and foremost, in the work's reliance on both comic and tragic modes.

Notes

1. I. S. Turgenev, *Polnoe sobranie sochinenii i pisem v 28–i tomakh: Pisma,* vol. 4 (Moscow-Leningrad: Nauka, 1960–68), 371. Further references to this edition of Turgenev's works will be indicated parenthetically within the text. References to *Fathers and Sons* are indicated by a single arabic numeral. Such references refer to volume 8 of the works. An arabic numeral followed by a comma and another arabic numeral indicates letters. A roman numeral followed by a comma and an arabic numeral indicates a volume of works. All translations are my own. The most accurate rendering of the title of Turgenev's novel would be *Fathers and Children,* but since the English-speaking world has known the work for over a century as *Fathers and Sons,* there seems little point in now trying to convert readers to a new title.

2. T. G. Brazhe, *Tselostnoe izuchenie epicheskogo proizvedeniya* (Moscow: Prosveshchenie, 1964), 19.

3. Joel Blair, "The Architecture of Turgenev's *Fathers and Sons*," *Modern Fiction Studies* 19, no. 4 (Winter 1973–74):556; hereafter cited in the text.

4. Vasily Gippius, "O kompozitsii turgenevskikh romanov," in *Venok Turgenevu* (Odessa: A. A. Ivasenko, 1919), 25–55; hereafter cited in the text. [Excerpts from Gippius's study are included in this volume.]

5. I wish to give credit here to Professor Roger Blakely of Macalester College, who in a course many years ago pointed out the possibility of identifying a comic structure in *Fathers and Sons*.

6. This is a reduction of Northrop Frye, *Anatomy of Criticism* (Princeton, N.J.: Princeton University Press, 1957), 43–52, 163–85.

7. As additional evidence that Arkady's role in *Fathers and Sons* is greater than secondary, it should be noted that many scenes in the novel are narrated from his point of view. In addition, Arkady's being caught between two women parallels the dilemma of such central heroes in other Turgenev novels as Lavretsky (*A Nest of Gentlefolk*) and Litvinov (*Smoke*). See also Gary Jahn, who in "Character and Theme in *Fathers and Sons*," *College Literature* 4 (1977):81, writes: "Arkady and Bazarov are the organizational focus of the novel." All in all, Arkady's role is considerably more central than that of the typical secondary hero in a Turgenev novel.

8. Alexander Fischler, "The Garden Motif and the Structure of *Fathers and Sons*," *Novel* 9 (1976):148; hereafter cited in the text.

9. F. D. Reeve, *The Russian Novel* (New York: McGraw Hill, 1966), 146.

10. Viktor Shklovsky, *Zametki o proze russkikh klassikov* (Moscow: Sovetskii pisatel, 1955), 221.

11. N. N. Strakhov, "Ottsy i deti," in *O Turgeneve: russkaya i zarubezhnaya kritika*, ed. P. P. Pertsov (Moscow: Koop. izd-vo, 1918), 40.

12. *Poshly* implies banality, mediocrity, self-satisfied complacency, poor taste, and other allied concepts. The English word "tacky" in its current popular usage perhaps comes closest to conveying the meaning of the Russian.

13. D. I. Pisarev, "Bazarov," in *Bazarov; Realisty* (Moscow: Uchpedgiz, 1974), 19. Pisarev's article originally appeared in *Russkoe slovo* 3 (March 1862).

14. I. A. Vinogradov, *Borba za stil* (Leningrad: Gikhl, 1973), 199.

15. Remarks on the nature of tragedy, unless explicitly stated otherwise, are based on material to be found in Frye, 35–43, 206–22; hereafter cited in the text.

16. Charles R. Bachman, "Tragedy and Self-Deception in Turgenev's *Fathers and Sons*," *Revue des Langues Vivantes* (Brussels) 34, no. 3 (1968):269.

17. Richard Freeborn, *Turgenev: The Novelist's Novelist* (Oxford: Oxford University Press, 1960), 121.

18. Helen Muchnic, *An Introduction to Russian Literature* (New York: Doubleday, 1947), 118.

19. Additional examples of such hesitation about calling the novel a tragedy include V. M. Fisher, "Povest i roman u Turgeneva," in *Tvorchestvo Turgeneva: Sbornik statey* (Moscow: Zadruga, 1920), 37 [reproduced in the present volume], who calls the novel an elegy, and Justus, 259, who describes it as an idyll.

INDEX